Network and Internet Security

Warning and Disclaimer

This book is designed to provide information about network and Internet security. The information is provided on an "as is" basis. In no event will the publisher or the author be liable or responsible to any person or entity with respect to any errors or omissions, or any loss or consequential, incidental, or indirect damages (including damages for loss of business profits, business interruptions, loss of business information, and the like) arising from the use or inability to use any information contained in this book, even if the publisher or author has been advised of the possiblity of such damages.

The opinions expressed in this book are those of the author and do not necessarily reflect the views or opinions of IBM.

Network and Internet Security

Vijay Ahuja, Ph.D.

Manager
Network Security Products
IBM Corporation

AP PROFESSIONAL

Boston   San Diego   New York
London   Sydney   Tokyo   Toronto

AP PROFESSIONAL
1300 Boylston Street, Chestnut Hill, MA 02167
World Wide Web site at http://www.apnet.com

An Imprint of ACADEMIC PRESS, INC.
A Division of HARCOURT BRACE & COMPANY

United Kingdom Edition published by
ACADEMIC PRESS LIMITED
24–28 Oval Road, London NW1 7DX

Ahuja, Vijay.
    Network and Internet Security / Vijay Ahuja.
        p.   cm.
    Includes bibliographical references and index.
    ISBN 0-12-045595-1
    1. Computer networks—Security measures. 2. Internet (computer network)—Security measures. 3. Computer
security.   I. Title.
    TK5105.59.A39   1996
    005.8—dc20   96-1378
                                                                                          CIP

Printed in the United States of America
96 97 98 99   CP 9 8 7 6 5 4 3 2 1

Dedication

To my dear wife, Neeta, and to my lovely children, Vini, Anant, and Devesh

Contents

3 Workstation Security   93

4 Distributed Security Services   133

5 Access Control   181

6 Internet Security   207

Acknowledgements

One of the more pleasurable tasks after finishing a book is to acknowledge the assistance of several people that have helped bring the project to fruition. First, I would like to thank my employer, the IBM Corporation and specifically my manager, Paula Lupriore for her encouragement and support of this endeavor. I would also like to thank my colleague, Ray Scanga and my daughter, Vinita Ahuja for their reviews and valuable comments on several sections of this book. A special thanks are due to Gael Tannenbaum and Barbara Northcott of AP Professional for their patience and excellent suggestions to improve the quality of this book. Finally, I must thank my respected father, Dr. Yog Dhyan Ahuja, for his guidance and moral support throughout this effort.

Preface

A secure network is critical for the survival and success of many businesses. The rapid evolution of client/server networks, the phonemenal increase in the number of networks attached to the Internet, the widespread use of Web browsers, and the growing commerce on the Internet each require that communication networks are secure. Security concerns for private networks as well as for the Internet range from exposures to computer viruses to break-ins by an intruder on the Internet.

The purpose of this book is to present the concepts in security and describe approaches to securing the networks. It introduces the risks to networks, followed by a review of basic security concepts such as passwords and encryption. For each concept, the book also provides an overview of the existing and emerging security technologies. In particular, it focuses on various security aspects of attaching to and communication over the Internet.

This book serves the growing need to understand and enhance the security of networks. The audience for this book is the computing professional who has the need or desire to understand the risks to networks and the approaches to addressing them.

Introduction

c h a p t e r

1

As networks grow in size, so do their risks. Network growth has vastly exceeded the corresponding improvements to ensure network security. In order to introduce various security technologies, this chapter begins with an overview of the client/server networks, followed by a description of security exposures and concepts in network security.

Background and Overview

History

Information processing entered the business world in the 1950s. However, the third-generation computers, such as IBM System/360, became the turning point in our transformation to the current age of information technology. The first signs of networking appeared in what was then called "time-shared systems." Some of the early operating systems that also supported time sharing were IBM's System/360 Model 65 and IBM Time Sharing System, DEC's PDP-8 Time Sharing System/8, and Honeywell's GECOS. By the end of 1960s, keyboard terminals and peripheral equipment had taken hold in numerous data processing installations. Next, the users on different time-shared systems wanted to communicate with each other. The time was ripe for the birth of networking!

During the same time, research had started in the area of resource sharing, under the auspices of the then known ARPA (Advanced Research Projects Agency, Department of Defense) network. ARPA network started in 1968 with four nodes, as shown in Figure 1.1. The objective of the project was to achieve resource sharing, but it also yielded some of the ground-breaking technologies such as packet switching, packet routing, and flow control.

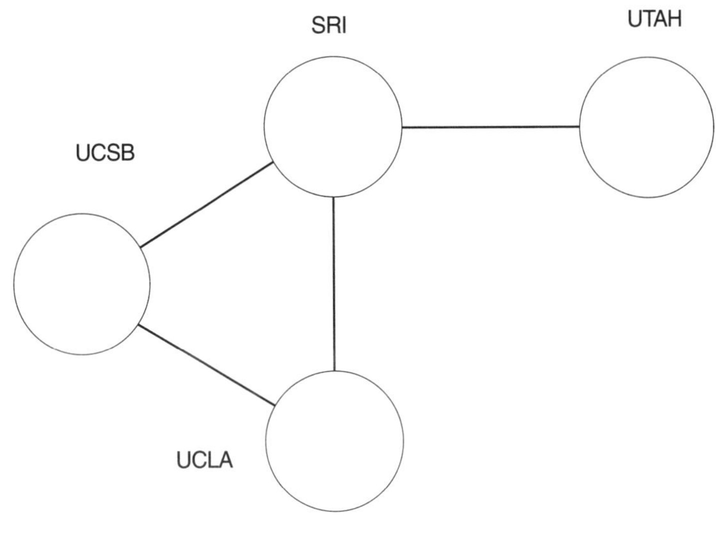

Figure 1.1: ARPANET, December 1969.

Source: "Queing Systems Volume II: Computer Applications," page 306 Leonard Kleinrock. Copyright© 1976 by John Wiley & Sons, Inc. Reprinted by permission of John Wiley & Sons, Inc.

During the early 1970s, several networking architectures were developed to incorporate the above concepts. The primary goal for these architectures was to define a common set of protocols that allow useful data interchange between communicating devices. Some of the well-known architectures include IBM's Systems Network Architecture (SNA), Digital Equipment Corporation's Digital Network Architecture (DNA), and Burroughs Corporation's Burroughs Network Architecture (BNA). As these architectures grew, there was the need to interconnect diverse vendor architectures through protocol gateways or "protocol converters." The international standards community introduced a comprehensive set of networking protocols under the title "Reference Model for Open Systems Interconnection," also known as the "OSI model." The OSI model is used as the reference model for the protocol layers in data networks. The international community has also agreed on standards for several specific networking services such as CCITT (International Telegraph and Telephone Consultative Committee) Recommendation X.400 for message handling and X.500 for directory services.

During the 1970s, it became obvious that there was a need for high-speed local interconnection and data exchange between several devices. The term "local area network" or LAN was coined in the mid-1970s. A LAN can be viewed as a collection of interconnected devices that can interchange data among themselves. The communication medium for the LANs can be a twisted pair of wire, a coaxial cable, a fiber-optic cable, or a wireless connection. Transmission rates from 4 megabits per second to more than 100 megabits per second were achieved. Several different LAN protocols were introduced, two of which became quite pervasive, namely the token ring and the Ethernet. The token ring uses the ring topology, while the Ethernet uses the bus topology.

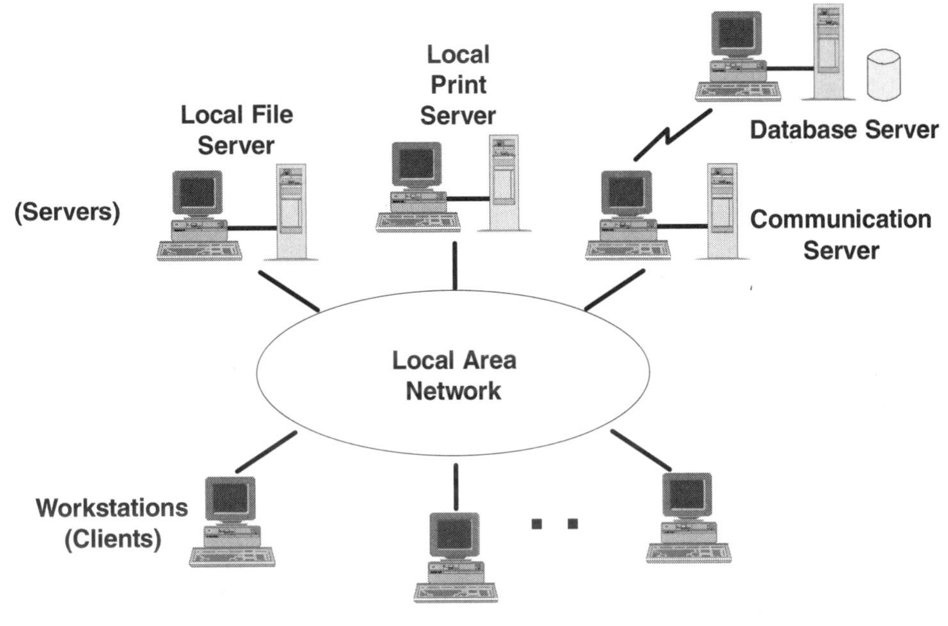

Figure 1.2: Local Area Networks

Client/Server Networks

During the 1980s, it also became apparent that a new networking approach was required to exploit the facilities of the local area networks. Furthermore, personal computers (PCs) were arriving at every office and household. The next challenge was to interconnect these workstations and provide a variety of functions and services to the individual users at the workstations. It was time to think of client/server networking. Novell introduced NetWare in 1983, and IBM introduced PC LAN in 1984.

As shown in Figure 1.2, a typical LAN consists of several work-stations and one or more servers such as a file server, a print server, or a communications server.

Client

A *client* is an entity that consists of an operating system and a collection of programs to perform a set of functions. The client functions include:

- Interacting with the user through a graphical user interface

- Preparing user inquiries and requests through standard interfaces for accessing the server

- Communicating with the server over a communications interface

- Performing analysis on the data received from the server to be presented to the user

Server

A *server* provides one or more services that may range from minimal server-based computing (such as for print server or file server) to intensive computing (such as for a database server or image-processing server). A server is a passive machine; it only responds to inquiries or requests from clients. A server does not initiate any communication on its own. It may, though, require access to another server. For example, a database server may need to access a directory server to locate some of the files. Servers should handle such interserver processing and communications without exposing it to the client.

The components of a client/server network are depicted in Figure 1.3.

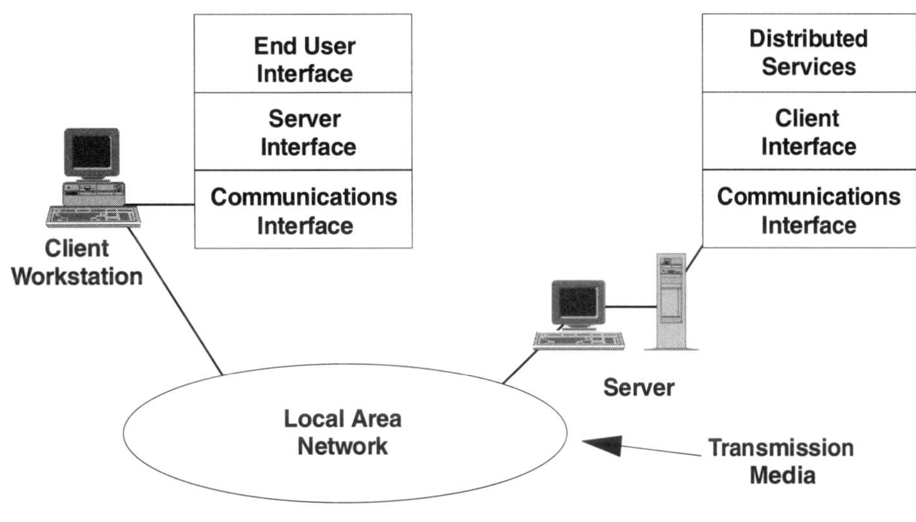

Figure 1.3: Components of a Client/Server Network

In a *client/server network*, each user has his or her own computing environment that consists of a desktop processor, a local operating system, and a local file system. Many tasks can be accomplished without requiring an external access to a server or a mainframe computer. However, certain tasks require access to servers such as for directory, security, print, time, and file.

In order to provide the security services, the client/server network may provide access to a security server. For example, each client workstation requires local security to encrypt the secret files or to protect the files from viruses. Similarly, each server requires access to security services in order to authenticate its clients. In this particular context, a server appears as a client to the security server. Furthermore, in order to send the requests and receive the security services, there needs to be a "security client code" residing in each client and each server.

The networking industry is experiencing constant evolution and change, accompanied by growth in the size and complexity of networks. The client workstations continue to improve, especially in terms of the processor performance, memory space, and software support. For the end user, the network should simply be a transparent connection with some value-added functions. In order to achieve these goals, several technologies and services are required.

To begin with, the applications and software systems need to support graphical user interfaces (GUIs). In some instances, support for more than one GUI may be required, depending on the underlying operating system and the user requirements.

Distributed Applications

A *distributed application* is defined as a collection of programs, where each program may reside in one or more workstations and collectively accomplish a related set of tasks. For a given distributed application to operate, there should be an underlying client/server network that provides the communication channel between the applications. The distributed application uses the communication interfaces to exchange information among its components.

Distributed Services

Next, we consider the services required for client/server networks. Distributed services may include directory services to locate the resources, security services to authenticate users and protect data, file services to provide access to data, and time services to synchronize time across the network. These services are required by each distributed application and each network user. Similarly, management services are required across the client/server network to allow for configuration, problem handling, and performance management of the clients and servers. Table 1.1 provides a list of various types of servers for client/server networks.

Server	Services
Security Server	Provides security services for the network such as data security, user authentication, and encryption keys
Directory Server	Provides location of users and resources
Time Server	Synchronizes time across the network
File Server and Database Server	Provides access to files and databases.
Communications Server	Provides access for remote servers
Print Server	Provides printing services
Management Server	Provides management of the client/server network such as configuration, problem handling, and performance

Table 1.1: Distributed Services for Client-Server Networks

Application Programming Interfaces

Finally, real networks are not homogeneous. Customers may buy the LANs, clients, servers, and distributed applications from different vendors. Given this freedom of choice for the customer, most private networks consist of software components from more than one vendor and in many cases several vendors. However, many network components from one vendor may not interoperate with those from another vendor. This leads to the need for supporting heterogeneous networks with components from different vendors and technologies. So, a given client/server network must support a variety of vendor software platforms including the underlying operating systems. In order to address this requirement, the networking industry continues to embrace open Application Programming Interfaces (APIs). An open API makes it easier to port applications over different software systems. A standard API for distributed security services is described in Chapter 4.

Additional information on design and analysis of data networks can be found in other references such as Sinha (1992), Comer (1991), and Ahuja (1982).

Security Risks and Break-ins

"By the year 2000, all white-collar crime will probably be computer crime."

James Settle, FBI Supervisory Special Agent
(Open System Today, November 8, 1993, p 10)

The ongoing growth in networks continues to expose new holes and vulnerabilities in network security. Network security is continually growing in importance and complexity. Networks are becoming such an integral part of our businesses that it is hard to separate the risks to networks from the risks to the businesses. Although there are great benefits to networking, many of these benefits wane in view of the security risks and exposures, threats, and many times even break-ins.

There are some startling statistics. By January 1995, the number of viruses had increased to approximately 6000, a 40 percent increase in 12 months. In 1992, check fraud cost the financial services industry over $1 billion, while credit card fraud cost the industry over $3.5 billion. The number of reported hacker invasions increased from 252 in 1990 to 2341 in 1994. The FBI estimates that a company loses approximately $500,000 each time a corporate computer is breached. It is estimated that downtime at a major banking data center costs approximately $5000 per second. (Sources: Sullivan 1993; Wagner 1993; FSTC 1994; Pounds 1995.)

This section begins with the classification of security risks, followed by a review of the motives behind network break-ins and a description of some of the recent security attacks.

Classes of Security Risks

Security risks can be divided into three categories: breaching secret data, unauthorized logons, and unauthorized denial of service.

Breaching Secret Data

The first class of risks pertains to breaching the secrecy of confidential data. A breach of this sort implies that an unauthorized person has broken into and revealed confidential data. Confidential data is often stored or transmitted in encrypted form. A weak encryption scheme or lack of protection for encryption keys may lead to a breach of secret data.

These attacks may be initiated by an intruder who can use a sniffer on a network connection and record the data during transmission. Assuming the data is encrypted using some standard encryption scheme, the intruder has two choices. First, the intruder can try to break the encryption code by attempting every possible hexadecimal combination as the encryption key. This is called "brute force attack." As will be presented in Chapter 4, there are certain computational limits to a brute force attack. The second choice, which is more common, is to steal the encryption key. In order to make the encryption key available to the client and the server, it is often distributed over the network. Unless schemes for key transmissions are designed to be especially secure, the encryption key may be easily stolen.

Unauthorized Logons

The second class of risks is from unauthorized logons resulting from the misuse of stolen or guessed passwords. Unauthorized logons can also occur due to a lack of appropriate authentication. Authentication, as defined in next section, is the process of verifying the identity of an individual or a program. It is often accomplished by sharing a secret code, such as a password, between the individual and the verifying system. A common security attack occurs when a hacker steals the password and misuses it to intrude into a computer system. Once a hacker has stolen a password, the hacker can impersonate the legitimate owner of the password. For example, if the hacker has determined the password for the administrator, the hacker can start the break-in and impersonate the administrator. Protecting passwords and securing transmission of passwords over the network has been a subject of study for several years. Some of the commonly used authentication protocols are described in Chapter 2.

Denial of Service

The third class of risks pertains to the *denial of service*. In this type of attack, the hacker is interested in shutting down the computer system, degrading its performance, or consuming some of the resources such as memory. The attack results in a lack of availability of the computer system or its resources for many users. Such attacks are often accomplished by injecting a virus, a worm, or installing a software time bomb into the computer system. The topic of malicious software is addressed in Chapter 3.

There is another type of attack, called *network spoofing*, which has been used to inflict denial of service. Network spoofing occurs when one host on the network is used to impersonate another host. In a TCP/IP network, such as the Internet, no validation is required for the source address field of the packet. By changing the source address, the packet may appear to be coming from another host. The Internet experienced a network spoofing attack in early 1995, described later in this section.

Motives of Security Attacks

So far we have been lucky; most of the known security attacks have been disjointed and sporadic. The motives for these attacks have been varied. In general, there are four types of motives behind security attacks: industrial espionage, financial gains, revenge, and publicity.

The first type of motive behind security attacks is industrial espionage. Here, the attacker gets into a company's private files, searches for the desired secrets, and delivers them to a competitor. Industrial espionage is particularly a threat for companies that have products requiring long lead times for research and development. One of the goals for such an attack is to prevent the attacked site from finding out about the attack.

The drive for financial gains can also be a motive for security attacks. In this case, the attacker attempts to steal money or steal resources to make money. The number of these attacks continues to increase. A greedy employee can attempt to transfer money to his or her account. Credit card frauds and telephone frauds are also well-known attacks of this sort.

Revenge is yet another motive behind security attacks. A disgruntled employee can seek revenge by installing a software time bomb or virus before leaving the company. When the software bomb explodes or the virus executes, it destroys key resources of the company.

Finally, the fourth type of motive behind security attacks is to seek publicity. There have been attacks on the Internet by individuals or groups in an attempt to be publicly recognized or to display their skills to other individuals and groups.

Chronology of Break-ins

Many security attacks take place on networks, although not all are reported. According to the Computer Emergency Response Team at Carnegie Mellon University (CERTB 1995), they receive an average of three new computer security incidents every day. In the following section, some of the well-known attacks are reviewed. The first few attacks relate to computer break-ins, followed by some Internet break-ins.

Computer Break-ins

September 1985: Software Time Bomb

A disgruntled programmer planted a software time bomb in his former employer's computer after being fired. The bomb went off on September 21, 1985, and deleted 168,000 employment records of USPA and IRA Company, an insurance and investment firm. The programmer, Donald Gene Burleson, was sentenced to 7 years probation and an $11,800 fine.

1986: Brain Virus

This first full virus was created in 1986. It spread on pirated copies of Lotus 1-2-3 and WordPerfect. This virus replaced the contents of a PC disk (boot sector) with the virus code and labeled three clusters as bad in a file table.

1992: Computer Fraud

On December 3, 1992, Julio Fernandez and John Lee pleaded guilty in a New York court. Their charges included breaking into computers that control telephone and credit card records. This attack was solely for the purpose of financial gains for the attacker and resulted in significant financial losses to some companies. Southwestern Bell alone estimated their loss at approximately $370,000.

1993: TREMOR Virus

This virus first appeared in March 1993 and quickly became quite pervasive. TREMOR virus modifies itself as it replicates, thereby making it difficult to be detected. TREMOR is a memory-resident virus and infects COMMAND.COM and EXE files of DOS systems. It results in a decrease in the available memory, shakes the display, and grows COM and EXE files. Sometimes this virus displays the message "Moment-of-terror-is the-beginning-of-life."

1993: INKY Virus

The INKY virus is also a memory-resident virus and infects the floppy-disk boot sectors, resulting in boot failures. When the user tries to boot from an infected disk, the following message is displayed: "Non-system disk or disk error. Replace and press any key when ready...." If the user replaces the boot diskette by another nonwrite protected boot diskette, INKY will also infect the boot sectors of the new diskette.

August 1995: Bank Fraud

On August 17, 1995, U.S. prosecutors asked a London court to extradite Vladimir Levin, a head of system operations of a St. Petersburg trading company. The charges included tapping into Citibank's fund transfer system in Manhattan more than 40 times during the previous year and shifting at least $10 million to other bank accounts. All but $400,000 of the money was recovered.

The above information on computer break-ins was obtained from Wagner (1993) for the software time bomb and computer fraud and Caldwell (1995) for the bank fraud. The brain virus is described in Sullivan (1993); the INKY and TREMOR viruses were quoted in PC Week (December 27, 1993/January 1994, p 81) to Patricia Hoffman's VSUM Report. These references also have additional information on computer break-ins.

Internet Break-ins

The *Internet* started with the ARPA network in 1968, as shown in Figure 1.1. It continues to grow rapidly and is claimed to be the largest network in existence. With such growth, the Internet has been faced with two major problems: usability and security. As more businesses and services attach to the network, there is a need for better usability and improved security. The recent emergence of the *World Wide Web* along with the web browsers and servers has started to address the usability issue. The security on the Internet, however, remains a lingering concern. Several Internet work groups are addressing this issue, which includes the need to support secure commerce over the Internet.

November 1988: Internet Worm

On November 2, 1988, Internet users experienced one of the worst attacks. The attack, called the *Internet Worm*, was a self-replicating program that spread within hours to several computers on the Internet. It affected only VAX and SUN 3 systems running BSD 4 UNIX operating system. The Internet Worm was developed by Robert T. Morris, a graduate student at Cornell University. It exploited weaknesses in three TCP/IP applications: FINGERD, RHOST, and SENDMAIL. The total extent of the attack is not known, but thousands of systems were affected, many systems were shut down, and many others experienced severe performance degradation. Some estimates state that as many as 7000 hosts were affected.

A trial for this case was held in January 1990. Mr. Morris argued that this was not an attack with any malice; instead he wanted to prove some of the security holes in the Internet. He was convicted under the Computer Fraud and Abuse Act (1986) and was given 3 years probation, a $10,000 fine, and 400 hours of community service.

This attack was well publicized and resulted in an increased awareness of risks to network security in the computer and business community. The CERT organization was formed as a result of this event. The above description used information from Clark (1991, 64) and Sullivan (1993).

1989: The Hacker in "Cuckoo's Egg"

In August 1986, Cliff Stoll, an astronomer, detected an intruder from East Germany attempting to gain access to U.S. military data. Stoll was working as a system administrator after his astronomy grant had run out. He was trying to track an accounting error of 75 cents. Over a period of 10 months, the intruder attacked approximately 450 computers belonging to the U.S. military or its contractors and successfully gained access to 30 of them. It is estimated that prior to the detection, the intruder was mounting attacks for as long as 1 year.

In this case, the intruder was looking for sensitive and classified data in each of these systems. The intruder seemed to be an expert in the field and was searching for passwords and key technical terms in the files. In order to hide the attack, the intruder probed the systems through multiple entry points. The intruder appeared to have long-term plans, as he or she set a trapdoor in one instance that was used a year later.

The investigation involved several governments and agencies of many countries. Stoll published his book, *The Cuckoo's Egg*, in 1989. In addition to Stoll's book, the above description included information from Clark (1991, 62), which has a good summary of this break-in.

1993: New York City Break-in

In October 1993, the system administrator of a New York public-access UNIX system reported that the security of hundreds or thousands of sites on the Internet could be compromised.

In this case, the intruder had found a security hole in the program *SENDMAIL*. This program is the same as that used in the Internet Worm, except that this break-in used a different security hole. The intruder intercepted the logon traffic from the Panix Public Access Internet system in New York City and recorded all the users' IDs and their passwords. The intrusion was discovered when the system administrator stumbled into one of the intruder's log files.

The above description is based on (OST 1993, 19), which has additional information on this attack.

1995: Internet IP Spoofing Attack

On January 24, 1995, USA Today carried the headlines, "High-Tech Crooks Crack Internet Security" (Steve Marshall). It was reported that more than 50 sites were affected, including the San Diego Center for Supercomputing and Stanford Linear Accelerator Computing Center. CERT issued a warning dated January 23, 1995 on the IP Spoofing Attack.

The intruder gained access through a firewall by using a technique called *IP Source-Address Spoofing*. Every packet on the Internet has a source address and a destination address. Unlike the telephone system, there is no validation of the source address on the Internet. Because of this, a host can modify the source address of a packet and make it appear as if it is coming from another host. This technique is documented in a report by Robert Morris (father of Robert Morris of the Internet Worm described earlier) and can be retrieved by anonymous File Transfer Protocol (FTP) from *research.att.com*.

The spoofing attack exploits the applications that perform authentication based on IP addresses. The attack can result in an unauthorized access and possibly root access to the target system. This attack can be resisted through an Internet firewall by not allowing any packet from the Internet that has a source address of a host from inside the secured network. Details of this attack are presented in Chapter 7.

Besides the CERT advisory, Jolitz (1995) provides a good description of the details of this attack.

Security Concepts

This section presents some of the most important concepts in network security. It introduces the various components of network security along with requisite technologies and approaches; the details are addressed in the remaining chapters of the book. We begin with a description of the basic concepts in network security.

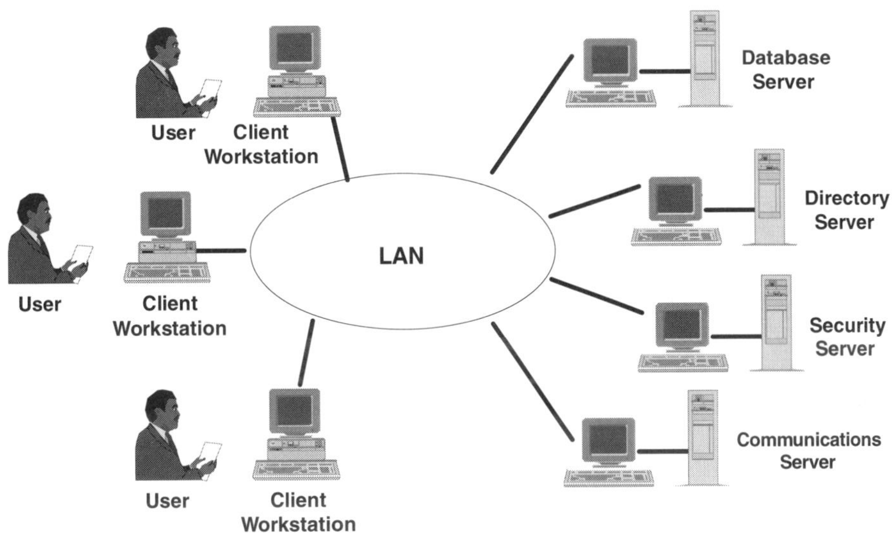

Figure 1.4: User Access to Servers

Identification

Users are identified to an application through a user identifier or *userid*. The userid is often referred to as simply ID. For the network shown in Figure 1.4, there may be one or more applications in each server. For each application, the user may have a different ID. Ideally, there should be one common ID for a given user to access all the applications in the network. However, a common ID requires coordination among users, system administrators, and security administrators.

Authentication

Authentication is the process used to verify the identity claimed by the user. This verification requires the exchange of shared secrets between the user and the application. Typically, this is a 6 or 8 character *password*. The user often memorizes the password or saves it securely. For the application, the password is saved in a secure database and made available to the application. The user sends the password to the application. The application verifies the user identity by comparing the received password with the password stored in its database for that userid.

Consider the network shown in Figure 1.4. The user logs on with the ID and the password at the workstation and intends to access the database. The database server receives the user's ID and the password. Next, the database server sends a request to the security server for verification of the user ID and the password. The security server compares the password from the database server with the password stored at the security server. If the two passwords match, then the security server informs the database server that the user is authenticated. If the passwords do not match, then the database server is informed to reject the logon. Alternatively, the authentication software may be integrated in the database server.

The above process for verifying the user identity is essentially a *one-way authentication*. This is true since the user is authenticated to the application, but the application is not authenticated to the user. When both the user and the application are authenticated to each other, it is called a *two-way authentication*. Two-way authentication is used to verify the identities of the two communicating entities.

Authorization

Authorization is the process of assigning access rights to each user (ID). The access rights include specification, such as whether the user is permitted to read, write, or update a given file.

Access Control

Access control pertains to the process of enforcing access rights for network resources. Access control grants or denies permission to a given user for accessing a resource and protects resources by limiting access to only authenticated and authorized users.

Access control is often specified by the system administrator or the owner of the resource. These specifications may include who can access the information in the resource, how it can be accessed, when it can be accessed, and under what conditions it can be accessed. For example, a user can access resources to modify the salary field only if it is being executed as part of a salary increase transaction initiated by the payroll change program.

Confidentiality

Confidentiality is the process used to protect secret information from unauthorized disclosure. Secret data needs to be protected when it is stored or when it is being transmitted over the network. When it is stored locally, such data can be protected by encryption or by enforcing access control. When secret data is to be transmitted over the network, it should be encrypted. The task of implementing encryption also requires secure distribution of the encryption keys to the sender and receiver of the encrypted data.

Data Integrity

Data integrity allows detection of unauthorized modification of data. Typically, data integrity detects whether the data has been modified during transmission. Such modification may be the result of an attack or a transmission error. Data integrity is accomplished by implementing a one-way hash function described in Chapter 4.

For the network of Figure 1.4, the secret files in the database server may be stored as encrypted text. In particular, the passwords at the security server must be stored as encrypted text in order to prevent theft of the passwords from the file. In addition, the passwords may be transmitted only as encrypted text or preferably not transmitted at all.

Nonrepudiation

Nonrepudiation is the capability to provide proof of the origin of data or proof of the delivery of data. It protects against any attempt by the sender to falsely deny sending the data, or the recipient to falsely deny receiving the data. Nonrepudiation is often required for handling commercial transactions over the Internet.

Denial of Service

A *denial of service* attack is one in which the attacker takes over or consumes a resource so that no one else can use it. Examples of such attacks include a virus consuming the memory of a system or an Internet attack where the attacking host takes over the legitimate host. Some of the denial-of-service attacks have been presented earlier in this chapter.

Secure Networks

A typical client/server network may include several end users with client workstations, a print server, a database server, a directory server, a security server, and a communication server for gateway to the Internet or other networks. The process of designing security for a typical client/server network consists of several steps. It includes authenticating the users, securing user workstations, defining and enforcing access control, implementing distributed security services, protecting the private network from unauthorized users on the Internet, and finally managing the security data as well as securing the management data. In the following, we outline the above aspects of network security. Additional details are provided in the remainder of the book in the corresponding chapters.

User Logon and Authentication: Chapter 2

To begin with, the end user needs to log on certain applications or servers in the network. As described earlier, the user must be authenticated using the ID and the password. Depending on the individual system, one of several authentication techniques can be implemented.

For each logon, the end user may be required to enter an ID and a password. There may be several servers and applications for a user to log on. For improved user productivity as well as network security, the security server should provide the user with the *single secure logon* feature.

The single secure logon works as follows. Consider an end user in the network depicted in Figure 1.4, and assume that there is more than one database server or application in this client/ server network. With single secured logon, the user logs on once to the security server by entering the ID and the password. The security server checks the ID and the corresponding password. Assuming that the password is correct, the user is presented a selection screen to choose a server (or application) for logon, and the user simply selects the desired server (or application). Subsequently, the user can go back to the selection screen and log on another server, without requiring reentry of IDs or passwords, and possibly without requiring retransmission of the password to each server.

Workstation Security: Chapter 3

Besides user authentication and single logon for the network, the end user's client workstation must also be adequately secured. There are a variety of problems associated with securing the client workstation.

First, there needs to be a screen lock that locks the screen when the user steps away for a long time. This mechanism ensures that an intruder cannot walk up to the workstation and access user data or open sessions. Next, if it is a multiuser workstation, it should provide partitioned access to its resources. For example, Tom and Sally both can log on the same UNIX machine, but Tom should not be able to access Sally's files. So a multiuser capability on workstations should ensure secured environments for each of its users. Finally, the workstation should be protected from viruses.

Distributed Security: Chapter 4

For a client/server network, such as the one in Figure 1.4, there may be several distributed applications. A distributed application may consist of two or more components residing in one or more systems. For these application components to communicate securely with each other, the network must provide access to security services such as data confidentiality and data integrity. The security services are often provided through an Application Programming Interface. Alternatively, the security services may be built into the communications access. Finally, the network must also provide for transmission and distribution of security data such as encryption keys and passwords.

Access Control: Chapter 5

Now consider the access from an end user to the files in local workstations or remote servers. The access control mechanism in each workstation and server should enforce access control and associated access rights for all of network resources. Furthermore, the access control rules should be enforced consistently across the entire network.

Internet Security: Chapters 6 and 7

Given the widespread use of the Internet, it is conceivable that many private networks will need to access the Internet to obtain information. Along with this attachment, there are the risks of attacks by hackers on the Internet. To protect from such attacks, a private network requires a specific type of gateway server, called a *firewall*. A firewall provides a secure barrier between a private network and the Internet.

As usage of the Internet grows, it is also expected to offer significant commerce. Commercial transactions over the Internet require secure transfer of sensitive information, such as credit card number or digital cash. In addition, there is the requirement for digital signature or nonrepudiation to avoid fraud over the Internet. Finally, users may also require security for their electronic mail (E-mail) over the Internet.

Security Management: Chapter 8

Implementation of the above security mechanisms is not sufficient to ensure that the network is secure. A secure network requires a coordinated policy and rules that are consistently enforced across the network. These policies require identification of critical assets or resources, a risk analysis to determine the areas of security exposure for these resources, and defining rules and procedures to address these exposures.

Finally, there is a need for coordinated management of security information for a given client/server network. *Security management* includes coordinating the various security databases including the IDs, passwords, access control lists, and access rights for the users across the network. Another aspect of security management pertains to securing management data such as Simple Network Management Protocol (SNMP) data units.

Evolution of Security Technologies

The challenges for the security industry are growing. Security technologies should be easy to implement and easy to use. With the electronic commerce spreading over the Internet, there are issues such as nonrepudiation to be solved. Financial institutions will have both technical concerns, such as the security of a credit card number or banking information, and legal concerns for holding individuals responsible for their actions such as their purchases or sales over the Internet. Issuance and management of encryption keys (or certificates, described later) for millions of users will pose a new type of challenge.

While some technologies have been developed, only an industry-wide effort and cooperation can minimize risks and ensure privacy for users, data confidentiality for the financial institutions, and nonrepudiation for electronic commerce.

With the continuing growth in linking individuals and businesses over the Internet, some social issues are starting to surface. The society may take time in adapting to the new concept of transacting business over the Internet. Consumers may take time to trust the network and accept it as a substitute for transacting business in person. Another class of concerns relates to restricting access over the Internet. Preventing distribution of pornography and other objectionable material over the Internet has already been in the news. We can expect new social hurdles over time and hope the great benefits of the Internet will continue to override these hurdles through new technologies and legislations.

Summary

Before presenting the concepts in security, it is important to give the readers a perspective on networking and network security. We began with a historical perspective on networking, followed by a review of the break-ins and the motives behind the break-ins. Network security is a broad topic, but there are some important concepts that help clarify the various risks and approaches to addressing those risks. We have presented those concepts here and will use them throughout the book. Another important purpose of this chapter was to provide the reader with an overview of the remainder of the book by relating various security concepts and issues to the chapter numbers.

Logon and Authentication

2

In this chapter, we present the various aspects of the logon process. In order to cover this broad topic, we include discussions on several related areas including passwords, authentication schemes, and approaches for single logon to multiple systems.

Logon Process

The user *logon* process begins with the user entering an identification (ID), followed by an exchange to verify the identity of the user.

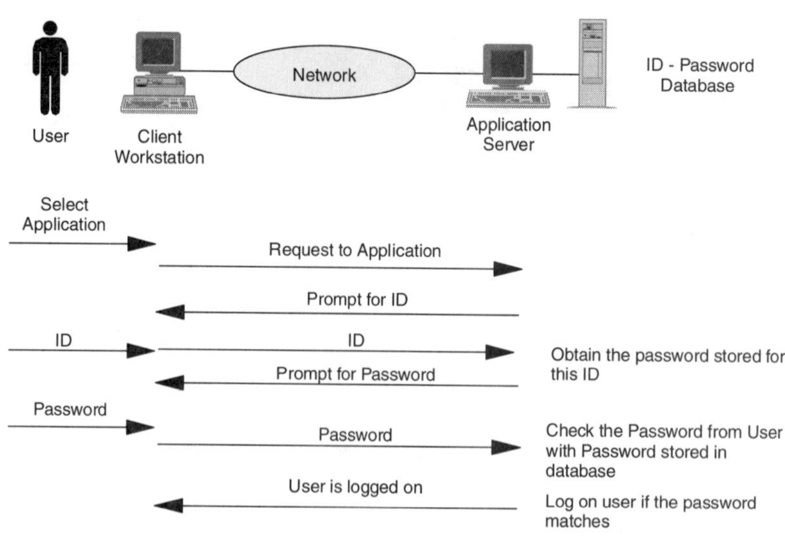

Figure 2.1: Basic Logon and Authentication Sequence

The basic exchange between the user at the client workstation and the application server is shown in Figure 2.1. First, the user selects the desired application to log on. The application prompts the user to enter an identifier (ID); the user enters the ID. Upon receiving the ID, the application prompts the user to enter the password. The user sends the password to the application. The application uses the ID to index into the application's database of IDs and passwords. Now the application compares the password it received from the user to the one retrieved from its ID-password database. If the two match, the user is logged on to the application; otherwise the application informs the user that the password or the ID is invalid.

The preceding description outlines the underlying exchange of information for the logon process. There are several security-related aspects of the user logon process. The following section presents an overview of some of the shared secrets for authenticating users. Another important objective for an authentication scheme is to secure the passwords during transmission or storage. Following the next section, we present the topics of password security and authentication procedures including the use of public key schemes. Finally, we discuss the approaches that offer single logon for user.

Authentication

According to Webster's Dictionary (Woolf 1977, 75), the word *authentic* means *being actually and precisely what is claimed to be*. Authentication is the process of verifying something, such as a user's identity, a network address, or the integrity of a data string. Furthermore, authentication establishes an association between two entities. For example, a client is authenticated to a server, so the client can access authorized services from the server, as shown in Figure 2.1.

In computer networks, users can be authenticated based on one or more of the following:

- Something the user knows
- Something the user has
- Something the user is

These secrets should be shared only between the user and the system. By presenting one of these secrets, a user can assure the system that he or she is a legitimate user.

Something User Knows

Users are often given a secret to memorize, such as a password. The password should be known only to the user and the system. A user can log on the system by entering the ID and password, as described earlier and shown in Figure 2.1.

Something User Has

Users may be given items such as keys, badges or other devices. These devices, in turn, help the system to authenticate the users. Users may also be given a hand-held device to be used during authentication. These devices are the size of a calculator or a credit card and consist of a processor and a display. There are many other kinds of user authentication schemes that deal with something the user has. A few of these are described below.

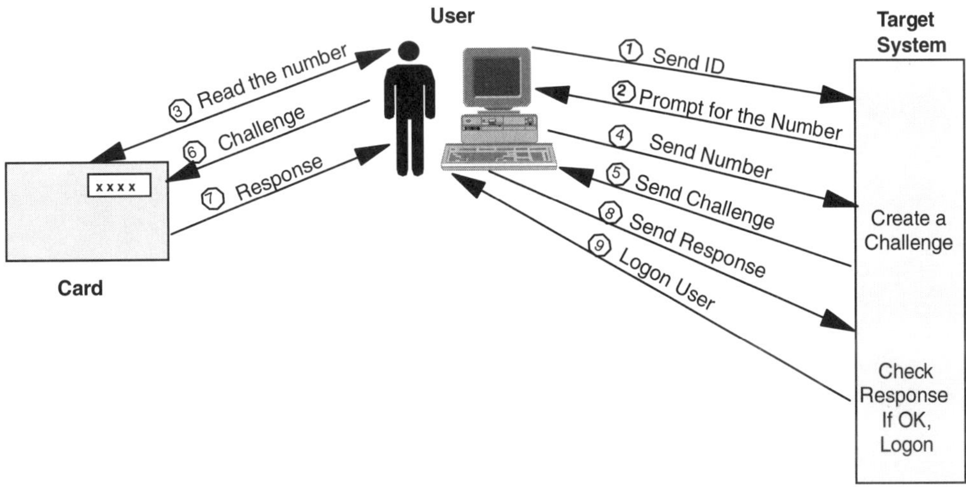

Figure 2.2: Challenge-Response Sequence.
User intends to log on to target system

Challenge-Response Authentication

In *challenge-response authentication*, the user is provided with a card. The card displays a number at all times; this number changes over time. Suppose a user wants to log on a target system. First, the target system authenticates the user. This authentication process is shown in Figure 2.2 and consists of the following steps:

1. The user sends his or her ID to the target system.

2. The system prompts the user to enter a number.

3. The user reads the number from the card.

4. The user sends the number to the system.

5. The system validates the ID with the number it received from the user. Assuming the ID and the number are valid, the system generates a number and displays it to the user. This is called a *challenge*.

6. The user enters the above challenge into the card.

7. The card calculates a number using this input and displays the result to the user. This is called the *response*.

8. The user sends this response to the system.

9. The system verifies whether the response is correct. If so, the user is authenticated and logged on to the system.

Digital Pathways Inc. markets a scheme similar to the challenge-response exchange.

Token Cards

In this approach, the user is given a *token card* that shares a secret key with the system. This key is called the *shared secret key*. The card displays a number that changes over time and uses the shared secret key. In some cases, the system clock is also (approximately) synchronized with the clock on the token card. The user authentication is achieved as follows.

1. The user provides the system with the identifier (ID) along with the number displayed by the token card.

2. The system computes a number using the received ID and the shared secret key.

3. If the number calculated by the system matches that entered by the user, then the user is accepted as the legitimate user and the authentication process is completed.

In order to enhance the security, the user may also be required to memorize a secret code, often called the *PIN* (personal identification number). In this case, the user is also required to enter the PIN to the system or on the card. The advantage of this scheme is that a lost token card cannot be misused by a hacker, since the hacker must also know the PIN.

The details of one such scheme are described in the next section under the topic of one-time passwords.

Something User Is

Every user has some unique physiological and behavioral characteristics that can be recorded and compared. In this approach, a particular characteristic of the user is observed and recorded by the system. Subsequently, the user is authenticated by observing the selected characteristic of the user and comparing it with that stored in the system.

There are two types of characteristics of interest for user authentication. The first are the *physiological characteristics* which include fingerprints, handprints and retinal patterns. The second are the *behavioral characteristics* such as vocal patterns, signature, and keystroke typing patterns.

Fingerprints are one of the most common characteristics used to authenticate individual users. Furthermore, fingerprints, and other physiological characteristics, can also help identify the hackers. In this scheme, the system records all the attempts by users to log on the system. As a result, all of the unsuccessful attempts are also recorded. Consequently, the system can identify the fingerprints of the persons attempting to break into the system.

For the behavioral characteristics, an *electronic signature* of the user is created and stored. The electronic signature may be a record of the keyboard typing pressure or the pen pressure while writing a specific word. For example, consider the keyboard typing pattern of each user. When the user first logs on, the user is required to enter the ID and the password a few times. Based on this, the user's typing pattern, such as the pressure on individual keys, is recorded as the electronic signature of the user. Subsequently when a user initiates a logon, the typing pattern is compared to the one stored under that user ID's electronic signature.

There are two types of errors that can result from the use of behavioral characteristics. The first type of error is *false positive*, where an individual is erroneously authenticated. The second type of error is *false negative*, where a valid user is erroneously rejected.

Authenticating users by verifying their behavioral or physiological characteristics has not yet gained significant popularity. At the present time, this approach is used in conjunction with password-based authentication. Such a two-stage authentication provides a higher level of security than that provided by either of the two approaches. Additional information on biometric systems is available in Russell (1991, 246).

Passwords

For several years, passwords have been used to authenticate users or applications. Although there are some exposures to password security, passwords are still by far the most commonly used authentication tool of choice.

Passwords may be compromised in two ways. First, the password can be stolen during transmission over the network. A password can also be stolen from the database where it is stored. The topic of protecting passwords is presented later in this section.

Second, a hacker can try to guess the password and use some type of attack to log on using the guessed password. A brute force dictionary attack includes attempting to match every available word against the secret password.

A hacker may also create a list of potential words that are likely to be used as the password. A portion of this list would be unique for each user and may include user's initials, names or initials of his or her immediate family members or friends, street or city names of their addresses, and dates of births or weddings. This list of potential passwords may also include names of sports, players, singers, politicians, TV stars, and movies. Many passwords can be guessed by using some of the personal information about the user.

Password Guessing

Klein has analyzed the ease with which individual passwords can be guessed. As described in Klein (1990), he collected lists of passwords from several of his friends, totaling approximately 15,000 passwords. Next, he collected the potential words to match the passwords by using the following steps:

1. List user's name, initials, account name, and other relevant personal information as a possible password. In all, he tried up to 130 different passwords for each user.

2. List words from various dictionaries including men's and women's names and their permutations; places; names of famous people; cartoons and cartoon characters; titles, characters, and locations from films and science fiction stories; sports names and terms; etc. He discarded all the duplicate entries. In all, he had a total of more than 60,000 separate words considered per user.

3. Include various permutations on the words from step 2.

4. List various capitalization permutations from step 2 that were not considered in step 3. For example, *michael* would also be checked as *mIchael*, *MIchael*, *mIcHael*, etc. The single-letter capitalization added 400,000 words to the list, and the various two-letter permutations of capitalized letters added another 1,500,000 words.

5. List foreign language words for foreign users.

6. List word pairs. This would increase the list by the order of 10^7, so this test was only partially executed.

The results of his tests are tabulated in Table 2.1. Table 2.2 lists the lengths of cracked passwords.

Type of Password	Size of Dictionary	Duplicates Eliminated	Search Size	# of Matches	Pct. of Total	Cost/ Benefit Ratio
User/account name	130*	–	130	368	2.7%	2.830
Character sequences	866	0	866	22	0.2%	0.025
Numbers	450	23	427	9	0.1%	0.021
Chinese	398	6	392	56	0.4%	0.143
Place names	665	37	628	82	0.6%	0.131
Common names	2268	29	2239	548	4.0%	0.245
Female names	4955	675	4280	161	1.2%	0.038
Male names	3901	1035	2866	140	1.0%	0.049
Uncommon names	5559	604	4955	130	0.9%	0.026
Myths & legends	1357	111	1246	66	0.5%	0.053
Shakespearean	650	177	473	11	0.1%	0.023
Sports terms	247	9	238	32	0.2%	0.134
Science fiction	772	81	691	59	0.4%	0.085
Movies and actors	118	19	99	12	0.1%	0.121
Cartoons	133	41	92	9	0.1%	0.098
Famous people	509	219	290	55	0.4%	0.190
Phrases and patterns	998	65	933	253	1.8%	0.271
Surnames	160	127	33	9	0.1%	0.273
Biology	59	1	58	1	0.0%	0.017
/user/dict/words	24474	4791	19683	1027	7.4%	0.052
Machine names	12983	3965	9018	132	1.0%	0.015
Mnemonics	14	0	14	2	0.0%	0.143
King James bible	13062	5537	7525	83	0.6%	0.011
Miscellaneous words	8146	4934	3212	54	0.4%	0.017
Yiddish words	69	13	56	0	0.0%	0.000
Asteroids	3459	1052	2407	19	0.1%	0.007
Total	**86280**	**23553**	**62727**	**3340**	**24.2%**	**0.053**

*Number of matches/search size

Table 2.1: Password Cracked from a Sample Set of 13,797 Accounts

Length	Count	Percentage
1 character	4	0.1%
2 characters	5	0.2%
3 characters	66	2.0%
4 characters	188	5.7%
5 characters	317	9.5%
6 characters	1160	34.7%
7 characters	813	24.4%
8 characters	780	23.4%

Table 2.2: Length of Cracked Passwords

Source for Table 2.1 and Table 2.2: "Foiling the Cracker: A Survey of, and Improvements to, Passward Security," Daniel V. Kline. UNIX Security Workshop, Portland, OR. 1990. Page 10, 11. Reprinted with permission from the USENIX Association, 1995.

Klein had access to four DECstation 3100s, each of which was capable of checking approximately 750 passwords per second. In all, approximately 25 percent of all the passwords were cracked after nearly 12 CPU months. However, 21 percent (nearly 3000 passwords) were guessed within the first week, and 2.7 percent (368 passwords) were guessed in the first 15 minutes.

In the world of password guessing, while the security technology is trying to innovate ways to make it harder to guess passwords, the computing technology is making it easier and faster to attempt long lists of words as potential passwords.

Klein's results demonstrate the ease with which passwords can be guessed using information about the user. We can also analyze the general probability of guessing the passwords. The probability of guessing a given password is simply:

$$P = \frac{L \times R}{S}$$

where P is the probability of guessing a given password, L is the password lifetime (see password aging later), R is the ratio to guess, i.e., the number of tries or guesses per unit of time; and S is the password space. So the probability of guessing a password decreases as the size of the password space increases.

For passwords of length k characters, and N as the size of alphabet, the password space is

$$S = N^k$$

Figure 2.3 shows the value of password space, S, for the size of alphabet, N, to be 10 (digits, 0–9), 26 (alphabets, A–Z), and 36 (digits or alphabets, 0–9, A–Z). If we allow hexadecimal passwords (that is, binary numbers), then the value of S for an 8-character (64-bit) password is 2^{64}. There are certain usability considerations in requiring users to remember hexadecimal passwords. Hexadecimal passwords are hard to memorize and hard to enter. So in order to remember such a password, users often have to write the password on a piece of paper or save it on some device. But for critical situations such as for use by system administrators, where security is a higher priority than usability, hexadecimal passwords may be the right choice.

Morris and Thompson (1979, 594–597) discuss the password security for UNIX systems and approaches to improve it.

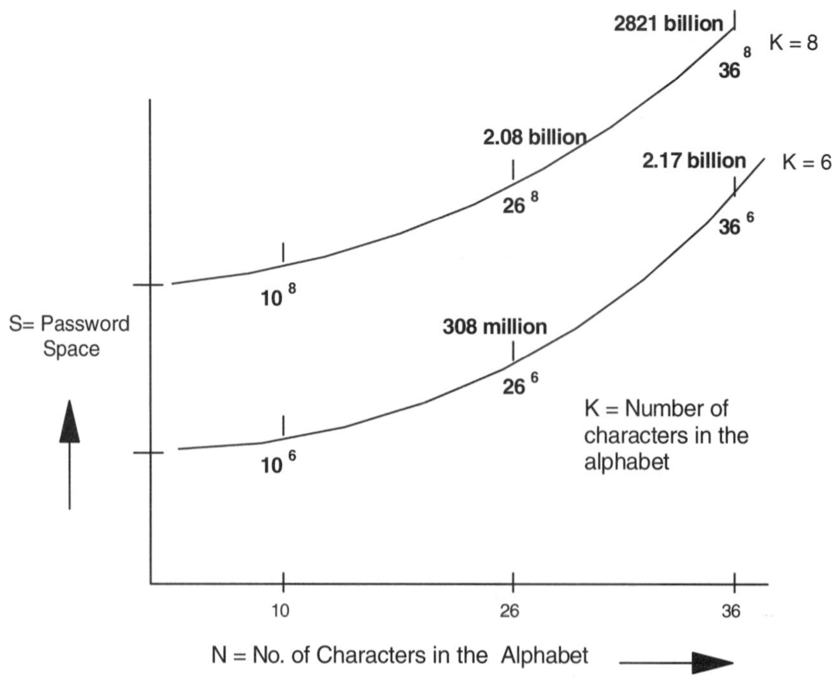

Figure 2.3: Password Space vs. Alphabet Size

Password Protection Strategies

As stated earlier, passwords should be hard to guess and difficult to steal. *Password protection* has been one of the key areas of research and analysis. Techniques to protect passwords range from imposing selection rules for passwords to rejecting passwords that can be easily guessed. These techniques can be classified in three categories. The first category describes some of the important password controls such as password selection and maintenance. The second category describes techniques to prevent password guessing by rejecting passwords that can be easily guessed. The third category describes strategies for securely storing passwords.

Password Controls

Passwords can be protected by imposing certain controls on the usage, maintenance, and changes of passwords.

System Messages

Most systems display a greeting message before and after a user logs on the system. Such messages often identify the system, thereby providing a clue to the intruder on the type of system being accessed. As such, these systems should provide an option to the system administrator to suppress these messages. In addition, the password should not be displayed during the time of entry. Otherwise, a bystander can look over the user's shoulder and read the password.

Limited Attempts

Many systems restrict the number of consecutive unsuccessful attempts to log on; typically this limit is set at 3 or 6. When the limit is reached, the system locks out the particular user ID and denies any more logon attempts. A locked-out user ID is reinstated only after the user has been authenticated to the system administrator through some other means than the password. In this way, a hacker cannot try a brute force attack to log on, since the system will lock that ID after the first few attempts. In addition, the system should also record all the unsuccessful attempts for further investigation.

Password Aging

Password aging implies that each password has a fixed lifetime, after which the password must be changed. Furthermore, most systems also allow users to change a password any time during this interval. For example, if a user suspects that someone has obtained his or her password, the user should be allowed to change the password without requiring any communication with the administrator.

Many systems do not allow a user to select the new password from one of the passwords most recently used by that user.

The system administrator should also have the authority to cancel an existing password, in order to respond to a security threat.

Two-Password Systems

Certain systems require more than one password to gain access to sensitive information. First, the user is prompted to enter a password at logon time. During the session, the user may choose to access some sensitive information. To allow that access, the system may require the user to enter another password.

Minimum Length

Since short passwords are easier to guess than long ones, many systems require that the passwords must be of a minimum length. Usually, passwords are required to be at least 6 or 8 characters long. The relationship of password length to the probability of guessing the password was provided earlier in this chapter.

User Lockouts

This feature allows the system administrator to lock out an ID that has not been used for a certain amount of time or that has not changed the password within the specified time limit. A locked-out user ID is reinstated only after that user has been authenticated to the system administrator through some means other than the password.

Root Password Protection

The *root password* is uniquely assigned to the system administrator for authentication. Since the administrator has significantly more access rights than a typical user, the root password is a common target of attack by hackers. As such, special precautions should be taken in selecting and communicating the root password. For example, it may be required that the root password must be a hexadecimal character string, as described earlier in this section. In addition, the root password should not be transmitted over the network and should be changed more frequently, such as once every week.

I once heard of an attack on an Internet firewall in a conference in January 1995. During late 1994, a firewall was attacked from the Internet side. The attacker tried various commonly used words and finally succeeded in guessing the root password. Given that the root password gave the hacker access as the administrator of the firewall, security of a large portion of the network was exposed.

System-Generated Passwords

Some systems do not rely on the user to select a *difficult-to-guess password*. These systems generate one or more passwords for the user that are difficult to guess as well as easy to remember. The user is allowed to pick one of the proposed passwords.

The first challenge for such an approach is to create easy-to-remember and difficult-to-guess passwords. For passwords that are not easy to remember, users may often write the password on a piece of paper, which in turn may compromise the security of the password. Another potential risk with this approach is that if the password generation algorithm is stolen, it may risk the security of a large portion of the network.

According to Russell (1991, 64), the VAX/VMS Version 4.3 system ensures that these passwords are pronounceable.

Password Checking: Reactive

Password checking can be performed in two ways. Passwords can be checked by running a program at frequent intervals. This *cracker* program can compare the existing passwords against a list of easily guessed passwords. The system cancels all the passwords that are found "guessable," and the users are informed.

In a tutorial I gave at ComNet in January 1995 on security, an attendee stated that they had run a password cracker program that could guess approximately half the passwords. This approach is called *reactive password checking*, since the passwords are checked after they have been entered and are already in use.

Raleigh and Underwood (1988) outline a password system called *CRACK*. This is used as a network service to test passwords. The service receives requests to crack a given password and responds with an indication that the password is crackable, along with the requisite level of cracking. Systems subscribing to the service notify users whose passwords have been broken to change them when they log on again.

Spafford (1992) describes the OPUS project at Purdue University. This project is an attempt to screen users' selection of passwords and prevent poor choices, with a focus on providing efficiency in disk space and time for workstations as well as mainframes.

There are certain drawbacks with a reactive password checking approach. First, this approach is resource intensive, since an attacker is going to comparably devote dedicated CPU for several hours and days to steal the passwords. This puts the cracker program at a disadvantage. Second, any existing passwords that are guessable remain vulnerable until the cracker program is executed and the user has changed the password.

Password Checking: Proactive

In this password checking scheme, the user is prompted to select a password. At the time of first entry of the password by the user, the system checks the password by executing an algorithm. The algorithm provides the indication if the password is easily guessable. The system rejects each of the guessable passwords and prompts the user to enter another password.

For such an algorithm, an important design consideration is to balance between usability and security (which is true for most security algorithms). If the algorithm is very restrictive, it will reject too many passwords, leading to user complaints that it is too hard to create an acceptable password. If the algorithm accepts most of the passwords, then it may make it easier for the hackers to guess the passwords and possibly the algorithm.

Next, an approach is outlined for designing a *proactive password checking* algorithm. The approach uses as input a list of common words that could be used for a brute force attack. Using this list, the proposed password is checked against the list. If the password is in the list, the proposed password is rejected. While this approach is feasible, the list can grow to be fairly large. Besides requiring large storage space for the list, it would also cost significant processing time to check a password against the list. An alternative to this approach is to develop a matrix of probabilities of occurrences of alphabet sequences. Then this probability matrix is used to obtain the probability of guessing the proposed password.

Additional details of approaches for proactive password checking can be found in Stallings (1995, 220-224).

Secure Password Storage

Every system has to provide for the storage and maintenance of its authentication data. Passwords are often stored using encryption. *Encryption* transforms the original password into a random set of bits that cannot be interpreted by an intruder. In order to decipher an encrypted password, the intruder requires the encryption algorithm and the encryption key. While most algorithms are available in public, the encryption key should be known only to the system administrator.

Many system use the *one-way hash* scheme for storing passwords. The password is stored after performing a one-way hash function (described in Chapter 4) on the password, as depicted in Figure 2.4. So even if the password is stolen, it is not available as clear text. This *one-way encryption* also implies that the original password cannot be derived from the encrypted password. So, in effect, a one-way encrypted password cannot be decrypted. On receiving a password from a user, the system first performs the same one-way hash function on the received password and obtains the encrypted password. Next, the system retrieves the encrypted password that is stored in the password database for this user (ID). Now the system compares the two encrypted passwords. If there is a match, the user is logged on to the system; otherwise the logon request is rejected. Note that the encrypted password is never decrypted during this process.

In this case, while the encrypted password cannot be decrypted, it can still be replayed. Such a replay can be prevented by adding another parameter to be sent from the user workstation to the system during the logon process. Such a parameter can be a random number or a time-based number generated by the workstation. Later, the receiving system can send the random number to the workstation for verification.

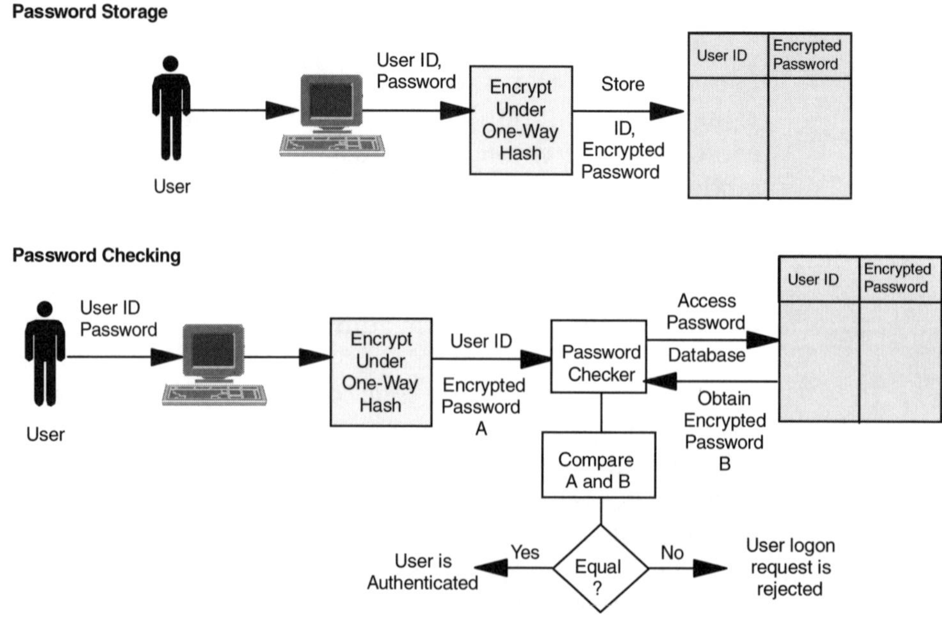

**Figure 2.4: Password Storage and Checking
Using One-Way Hash Function**

Password Storage In Unix Systems

Let us review a scheme commonly used to store passwords in
UNIX systems. The password is not stored in the clear; instead
the following scheme is employed.

A user selects an 8-character password. This password is converted into a 56-bit key, using 7-bit ASCII (7 bits for each character). This 56-bit string is then used as the key input to an
encryption algorithm. The encryption algorithm is based on
DES (Data Encryption Standard), described in Chapter 4. The

E-table (see Chapter 4) for the DES algorithm is modified using a 12-bit *salt* value (a value typically related to the time at which the password is assigned to the user). This modified DES is executed with the data input of a 64-bit block of zeros.

The output of this algorithm is used as the input for a second encryption. This process is repeated 25 times. The resulting 64-bit string is then coerced into an 11-character sequence using 64-character alphabet (A–Z, a–z, 0–9, ".", "/"), by mapping several bit values into the same character. Since this conversion is mapping many values to one, it is not reversible. So the 64-bit string cannot be derived from this character sequence. This encrypted password and the salt value are stored in the password database for the corresponding user ID, as shown in Figure 2.5. Although for convenience we called this string the encrypted password, the password was used only as the key to encrypt a bit string that started with all zeros.

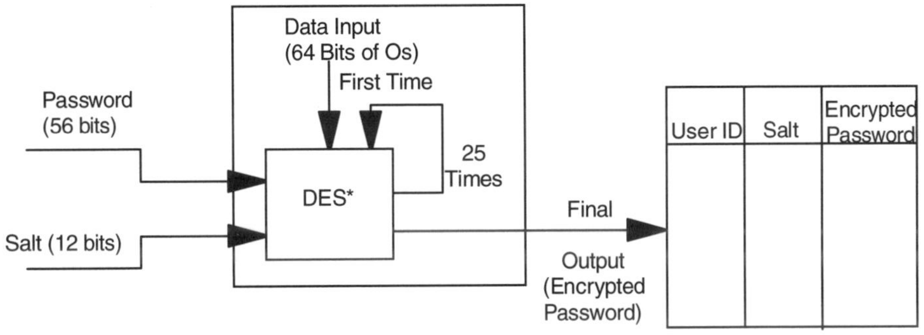

Figure 2.5: UNIX Password Storage

While initiating the logon process, the user provides the ID and the *plaintext password*. The UNIX system uses the user ID to index into the password database and retrieves the encrypted password and the salt value for that ID. The system then uses the plaintext password (received from the user) along with the salt value to execute the above encryption scheme. The resulting encrypted password is compared with the one retrieved for this ID from the password database. If the two passwords match, the user is authenticated and logged on; otherwise the logon request is rejected, as shown in Figure 2.6.

The use of salt provides certain benefits. First, if two users select the same password, it will still result in different encrypted passwords. This is true because the salt value is based on time; so the two users with the same password will still have different salt values, leading to different encrypted passwords. Second, the length of the password is effectively increased by two additional characters of salt value, without requiring the user to memorize two additional characters.

For additional details of this topic, see Stallings (1995, 214) and Curry (1992, 147–148).

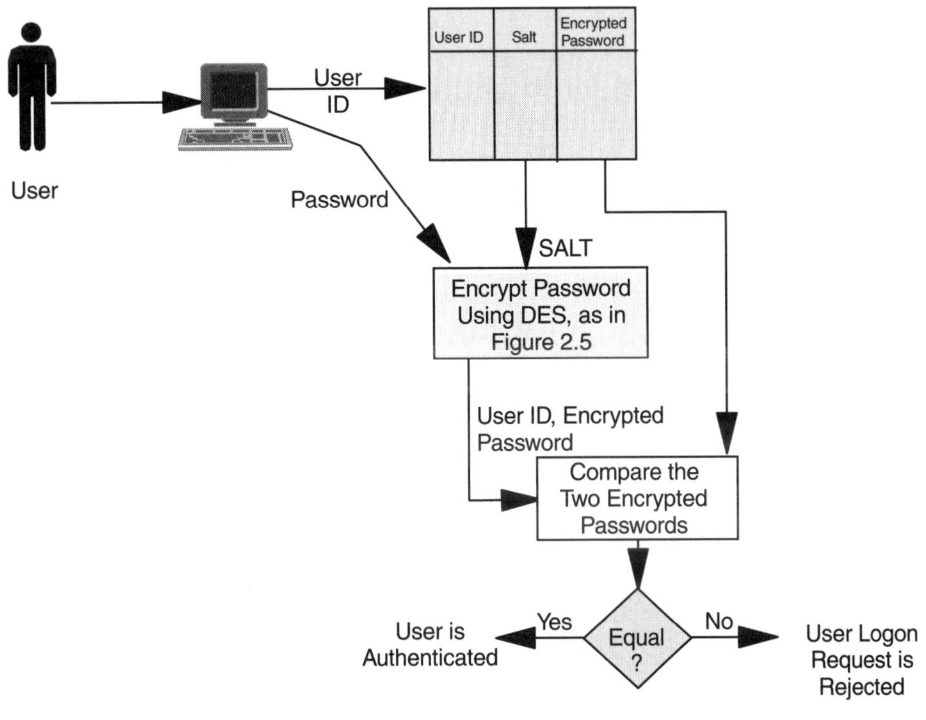

Figure 2.6: UNIX Password Checking

Brute Force Attack

In certain ways, password cracking is a computational challenge! Stallings (1995, 215) describes one of the fastest password crackers. Quoting (J. Madsen, "World Record in Password Checking," Usenet, comp.security.misc newsgroup, August 18, 1993), a performance of 1560 encryptions per second was achieved on a parallel computer from Thinking Machines Corporation. Using 4 vector units per processing node, it comes to 800,000 encryptions per second for a 128-node machine and 6.4 million encryptions per second for 1024-node machine. Even these rates are not sufficient to launch a brute force attack for deciphering user passwords. For example, for an 8-character password using an alphabet size of 36 (36 for A–Z and 0–9, while ignoring the lowercase letters), there are 36^8 or 2821 billion combinations. In the above case, we concluded that the fast machine would yield approximately 6.4 million encryptions per second, while it would require approximately 25 encryptions to check each possible combination for the password. As such, it would take approximately 4 seconds to check 1 million combinations for a password. Then for 2821 billion combinations, it should take approximately 4 months to launch a brute force attack

One-Time Passwords Using Token Cards

The concept of *one-time password* is based on generating passwords that can be used only once. After its first use, the one-time password becomes invalid. As such, theft of such passwords is of no significance to the network. The one-time passwords are essentially pseudorandom numbers generated at the client workstation and verified at the target server.

One-time passwords can be generated in software, such as in a security server. One such scheme works with using a *third-party authentication* scheme. The topic of secure single logon using software-generated one-time passwords is described at the end of this chapter.

Now consider the one-time passwords generated by hand-held devices. This approach is based on the concept that traditional passwords, if stolen, can be replayed and thereby expose the

network security. To avoid this exposure, the password is generated from a token card possessed by the user.

Consider the network shown in Figure 2.7. To begin with, the
individual user possesses a *token card*. The token card is of the
size of a credit card or a pocket calculator and contains a processor that generates and displays a code at fixed time intervals
such as every minute. Each token card generates its own
unique sequence of codes; this code is used as the one-time
password.

Besides the token card, the user may also be provided with a
PIN (personal identification number). In this case, the user
needs to enter the PIN through a keypad on the card. The processor on the card uses the PIN to compute a code, and the
code is displayed to the user. The user enters this code in the
system as the one-time password. An alternative approach is to
enter the PIN as an extension to the password.

At setup time, the token card is initialized with the user verification software located in the server. The target application
receives the user ID and the one-time password. The application contacts the user verification software at the server with
the ID and the one-time password. The verification code determines if the user has entered the correct ID and one-time password. If the one-time password is valid, then the user is logged
on to the server application.

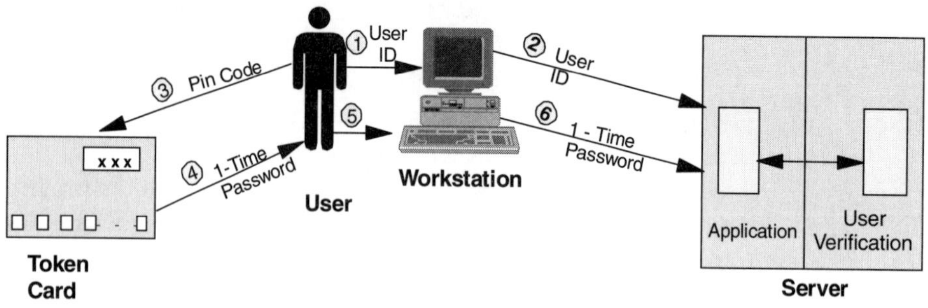

Figure 2.7: Token Card Authentication

There are several benefits to this approach. First, the one-time password changes frequently, such as once every minute. So, if this password is stolen, it cannot be legitimately reused after 60 seconds. Second, the user must enter the PIN, which is known only to the user. Therefore, even if the user loses the token card, the hacker cannot misuse the token card since the hacker does not know the PIN.

The above description is based on the approach used by Security Dynamics Inc., which markets a SecureID card. Optionally, the SecureID card also offers a keypad to allow the user to enter the PIN on the token card. Note that even the administrator does not need to be aware of the PINs assigned to the users. There are other variations by different vendors. In some cases, the user may engage in a challenge-response sequence with the token card, as described earlier in this chapter.

Johnson and Tolly (1995) provide an extensive overview of token authentication schemes.

Authentication Procedures

"Who are you?"
"I am your new chef, Sir!"
"How good is your cooking?"
"I am what I am Sir."
"Are You?"

Authentication is the process of verifying the identity of a user. This section addresses the procedures used to verify the identity of a user. These procedures assume that the user or the process is in possession of a password that is shared between a user and an application or a system.

In a given distributed network, clients as well as servers need to be authenticated. Consider a network where a user A needs to request services from server S. Then user A has to be authenticated to the server S, and optionally, the server S has to be authenticated to user A. This is called *two-party authentication* and is shown in Figure 2.8.

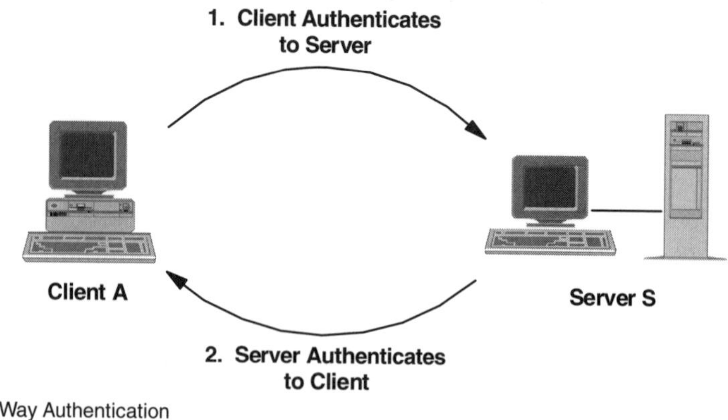

Figure 2.8: Two-Party Authentication

As described earlier, many environments require a trusted third party for authentication. This third party ensures the identities of the client and the server. It is often called a *security server* that provides storage for the passwords and uses these stored passwords to verify the identities of the users and servers. This is called *third-party authentication*. Procedures for achieving two-party authentication are presented below, followed by various schemes for third-party authentication.

Two-Party Authentication

Two-party authentication is used for achieving *one-way authentication* as well as *two-way authentication*.

One-Way Authentication

Consider the simple case in which a user wishes to log on to a host application. In this case, let us assume that only the user needs to be authenticated to the application. Therefore, the host application is not to be authenticated to the user. Then the authentication procedure simply involves the user sending his or her ID and the password to the application. The application verifies the password for the received ID, thereby authenticating the user. One-way authentication accomplishes the following:

1. It confirms that the application has authenticated the user's ID.

2. It assures the application that the ID and password was indeed sent by the legitimate user (no one else has the user's password).

This one-way authentication is shown in Figure 2.9.

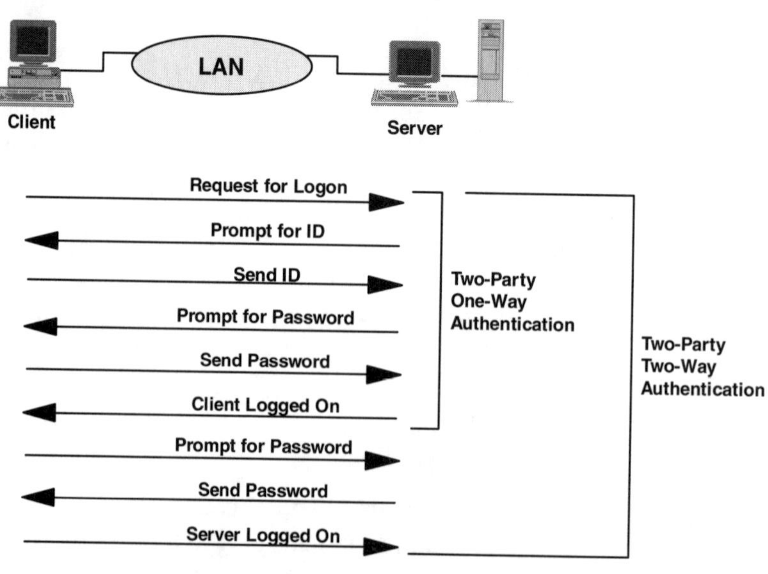

**Figure 2.9: Two-Party One-Way Authentication
and Two-Party Two-Way Authentication**

Two-Way Authentication

For two-party two-way authentication, both parties are authenticated to each other. This is also shown in Figure 2.9. So in
addition to the two items listed under one-way authentication,
two-way authentication also accomplishes the following:

3. The server has also been authenticated to the user.

4. The password for the server was sent by the legitimate server (since no one else has the server's password).

The two-party two-way authentication is not commonly used due to some practical problems. Consider a network where there are 50 users (or applications), and every user can communicate with any other user. So every user should be capable of authenticating every other user. Furthermore, for security reasons, we want each user to have a private password. In this case, every user has to store a password for each of the other users. This results in storing 49 passwords at every user workstation. Now consider the case in which a user is added or deleted or a password is changed. Such a change requires coordinating an update to the list of stored passwords for each of the 50 users. As such, maintenance of passwords for a two-party, two-way authentication scheme becomes cumbersome and inefficient.

Third-Party Authentication Schemes

A natural extension to the two-party two-way authentication is to use a *trusted third-party* that stores all the passwords. This trusted third party is the only location where passwords are stored and maintained. Every user or application will send the ID and the password to the trusted third party for authentication. This approach improves the security and simplifies the storage and maintenance of passwords.

Before proceeding to describe a third-party authentication scheme, we summarize the basic requirements for a third-party authentication scheme.

1. The scheme should provide two-party two-way authentication; the third party should provide centralized storage and maintenance of the passwords.

2. The scheme should not transport passwords over the network. This is desirable since a plaintext or

encrypted password can be copied from the network and replayed at a later time.

3. The passwords should not be stored at the client workstation. A stored password can be retrieved by an intruder when the user has stepped away from the workstation.

4. Once a user is logged on, the authentication scheme should provide a temporary secret to represent the user. In this way, repeated entries of passwords are not required. For example, a user may want to access the mail server to check the mail about six times in a day. It is desirable that the user not be required to enter and transmit the password six different times. Instead, the client workstation should use a temporary secret on behalf of the user to access the mail server.

5. The security system should be capable of securely transmitting encryption keys among the clients and servers.

Kerberos

Kerberos is a two-way third-party authentication and key distribution system that was developed at the Massachusetts Institute of Technology (MIT). The protocols are based on the model developed by Needham and Schroeder (1978). The following description begins with the concepts behind the Kerberos protocols, followed by some details; additional details can be found in Kohl (1993), Steiner (1988), Curry (1992), and Stallings (1995). Lunt (1990) provides experiences with Kerberos.

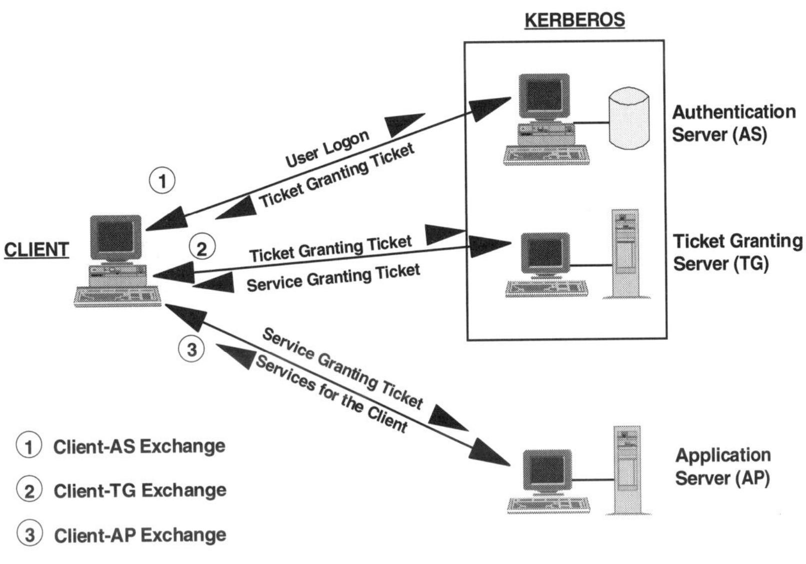

Figure 2.10: Kerberos System

Exchange	Frequency
1. Client-authentication server exchange	Once per user logon
2. Client-ticket granting server exchange	Once per type of service required
3. Client-application server exchange	Once per service request to any application server

Table 2.3: Kerberos Information Exchange

Four entities are used in the Kerberos system as shown in Figure 2.10.

1. **Client Workstation:** Client workstation is where the user interacts with the workstation and enters the ID and the password. For simplicity, we use the word *client* to represent the user at the client workstation.

2. **Authentication Server (AS):** The *authentication server* provides the password storage and interacts with the client in authenticating the user. This interaction also includes providing a ticket-granting ticket to the client. The ticket-granting ticket is used by the client to obtain a service-granting ticket from TG (described below). The service-granting ticket is a temporary secret to be used by the client to achieve authentication with the application server.

3. **Ticket-Granting Server (TG):** The *ticket-granting server* provides a service granting ticket to the client for receiving services from an application server.

4. **Application Server (AP):** The *application server* provides the desired services to the user through the client workstation.

The authentication procedure is accomplished in three sets of information exchanges as listed in Table 2.3 and outlined next.

The first exchange is between the client and the AS. In this exchange the client is authenticated by the AS. The AS also provides the client with information to initiate the next exchange with the TG. The second exchange is between the client and the TG. In this exchange, the client obtains a ticket for accessing a specific AP for services. The third exchange is between the client and the AP. In this exchange, the client uses the ticket from the second exchange to assure the AP that it is a legitimate user.

Details of these protocols are presented next. A casual reader may not need to review details of Kerberos and can skip this part of the section.

I. Client–Authentication Server Exchange

The objective of this exchange is to authenticate the user to the AS and allows the AS to provide the client with the capability to obtain a service-granting ticket from the TG. This is accomplished in such a way that the password is not transmitted over the network, and secret keys are securely distributed between the client and the TG to prevent replay of the ticket-granting ticket by a hacker. This exchange takes place every time the user logs on to the security system.

To begin with, the client sends the AS a request that consists of the IDs of the client (itself) and the TG and a *time stamp*. The ID of TG is sent to the AS to request a ticket-granting ticket for the identified TG. The purpose of the time stamp is to use this time value to synchronize the AS clock with the client clock.

Now the AS derives an encryption key from the user's password and uses it to encrypt a packet for the client. The packet consists of TG's ID, a *time stamp*, a *lifetime value*, a *session key*, and a *ticket-granting ticket*. The time stamp informs the client of the time this ticket-granting ticket was issued. The lifetime parameter informs the client of the duration of the validity of this ticket-granting ticket. The session key is described later.

The ticket-granting ticket is additionally encrypted using an encryption key shared only between the AS and the TG. As a result, the ticket-granting ticket can be decrypted only by the TG. The ticket-granting ticket includes the IDs of the client and TG, the session key, a time stamp, and a lifetime parameter. Note that both the client and TG will get the same session key. The client will decrypt its session key using the encryption key derived from the password. The TG will get the session key as part of the ticket-granting ticket. The TG decrypts the ticket-granting ticket using the encryption key shared between TG and AS. In this way, the session key has been distributed securely.

Now it is possible that an intruder can copy the ticket-granting ticket and use it before its lifetime has expired. In this way, the intruder can access the TG and obtain valid tickets. In order to avoid this attack, AS sends a session key to be shared between the client and TG. The client establishes its authenticity to the TG using this key. As will be shown in the next exchange, TG uses this session key for encrypting the service-granting ticket, which only the client can decrypt.

Upon receiving the above packet from the AS, the client prompts the user for the password. The client receives the password, derives the encryption key from the password, and attempts to decrypt the packet from the AS. The ticket is successfully recovered only if the correct password was supplied by the user. So now the client has the ticket-granting ticket that it can use for requesting the service-granting ticket from the TG.

Note that this exchange did not require any transmission of a password over the network. Additionally, it prevents replay of the ticket-granting ticket.

II. Client–Ticket-Granting Server Exchange

The purpose of this exchange is for the client to send a request to the TG to obtain a service-granting ticket for a desired application server, such as a mail server or a file server. This exchange takes place once for every type of service requested by the user.

To begin this exchange, the client sends TG with the ID of the desired AP, the ticket-granting ticket, and an *authenticator*. The authenticator consists of the client (user) ID and address, and a time stamp. Although the ticket-granting ticket can be reused, the authenticator cannot be reused and has a very short life span. This prevents replay of the packet by an intruder.

TG uses the secret key (shared between the TG and AS) to decrypt the ticket-granting ticket. This ticket assures the TG that the client has been provided with the same session key and that the packet is indeed from the client. Then TG sends the client a packet that includes an encryption key to be shared between the client and the AP, the ID of the AP, a time stamp, a lifetime parameter, and a service-granting ticket. The packet is encrypted using the session key shared between the client and TG.

The client now has the service-granting ticket that it can repetitively use to gain access to the same AP.

III. Client–Application Server Exchange

This exchange takes place every time the user desires to obtain services from any AP. The objective is to assure the authenticity of the client to the AP. Additionally, the client needs to supply the service-granting ticket to the AP. Finally, this exchange must optionally allow for the AP to authenticate itself to the client.

Note that the client can reuse the service-granting ticket for the same application server. For example, once the client has obtained the service-granting ticket for a mail server, the client can subsequently resend the same ticket for accessing the mail server within the ticket's lifetime. In this way, the user is not required to reenter the password every time she or he wants to check the mail.

The exchange begins with the client sending the service-granting ticket and an authenticator to the AP. The authenticator consists of the ID and address of (the user at) the client and a time stamp. The authenticator is encrypted using the encryption key shared between the AP and the client. Since the authenticator includes the time stamp, a replay of this packet will be detected and rejected by the AP.

If the client desires that the AP also be authenticated, then the AP responds with a packet to the client. This packet is encrypted using the session key shared between the AP and the client. It includes the time stamp received from the client, incremented by 1. The client can decrypt this packet using the shared session key. This authenticates the AP to the client, since only the legitimate AP knows the shared encryption key.

Kerberos has significantly enhanced client/server security through the use of a trusted third-party. It is an accepted security standard for the Internet. However, there are some shortcomings with the Kerberos scheme, as described in Curry (1992, 151–152). Kerberos requires the storage of all the keys as plaintext. Therefore, if the security of the authentication server is compromised, so is the security of the entire network supported by Kerberos. Second, the Kerberos system relies heavily on the clock synchronization between the client and the AS. An inadvertent or malicious discrepancy in the clocks may permit attacks. It is also cumbersome to synchronize clocks when the network is spread geographically; a network-wide secure time service can address this deficiency.

The most pervasive commercial levels of Kerberos are Version 4 and Version 5. Version 4 uses Data Encryption Standard (DES)[1] for encryption. Version 5 provides some enhancements, such as support of a standard security API, namely GSSAPI (Generic Security Services API).*

---

1. DES and GSSAPI are described in Chapter 4.

Kerberos is available as a software product from several vendors, such as OpenVision's OpenV*Secure (OpenVision 1994, 4). OSF's (Open Software Foundation's) DCE (Distributed Computing Environment) has adapted Kerberos for its underlying third-party authentication scheme. Kerberos source code is freely available from the Massachusetts Institute of Technology.

Public Key Authentication

In order to describe the topic of public key authentication, we first present some of the concepts of a *public key* scheme. Traditional encryption systems require a common secret key that is used for both encryption and decryption, as shown in Figure 2.11. As noted in the preceding section, third-party authentication requires a security server that stores all the secret keys. Diffie and Hellman (1976) achieved the most remarkable breakthrough in cryptology. The public key approach proposed by them is radically different from the traditional encryption systems. As described later, the public key scheme does not require users to share or store their secret keys with any system.

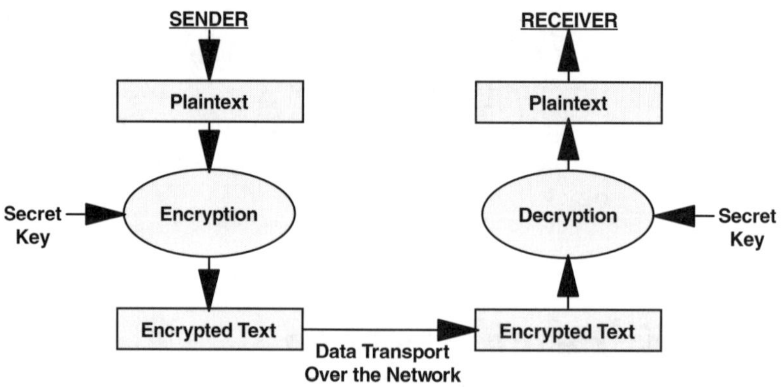

Figure 2.11: Data Encrypton and Decryption

For many of the encryption schemes, the key used for encryption is the same as that used for decryption. This is not necessary. In fact, it is possible to devise a scheme which uses one key for encryption and a different but related key for decryption. This approach is called *asymmetric key encryption* and is the basis of the public key schemes. In contrast, a *symmetric key encryption* scheme uses the same key for encryption and decryption.

Public key systems have the following two important attributes.

First, it is computationally infeasible to derive the decryption key, given only the knowledge of the encryption key and the cryptographic algorithm.

In this approach, every user has two keys; a *private key* (known only to the user) and a *public key* (known to everyone). So the public key of each user is published in *yellow pages* or made available through other means. If A wishes to send an encrypted packet to B, A can use B's public key to encrypt the message. B will use its private key to decrypt the message. No other recipient can decrypt this message, since only B knows B's private key. This is shown in Figure 2.12a.

The second attribute of some of the public key schemes is that either of the two keys can be used for encryption and the other key for decryption. The public key algorithm by RSA, described later in this section, exhibits this useful attribute. This attribute allows encryption as well as authentication using the public key and the private key, as described below.

Consider user A and user B as shown in Figure 2.12a. User A encrypts the message using B's public key. However, any other user with the knowledge of B's public key could have sent this message. This is true since B's public key is published and available to all the users. So although this exchange provides confidentiality of the message, it does not authenticate the sender (user A).

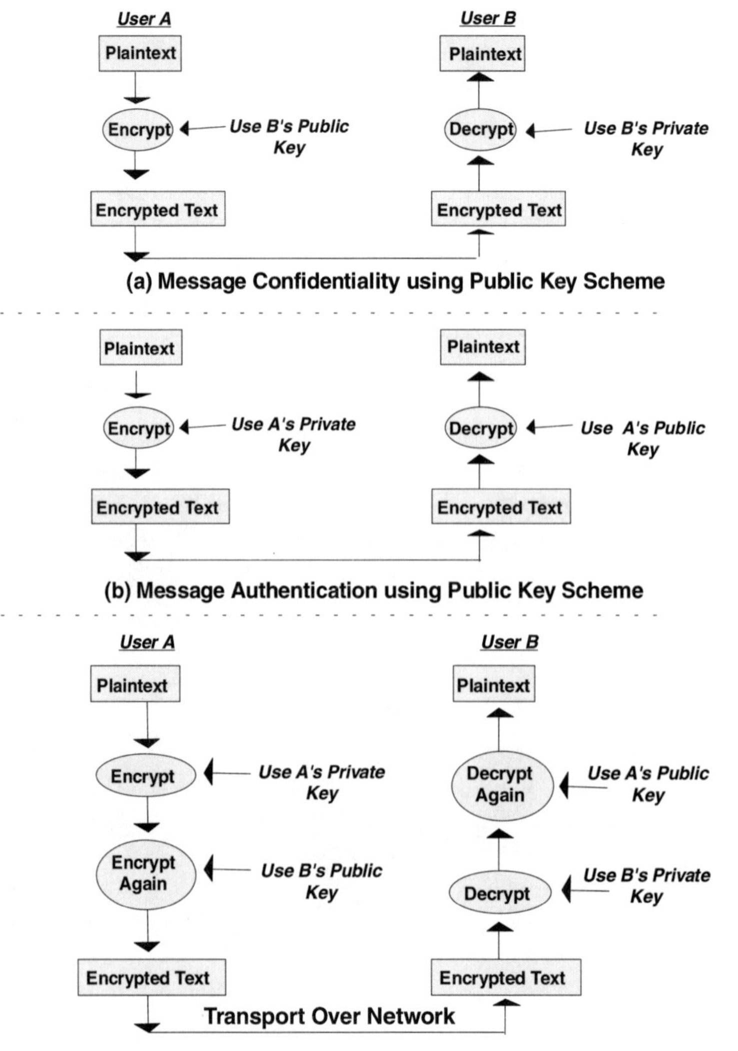

Figure 2.12: Message Confidentiality and Authentication

The sender of a message can be authenticated as follows. A can encrypt the message using A's private key, which is known only to A. The recipient, B, can decrypt the message using A's public key, as shown in Figure 2.12b. So B is assured that it is indeed A that sent this message, since only A knows A's private key. In this approach, we have achieved A's authentication, but it does not provide confidentiality (privacy) for the message. The reason is that any user can decrypt the message by simply using A's commonly available public key.

The above two approaches can be combined to provide privacy as well as authentication. First, A encrypts the message using A's private key. This step ensures A's authentication, since only A knows its private key. Next, A takes this encrypted message and encrypts it again using B's public key. This step ensures privacy, since only B can decrypt this message using B's private key. When the message arrives at user B, B first decrypts it using B's private key. Next, B takes the output of this decryption and decrypts it again using A's public key, as shown in Figure 2.12c.

One-Way And Two-Way Authentication

Public key systems provide both one-way and two-way authentication. Figure 2.12b shows one-way authentication using a public key scheme. When A sends a message to B, A encrypts it using A's private key. B decrypts the message using A's public key. So B is assured that the message came from A, since only A knows its private key. B can also send a message to A using A's public key, and A can decrypt it using A's private key. This exchange has accomplished one-way authentication, since only A has been authenticated to B.

Now consider again the message from B to A. Instead of B encrypting the message using A's public key, B could encrypt it using B's private key. Then A decrypts the message using B's public key. This assures A that the message was indeed sent by B, since only B knows B's private key. So B is also authenticated to A. In this way, we have achieved a two-way authentication using public key system. This exchange using B's private key and public key is, however, not shown in Figure 2.12.

RSA Public Key Algorithm

The RSA public key algorithm was developed by Rivest, Shamir, and Adleman (1978). This public key algorithm is in common use on the Internet to provide confidentiality and authentication.

In this algorithm, the plaintext is encrypted on blocks of characters. Each block has a binary value that is less than n. Let P be the block of plaintext and C the resulting encrypted block of characters. Then the algorithm is

$$C = P^e \bmod n \,,$$

$$\text{and} \quad P = C^d \bmod n \,,$$

$$= (P^e)^d \bmod n,$$

$$= P^{ed} \bmod n.$$

To begin with, this algorithm is implemented in the sender and the receiver workstations. Additionally, the sender knows the value of e, while the receiver knows the value of d. So the sender can encrypt by using the expression $C = P^e \bmod n$, using P as the plaintext block and by applying the values of e and n.

The receiver can decrypt by using the expression $P = C^d \bmod n$, using C as the received encrypted text and applying the values of d and n. This description assumes that the receiver's public key is (e, n) and private key is (d, n).

The topic of generating the public keys and the computational complexity required to break the public keys are not addressed here. The reader is recommended to consult Stallings (1995, 123–128) for these details.

X.509 Directory Authentication

X.509 directory authentication specifies authentication approaches using a public key scheme. CCITT (International Telegraph and Telephone Consultative Committee). Recommendation X.509 is part of CCITT's X.500 series of recommendations. *X.500* specifies the directory service, while *X.509* specifies the framework for providing authentication services by the X.500 directory for its users. X.509 uses the X.500 directory to store the information about users, as described later.

X.509 Certificates

X.509 authentication is based on the use of X.509 certificates. An *X.509 certificate* is issued to each user by a *Certification Authority* (CA). It may be viewed as a person's electronic *driver's license* for authentication on the Internet. The user or the CA stores this certificate in the *X.500 directory*. The X.500 directory simply provides a central storage for user certificates. X.509 uses public key encryption scheme and digital signatures. The RSA algorithm for public key is recommended but not required.

The format of the X.509 certificate is shown in Figure 2.13.

<table>
<tr><td>Version</td></tr>
<tr><td>Serial
Number</td></tr>
<tr><td>Algorithm
Identifier</td></tr>
<tr><td>Issuer</td></tr>
<tr><td>Period of
Validity</td></tr>
<tr><td>Subject</td></tr>
<tr><td>Public Key
Information</td></tr>
<tr><td>Signature</td></tr>
</table>

Figure 2.13: X.509 Certificate

Version: Relates to the version of the certificate format. Default is the 1988 format.

Serial Number: Number assigned to the user (certificate) by CA. This number is unique within the CA.

Algorithm Identifier: The algorithm used to sign the certificate, including any associated parameters.

Issuer: The CA that created and signed this certificate.

Period of Validity: The period of validity is specified in terms of two dates. The certificate is not valid before the first date and after the second date.

Subject: The user to whom this certificate is issued.

Public Key Information: Public key of the user and an identifier of the algorithm for which this key is to be used.

Signature: Apply a one-way hash algorithm (see Chapter 4) to all the fields of this certificate, except the signature field, and encrypt the result using CA's private key. Any user can decrypt this signature by using CA's public key. The signature ensures that this certificate was indeed issued by the CA identified in this certificate. As such, the signature authenticates the originator (CA) of the certificate.

A new user accesses the CA and obtains an X.509 certificate. The certificate is stored in the X.500 directory. Any user can access the X.500 directory and obtain the public key of another user. CA maintains the validity of the certificates. CA also maintains the list of all revoked certificates and updates the X.500 directory with that information. A certificate may be revoked before it expires for the following reasons:

1. The user's or CA's private key is assumed to be compromised.

2. The user is no longer certified by this CA.

X.509 certificates are used by Privacy-Enhanced Mail (PEM), Pretty Good Privacy (PGP), Secure Sockets Layer (SSL), and Secure HyperText Transfer Protocol (S-HTTP) (see Chapter 6). I expect that X.509 certificates will become pervasive for user authentication and nonrepudiation as part of electronic commerce over the Internet.

Other X.509 Authentication Schemes

X.509 also specifies three alternative ways of authenticating users.

I. X.509 One-Way Authentication

For one-way authentication, authentication information is sent from one user (A) to another user (B). This information includes:

- Identity of A.

- Identity of B (destination of the message).

- Time stamp that includes an optional generation time and an expiration time. This prevents delayed delivery of the message.

- A *nonce*, or a random number generated by A. This number is unique within the expiration time. B saves the value of the nonce for the period that the message is valid. Any message received within the valid time period including the same nonce is rejected. In this way, a hacker cannot replay the same message.

- A message signature signed by A's private key; similar to the signature process described earlier for signing X.509 certificates. This signature process establishes A's authenticity, since only A knows his or her private key.

The sender may also want to send some information in addition to the authentication information. Optionally, the message may include data that is signed by the sender. It may also include a session key shared between A and B, which is encrypted using B's public key.

2. X.509 Two-Way Authentication

For one-way authentication A is authenticated to B; for two-way authentication, B also needs to be authenticated to A. The message from B to A includes information equivalent to that sent by A to B. It will also include the nonce sent by A to B to validate the reply. In addition, B creates another nonce and includes it in the message to A. Optionally, the message may also include signed data from B and a session key encrypted using A's public key.

3. X.509 Three-Way Authentication

In three-way authentication, a final message is also included from A to B. This message includes a signed copy of the nonce that A received from B.

In this three-way authentication, the time stamp checking is not required. Instead, the three-way authentication uses nonces that are signed and returned by each party. Each party creates a nonce and receives verification from the other party. This approach is useful where synchronization of clocks is not available.

Single Logon

A client/server network offers access to resources over mixed platforms and diverse applications. Such networks are offering unprecedented user access to information; it can also imply new problems for user productivity and network security.

The concept of *single logon* is simple to describe but hard to achieve. In practice, a typical user logs on 4 or 6 systems in a day. In order to log on each system, the user is required to enter the ID and the password every time. This leads to loss of productivity due to the time spent in entering the IDs and passwords. There is additional productivity loss resulting from user errors in entering wrong IDs and passwords.

Single logon means that a user should enter the ID and the password only once. Once the user has been authenticated by a system, there should be no need to enter any more IDs and passwords. This concept pertains to a *single system image* for users.

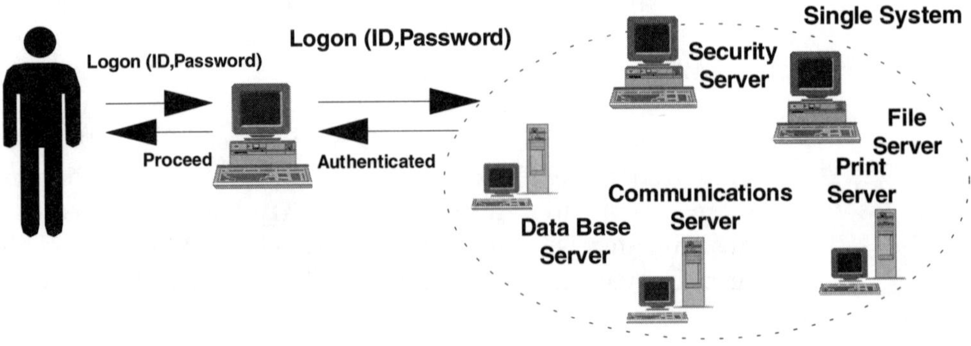

■ **Logon once to the security server, then access any server in the system.**

Figure 2.14: Single System Image for User Logon

Figure 2.14 depicts the concept of a single system image for single logon. For example, a user may need to check the E-mail several times during the day. In addition, the user may log on a file server or a database server to obtain some data. Finally, the user may also access the print server several times during the day to print some E-mail or reports. To the user, a single system image appears as a single interface (logon) for accessing a collection of servers.

Any single logon solution should also provide secure transport of passwords to the servers; this is called *secure single logon*. So in order to provide secure single logon, the following problems are to be addressed:

- For each user, coordinating and maintaining the (different) user ID and the password for each server accessible to the user.

- For each user, securely storing the IDs and passwords.

- For each user logon, secure transport of the IDs and passwords to each system.

In the remainder of this section, we cover the requirements for single logon and review various single logon schemes.

Requirements For Single Logon

There are two types of requirements for single logon: productivity and security.

Productivity

As mentioned earlier, users often have to remember and securely protect a large number of passwords. It can be expected that users may frequently forget one or more of their passwords. Assuming a given company requires users to remember four to six passwords, a rough estimate is that each user forgets one password every month. Every time a user forgets a password, the user contacts the administrator to obtain the current password or a new password.

For example, consider a company with 500 users where each user has to log on 10 times every day. Assume that each user forgets one password every month, which leads to a loss of 1 hour of user time or administrator time. Then at the rate of $30 per hour, it would cost the company approximately $180,000 per year.

In Hurwicz (1995), a credit card company adviser is quoted as saying that there are users at the company requiring more than 50 IDs. In Edwards (1993), the information security officer of a life insurance company stated that often their users had to remember as many as 10 passwords.

There is another aspect of productivity related to single logon. It takes a certain amount of time for a user to enter the ID and the password to each system. If the user had a single logon, then there would be no need to enter an ID and a password for each server. We again consider the earlier example of a company with 500 users and assume that each user has 10 IDs and passwords. Then a single logon approach would save nine entries of IDs and passwords per user per day. Let us assume that it costs 1 minute of user time entering an ID and a password. Then it amounts to a savings of 75 hours per day or approximately $2000 per day at $30 per user-hour.

According to the Aerospace Industries Association, as quoted in Brown (1994), companies with single sign-on environments can save $677 per user annually.

Security

There are certain security exposures associated with multiple logon environments. First, users with several IDs and passwords may write their passwords on a piece of paper, since it is difficult to remember several passwords. Some users even paste their passwords on the monitor. Finally, many users would create simple (easy to guess) passwords and their variations for their several systems. With a single logon, the user is required to memorize only one password. As a result, the user can be asked to select and memorize a complex password that cannot be easily guessed by a hacker.

Consider the security aspects of storing the passwords. It would be cheaper and easier to have a single password database, which can be secured and protected. Securing multiple password databases may reduce security and increase potential penetration by hackers.

Single Logon Schemes

A single logon scheme can be developed in several ways. However, the single logon scheme must accomplish a basic sequence of exchange between the user, the client workstation code, and the applications. This is shown in Figure 2.15 and described next.

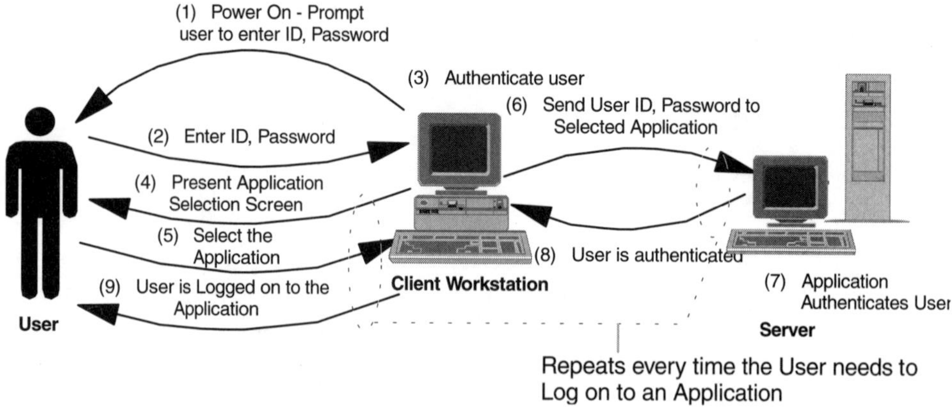

Figure 2.15: Basic Single Logon Exchange

1. When the workstation is powered on, the user is prompted with a screen to enter the ID and the password.

2. The user enters the ID and the password.

3. The single logon code at the workstation authenticates the user by verifying the password for the ID.

4. The single logon code at the workstation presents the user with an application selection screen. This screen includes all the applications that the user is authorized to access.

5. The user selects the desired application.

6. The single logon code at the workstation sends the ID and the password to the selected application.

7. The application authenticates the user ID and the password.

8. The application informs the client workstation that the user is authenticated.

9. The client workstation informs the user that logon is completed.

Steps 4–9 are repeated each time the user desires to log on another application. Note that this process required only a single entry of the ID and password by the user.

Some of the single logon schemes provide security in addition to that in the above steps. In those schemes, the password is not sent to the applications in steps 6 and 7. Instead, a temporary secret is sent from the workstation to the applications, such as that described for Kerberos earlier in this chapter.

Single Logon Using a Local Workstation

In this approach, the ID and the password for the user are stored at the workstation. In addition, the single logon processing is handled by the client code at the workstation.

To begin with, the workstation is powered on and the user is prompted to enter the ID and the password. Upon receiving the ID and password from the user, the single logon code at the workstation compares the ID and the password entered by the user to that stored at the workstation. Assuming that there is a match, the user is presented with a list of all the authorized applications. The user selects the desired application for logon. At this time, the single logon code at the workstation sends the appropriate user ID and the password to the selected application. As a result, the user is logged on the selected application. Subsequently, the user may select any other application at anytime, which results in transmission of the corresponding user ID and the password to the application, without requiring any additional entries of ID and password by the user.

This approach has several pros and cons. Clearly, it yields the productivity gains by avoiding the multiple entries of IDs and passwords by the user. But there may be some security exposures to this approach depending on the underlying design. First, since the password is stored in the client workstation, it may be exposed to theft, such as when the user has stepped away. Note that this exposure did not exist in the environment where the user had to enter multiple IDs and passwords. Second, a loss of this password would give a hacker access to all of the user's systems. To address this concern, one approach is to store the password in an encrypted form using a one-way hash function. Finally, the number of password transmissions for this approach is the same as for the network without single logon. So this approach does not enhance the security of the password transmission over the network.

In this scheme, the single logon code at the workstation can be implemented using *scripts*, which are sequences of encoded commands. These scripts are executed by the single logon code as if these were commands entered at the user console.

Secure Single Logon Using Local Workstation and Third Party

This approach enhances the security of the preceding scheme by using the services of a third-party security server. Here, the password is not kept at the client workstation; instead, the password is stored in a trusted third-party security server.

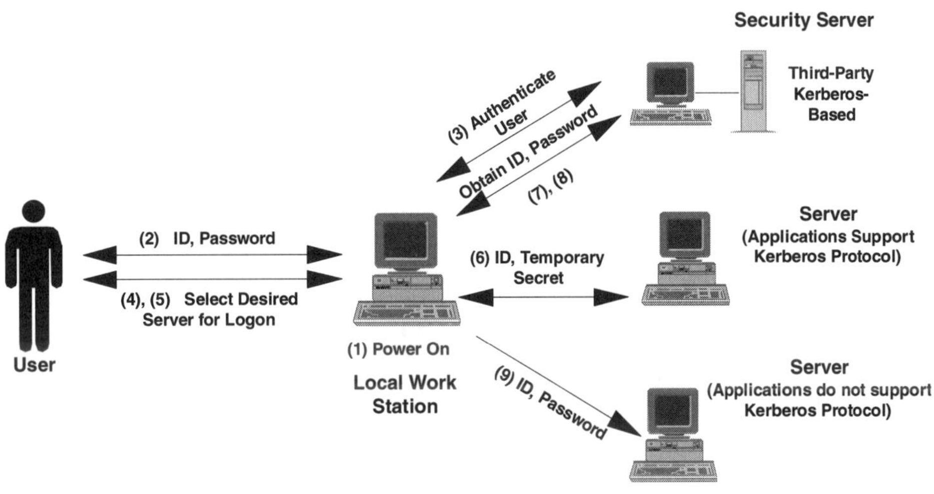

**Figure 2.16: Secure Single Logon Using Local Workstation
and Third-Party**

The logon sequence is outlined in Figure 2.16 and consists of
the following steps:

1. User powers on the workstation.

2. The single logon code at the client workstation
   prompts the user and receives the ID and the password.

3. A third-party authentication, such as Kerberos
   (described earlier), is used to securely authenticate
   the user. The password is not transmitted over the
   network.

4. Now the user is presented with an application selection screen. This screen has the list (or icons) of all the
   applications this user is authorized to access.

5. User selects a desired application.

6. If the selected application supports the third- party authentication scheme (such as Kerberos), then follow the steps for logging on using that third-party protocol. Otherwise, proceed to step 7.

7. The code at the workstation accesses the security server for the password (and optionally the ID) for the selected application. The ID is required if it is not the same for all the applications.

8. The security server returns the password and (optionally) the ID.

9. The code at the workstation transmits the ID and password to the selected application. The user is now logged on the application.

At any time after the above sequence, the user can go back to step 4 for the application selection screen and log on another application or server without requiring entry of any more IDs or passwords.

In this scheme, each password is stored at the security server. The initial authentication is accomplished securely using the underlying third-party authentication scheme, and no password is stored at the workstation. However, this scheme requires the security server as well as additional transmission of passwords from the security server to the client workstation. Finally, the security server requires storage of additional IDs and passwords for applications that do not support the third-party authentication scheme.

Secure Single Logon Using One-Time Passwords

This approach employs the third-party security server to provide one-time software-generated passwords. It is particularly attractive since the one-time password can be used for each selected application, without requiring user intervention.

The user initially logs on with the ID and the password. Assume that the user entered the correct ID and password and is therefore authenticated by the security server. Next, the single logon code presents the application selection screen and the user selects the desired application. Now the single logon code at the workstation accesses the security server to obtain a new one-time password for the selected application. The security server sends back the one-time password to the client workstation. The client single logon code sends the user ID and this one-time password to the selected application. The application forwards this information to a password verification code that verifies whether the one-time password is valid.

There are some inherent advantages and limitations with this scheme. First, the one-time password is valid for a short time interval, so it cannot be reused by a hacker. This addresses the risk of passwords being stolen during transmission. A limitation of this scheme is that the applications need to implement and support the one-time password verification code.

The one-time password generated in the software, as outlined above, is offered by IBM as part of the Resource Access Control Facility (IBMRACF 1993). The complementary security server and the single logon code for the client workstation are provided by IBM's Network Security Product Secured Logon Coordinator (IBMSLC 1994).

Summary

We have reviewed the topic of logon and authentication in this chapter. The first important concept for logon is the management of the passwords. Besides various approaches to securing the passwords, the use of one-time passwords is becoming critical. We have presented various approaches for implementing one-time passwords. Another area of growing concern is the need for a user to enter multiple IDs and passwords to access different systems. We have described some approaches to providing secure single logon.

Workstation Security

"Bolted doors don't always secure data."

PC Week, August 8, 1994. p 8. (Peter Coffee)

Several years ago, a computer system was accessed by the users through display terminals such as the IBM 3270s. While the users could access the system through the display terminals, the system consoles were often secured in the locked computer rooms. In this way, the access to control and modify the system was restricted. Today, a workstation is the most common and convenient way to access and control the network.

Network security relies on the assumption that the underlying software on the client workstations and the servers is secure. For example, data encryption over the network is of little value when it can be easily copied or stolen as plaintext from the client or the server. So securing each workstation and server is critical for protection of the entire network.

We begin by presenting two basic aspects of workstation security: workstation access and workstation monitoring. Workstation security also requires protection from viruses. After reviewing the topic of viruses, we describe approaches to classifying computer systems based on their security levels.

Workstation Access

Power-On Password

Workstations should be protected from unauthorized user access. At power-on time, the workstation software should prompt the user to enter a password. In the absence of such a requirement, an intruder can walk to the workstation, power it on, and attempt to steal or damage the workstation resources as well as other network resources accessible through the workstation.

Screen Lock

Screen lock is perhaps the single most valuable feature to protect the workstation. After a certain inactivity time-out, this feature automatically locks the workstation screen. The screen can be unlocked by entering a password that is known only to the user. This is clearly of significant value, since it protects the workstation when the user has stepped away for a long time.

Additionally, the workstation may present a locked screen at the time of power on. In this way, even if an intruder walks to a workstation and powers it on, he or she still cannot unlock the screen.

Old Accounts

A large system may contain many user accounts whose owners have since left the organization. Such accounts may be broken into by an intruder if the power-on logon password is easy to guess. Furthermore, breaking into these accounts may go unnoticed because the legitimate user is not around any more.

A simple precaution is to identify and delete all the idle accounts at frequent time intervals. To implement this function, each user account is assigned an expiration date. For example, for a student account in a university system, the expiration date may be the end of the academic year. At the beginning of every month, the system (administrator) can check the accounts that are due to expire that month and delete accounts that are not required anymore.

Single-User And Multiuser Modes

UNIX systems can operate in a *single-user mode* or a *multiuser mode*. In the multiuser mode, most of the system services are running. Users can access these services through a terminal, modem, or a network connection. A UNIX system is changed to a single-user system in order to repair the system after a crash, back the system on a tape, or install new hardware or software. When the UNIX system is booted in a single-user mode, a shell (sequence of commands) is started. In many systems, the *root* password is not required before this shell is started. So if the intruder has access to the system console and can place the system in a single-user mode, the intruder can gain access to the system without providing the root password. However, this shell has privileges associated with a superuser. With superuser access, an intruder can modify critical data such as user passwords. This security hole has been recognized by various vendors (Curry 1992, 105–106), and many systems have been changed to require the user to enter the root password before starting this shell.

Details on UNIX security can be found in Curry (1992), Carlin (1993) and IBMAIXS (1991).

Workstation Monitoring

Workstation monitoring consists of tracking and investigating the history of significant events. We divide this discussion into two parts, audit trail and intrusion analysis.

Audit Trail

There are several significant events that should be recorded for potential review at a later time. For example, consider a system where an intruder is persistently attempting to log on by trying different words as the password. The intruder tries a few times every few hours, bypassing checks by the system for a persistent user. Assume the worse case that the intruder has ultimately succeeded in logging to the system. Then for the purposes of investigation, it is desirable to maintain a record of all logon activities. This record should include network addresses of the workstations from which each user (including the intruder) has tried to log on the system. In addition, the record should indicate the time at which the logon was attempted.

The example above relates to user activity, but it is also important to record administrative activities. In case of a break-in, a record of all the user and administrative actions may be required to investigate the break-in. A break-in can occur as a result of an inadvertent action by the administrator, such as erroneously giving root access to another user.

Audit trail pertains to automatic recording and saving of significant system events. Auditing requires the use of procedures that automatically create a record for every security-sensitive workstation event and store the record in a secure log.

The creation and recording of audit records for logon attempts are shown in Figure 3.1. It is a common practice for the logon products to offer an option for recording all logon attempts. At a minimum, it should record all the unsuccessful logon attempts.

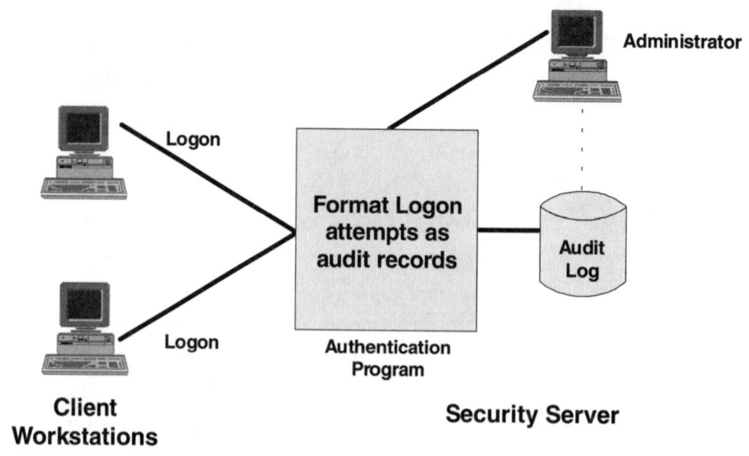

Figure 3.1: Audit Log of Logon Attempts

Audit Requirements

Some of the important requirements for an audit system follow:

- Automatically collects information on all the security-sensitive activities. These activities are often selected by the administrator at installation time.

- Stores the information using a standard record format. A format for an audit record is shown in Figure 3.3.

- Creates and saves the audit records automatically without requiring any action by the administrator.

- Protects the audit records log under some security scheme. For example, encrypt the audit log using the root password as the encryption key, or require entry of the root password to access the audit log.

- Minimally affects the normal computer system operation and performance.

Audit System Design

Implementation of an audit system can be achieved in several steps. In short, it consists of determining what events must be audited, creating the software to record those events, and then saving these records in a protected log.

To begin with, there must be some audit mechanism that is monitoring the system activities. This mechanism also logs details of each activity in the form of an *audit record*. Such activities may include logon attempts (successful and unsuccessful), read or write of sensitive files such as changes to the password database, deletion or creation of files by the administrator, and delegation of access rights by the administrator. The system administrator selects these activities at the time the audit system is installed or configured.

The audit records are saved in a secure log. Most systems work with two log files. When one of the log files is full, the audit mechanism informs the administrator to dump or print the current log file and starts writing to the other log file. This gives the administrator time to copy the audit records from the current log file to a tape or other backup medium. Alternatively, this backup process can be automated so that when a log file is full, it is programmed to be copied to the backup storage medium without requiring any administrator actions.

Intrusion Detection

Concepts

Intrusion detection is the process of detecting and identifying unauthorized or unusual activity on the system. By using the audit records, the intrusion detection system should identify any undesirable activity. Such a scheme requires specification of what constitutes an undesirable activity and a means of automatically detecting such activity as it occurs.

For example, consider a real estate agent who works 9 AM to 5 PM every weekday. The agent logs on the real estate database at about 9 AM and logs off around 5 PM. Let us assume that an agent lists or sells no more than one or two properties in a day. Then we also know that the agent would write to the database at most two times a day. These characteristics, put together, constitute a user profile that can be used to identify any unusual behavior. If it is found that the agent logs on late in the night and writes several records on the real estate database, then this activity may be considered suspicious. But in order to automate the system, some thresholds should be specified. For example, the threshold may specify that based on the profile for the agent, more than two logons per week outside 9 AM to 5 PM or more than 20 updates to the real estate database per week should be identified as an unusual activity.

Design

Intrusion detection design consists of two basic steps. The first step is the creation of audit records. The second step is checking the audit log against the intrusion thresholds. This design is depicted in Figure 3.2 and is outlined below.

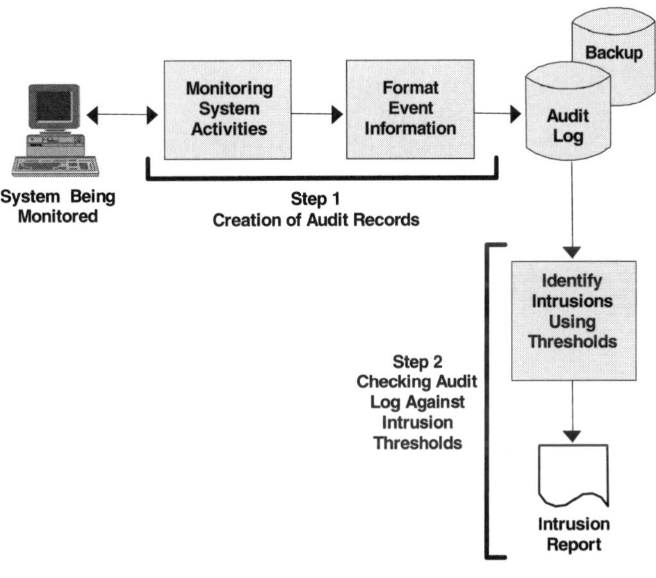

Figure 3.2: Intrusion Detection Design

The creation of audit records was described under the topic of audit trail. In the second step, the audit records are checked at frequent intervals for any activity that has exceeded the specified thresholds. Finally, an intrusion detection report is generated for review by the system administrator or investigators for potential break-ins under way.

Intrusion Detection Model

Dorothy Denning (1987) has published an Intrusion Detection Model that provides a comprehensive approach for intrusion detection. Denning's model consists of subjects, objects, audit records, profiles, anomaly records, and activity rules as described below.

Subjects, Objects, And Audit Records

Each audit record consists of six fields; subject, action, object, exception condition, resource usage, and time stamp, as shown in Figure 3.3.

Format	Example
Subject	Joe
Action	File Write
Object	Employee Record File
Exception Condition	No
Resource Usage	10
Time Stamp	0800 112795

Example: Joe wrote 10 records to Employee Record File at 8 AM on November 27, 1995.

Figure 3.3: Format of Audit Record

The *subject* field identifies the initiator of actions on the system. A subject can be a terminal user or a process acting on behalf of a user.

The *action* field describes the action taken by the subject. Examples include log on, log off, read or write on a file, or execute a program.

The *object* field identifies the receptors of the action by the subject. Examples include files, databases, messages, terminals, printers, and user- or program-created data structures. When a subject is the receptor of an action such as for electronic mail, then that subject is considered as the object.

The *exception* field indicates which, if any, exception condition was detected as a result of this action.

The *resource usage* field includes the amount of resource used by this action. For example, it may be the number of lines printed on a printer, number of records read or written on a file, or the amount of CPU time used by a program.

The *time stamp* field identifies when this action took place.

Profiles

Profiles characterize the behavior of a subject (or a group of subjects) on an object (or a group of objects). Profiles include the description of normal behavior of subjects with respect to the objects. So profiles can be used to detect and report any abnormal activity as recorded in the audit records.

Three candidate profiles are described, one each for measuring logon and session activity, command or program usage, and file access activity.

Logon and Session Activity

Logon and session activity is represented in the audit records as follows. The subject is the user, the object is the user's logon location, and action is log on or log off.[1]

Several profiles may be created, such as for the *logon frequency, location frequency, last logon,* and *session elapsed time.* Logon frequency is measured by time or day. This measure is useful in identifying an intruder attempting to log on during off-hours when the legitimate user is not expected to be logged on the system. The location frequency measures the frequency of logons at different locations. This can help identify a hacker location, especially when the hacker is using a location that the legitimate user never uses. The last logon measure provides the elapsed time between two consecutive logons. The session elapsed time measure provides the amount of elapsed time per session.

An observation is accepted as abnormal if it is considered to be significantly different from the profile (using some statistical analysis). According to Amoroso (1994, 198), experience has shown that such measures are surprisingly regular for most computing environments.

Command or Program Execution

For these profiles, the audit records show the subject as a user, the object as the name of the program, and the action is execute. Measures for these profiles include *execution frequency, resource usage,* and *execution denied.*

Execution frequency measures the number of times a program is executed during some time period. Resource usage provides

---

1. Log out and log off are used synonymously. Some systems use log out and others use log off.

the amount of CPU utilization or the number of file input/output operations during an execution. This measure is also quite regular and predictable for different systems. For example, an E-mail server will have little CPU utilization in receiving or sending an E-mail. On the other hand, a scientific computer system may have a high CPU utilization for every execution of its applications. The execution-denied measure records the number of times attempts were made to execute an unauthorized program during a time period such as a day. This parameter may help in identifying if someone is trying to execute an unauthorized program repeatedly.

File Access Activity

File access activity is reflected in audit records where the subject is a user, the object is the name of a file, and the action is *read, write, create, delete,* or *append.*

Measures for these profiles include the number of file accesses of specific types (such as reads or writes) during the day (or some other time period) and the number of access violations during the day. Consider the example of a password file. It may be normal for an average user to access and update the password, which leads to reading (to validate the existing password) and writing (to add the new password) the file with, say, eight or less characters. On the other hand, copying of the password file by an unauthorized user may be considered a suspicious activity.

Anomaly Records

An *anomaly record* is created when the audit records show some abnormal behavior compared to that in the profiles.

An anomaly record consists of three fields: *event, time,* and *profile*. The event indicates the system action, the time field shows the time when the event took place, and the profile field identifies the profile that was not matched. For example, all users in an office log on between 7:45 AM and 8:20 AM. One audit record, however, indicates a user who logged on at 1 AM. So the anomaly record would consist of the event as logon, time as 1 AM, and the profile field will have the logon profile.

ComputerWatch: An Audit Trail Analysis Tool

As described in Amoroso (1994, 201), ComputerWatch is an audit trail analysis tool reported by Cheri Dowell and Paul Ramstedt of AT&T Bell Laboratories. The tool is compatible with many UNIX-based audit trails and has been used by many government and commercial computing establishments to perform audit analysis.

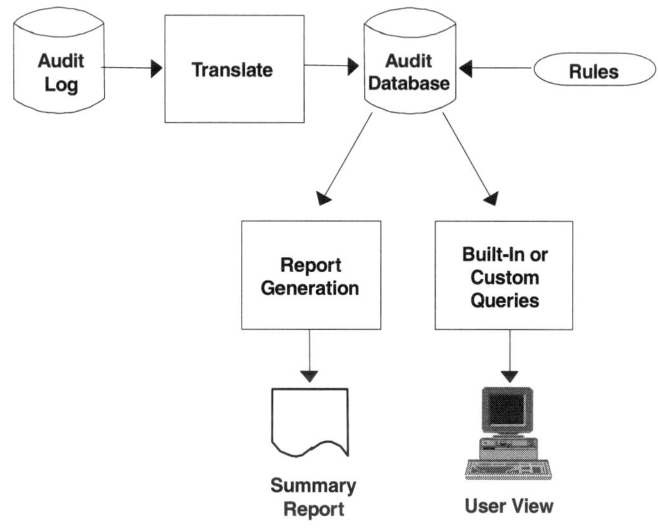

Figure 3.4: ComputerWatch System Components

Source: Amoroso, Edward, Fundamentals of Computer Security Technology, ©1994, p. 201. Adapted by permission of Prentice Hall, Upper Saddle River, New Jersey.

The components of ComputerWatch are depicted in Figure 3.4. First, the audit log is translated into a database format. The database format makes it easier to analyze the audit information against rules. Next, the rules are provided by the administrator to perform heuristic analysis in identifying abnormal activity. Finally, the report generation component presents the summary reports by the system.

Viruses

"This advisory warns users of a PC virus called Michelangelo. The virus affects IBM PCs and compatibles, and has a trigger date of March 6 (any year)."

CA-92:02.Michelangelo.PC.virus.warning CERT Advisory February 6, 1992.

Politically Correct Virus:
Never identifies itself as a virus, but instead refers to itself as an electronic micro-organism.

Brad Wood. Virus Alert (joke). May 5, 1995.

Background

According to The Complete Medical Guide (Miller 1967, 127–128), a *germ* is a microorganism that is too small to be seen by an unaided eye. A *virus* is one of five types of microorganisms that cause communicable diseases. While viruses are very hard to grow in an experimental environment, they are very potent, and a very small number can start a disease. Viral diseases include polio, yellow fever, smallpox, and the common cold.

The scientifically correct definition for a computer *virus* is *self-reproducing automaton*. Viruses often have the capability to gain control of the computer. When it is executed, a virus makes one or more copies of itself, and when these copies are executed, more copies are made, ad infinitum. A virus is not an independent program. A virus executes when its home program executes, as explained later.

Thompson (1984) developed a program that is perhaps the first virus program ever developed, although he did not give it that name. He first wrote a self-reproducing program in C language. Next he inserted a Trojan horse (defined later) that would look for the code pattern of a UNIX logon command. On detecting that pattern, it would deliberately miscompile the UNIX logon command so the UNIX code would accept his intended encrypted password or a particular password. As a result, he could log on as any user. Then he added another Trojan horse targeted at the C compiler. He modified the source, used the official C to compile, and produced a bugged binary. He installed the bugged binary as the official C and removed the bugs from the source of the compiler. So whenever new source of the compiler was compiled, the new binary reinserted the bugs with no trace in the source code anywhere.

By and large, the main route for virus distribution is through the diskettes distributed through homes. According to S&S Software International, as quoted in INFOWEEK (1995, 12), the number of computer viruses had grown to 6000 by January 1995, an increase of 40 percent in just 12 months.

Taxonomy of Malicious Programs

There is a variety of malicious software that can attack computer systems. Almost everyone has heard about viruses, but many people are not aware of other kinds of vandal programs and how they differ from each other. In the following, we present the different types of malicious software.

Malicious programs can be divided into two types; programs that must require a host program and programs that can exist independently. Programs of the first type are really fragments of software. These programs cannot exist by themselves; they need some application, utility, or system program. Viruses, for example, need a host program and can also replicate themselves, as described earlier. The second type of program is self-contained and can be scheduled and run independently. Another approach to classifying the malicious programs is based on whether they can replicate themselves. Both classifications are shown in Table 3.1.

	Can Replicate Itself	Host Program Required
Viruses	Yes	Yes
Bacteria	Yes	No
Worms	Yes	No
Trapdoors	No	Yes
Logic bombs	No	Yes
Trojan Horses	No	Yes

Table 3.1: Classes of Malicious Programs

Bacteria

Bacteria are programs that duplicate themselves. While these programs do not directly attack any software, they consume resources simply by replicating themselves. For example, a bacteria program may create two new files by copying its own source file. These source files execute again to replicate themselves, and so on. So, bacteria grow exponentially, eventually consuming all the processor capacity, system memory, or disk space.

Worms

A *worm* is an independent program that can replicate itself and often spreads to different sites over a network. Since it is an independent program, it does not need another program to spread itself. A worm usually does not attack other programs or files. At the same time, it is not benign; it consumes network resources and can bring the network to a near shutdown. The famous Internet Worm is described in Chapter 1.

Trapdoors

A *trapdoor* is an undocumented entry point into software that circumvents the normal system protection. Trapdoors have been used legitimately by programmers to test, monitor, trace, debug, and sometimes even fix programs. Mostly, trapdoors are used during software development. But sometimes the trapdoors are left in the programs by design or oversight.

When a programmer inserts a trapdoor, usually the programmer does not expect others to find out the method of access to the trapdoor. It may be a special keystroke or a special command. If another programmer finds out the trapdoor, then that programmer has instantly gained special privileges to change or modify the program.

In the 1983 movie *WarGames*, the hero gains access to a NORAD computer system by inadvertently entering a trapdoor planted by its creator. This allows him to log on the system, leading to a global thermonuclear war game that became all too real.

Logic Bombs

A software *logic bomb* or a *time bomb* is a fragment of software that is set to inflict damage when a certain set of conditions exist.

A logic bomb needs a host software program to carry the bomb. The conditions that would trigger the bomb may include the presence or absence of a file, a particular user accessing a file or logging on, or a particular day of the week or a date. Once triggered, a bomb may modify or delete data, delete an entire file, cause the machine to halt, or inflict some other damage.

An example of a computer break-in using a time bomb was described in Chapter 1. Another interesting example is described in Stallings (1994, 240, referencing Time Inc., *Computer Security, Understanding Computer Series*, Alexandria, VA. Time-Life Books. 1990). A software contractor supplied the computerized circulation system for Montgomery County, Maryland. In the program, the contractor had planted a logic bomb that would disable the system on a certain date unless the contractor had been paid. So when the library withheld the payment to the contractor due to poor response time, the contractor informed the county of the existence of the bomb and threatened to let it go off unless the payment was forthcoming.

A legitimate use of logic bombs is in the area of software distribution. A software vendor may provide a customer with free software for trial use for a fixed period of time. At the end of that period the logic bomb sets off, disabling the software from the customer's system. In some cases, the vendor may also provide the customer with a password to diffuse the bomb after the customer has bought the software and made the payment.

Trojan Horses

In classical mythology, a *Trojan horse* was a large hollow horse made of wood in which the Greeks hid their soldiers and left it at the gates of Troy. When the Trojans brought the horse inside Troy, the hidden soldiers came out and opened the gates for the rest of the Greek army, which led to the Greeks winning the war.

For computer systems, a *Trojan horse* is a piece of code that hides inside a program and performs a disguised function. This piece of code does not exist independently and needs to be planted in another program for disguise. Thompson (1984) used the concept of a Trojan horse in modifying the C compiler, as described earlier.

Types Of Viruses

For IBM PCs and clones running PC-DOS or MS-DOS, all the data and programs besides the operating system are stored as files. The data can be stored under an 8-character file name and a 3-character extension, such as STORAGE.TXT. All the programs are stored with the extent words of COM, EXE, and SYS. Under DOS, only those files with the three-letter extent field are executed.

There are three types of viruses that run on IBM PCs and clones. The first type of virus attaches itself to EXE, COM, or SYS files and is executed whenever that particular file is executed. The second type of virus attaches to a specific file, rather than attacking any file of a given type. For this type of virus, the creator must gain extensive knowledge of the particular file. A virus of this type can then hide inside the file, such as in the data area. The third type of virus is called a *boot sector virus*. Here the virus resides on the boot sector of the disk drive. When the computer is powered on, it loads the boot sector before executing any other program. In this way, the virus is executed before any other program can execute and detect the existence of the virus.

Viruses can infect several kinds of computer systems. Although many viruses are designed to attack IBM PCs and their clones, there exist viruses that infect Macintosh and UNIX systems.

Designing A Virus

Consider a virus that is designed to infect an assembly language program. It must execute a sequence of steps to effectively plant the virus code for execution. These steps are listed below.

1. Locate the first executable instruction in the target program.

2. Replace that instruction with an instruction to jump to the memory location next to the last instruction of the target program.

3. Insert the virus code for execution at the end of the target program.

4. Insert an instruction at the end of the virus program to simulate the original first instruction of the target program that the virus replaced in step 2.

5. Add another instruction at the end of the virus code to jump back to the second instruction of the target program.

Elements Of A Virus

Any virus must consist of some basic functions. It must be able to locate new areas of target, must be able to copy to those new areas, must have executable code to inflict the damage, and must have a set of antidetection routines to protect all of the virus code from being detected.

To begin with, the virus needs a *search routine*. The search routine finds new areas for the virus to extend, such as disk space or programs. These are the areas that would be the next targets for the virus to locate its copies. The search routine finds safe areas where the virus can hide its copies. There is a tradeoff here between the size of the routine and the search for target areas. A good search program will quickly find new target areas. However, this may lead to a large search routine, which leads to a larger size for the virus code, thereby increasing the chances of the virus being detected.

Next, the virus must include a *copy routine* to copy the virus to new target areas. The size of the copy routine depends on the complexity of the virus code and the target area. The copy routine must also be as small as possible to avoid detection.

Additionally, the virus must include a *viral routine* that executes the unauthorized actions such as deletion of records from a particular file or preventing the user from accessing computer resources.

Finally, the *antidetection routine* is embedded all through the virus code and protects the virus from detection. This routine, as well as the rest of the virus code, should add up to a small piece of code. A smaller code size makes it easier to hide and reduces the chances of being detected. Antidetection routines may also control the timing of the execution of the virus code. For example, it may not let the virus code access a file continuously over a short period of time, in order to avoid arousing the user's suspicion by noticing unauthorized file accesses. On the other hand, the antidetection routine may let the virus access a particular file when the user is accessing some other file, so the file access by the virus code may go undetected.

Virus Precautions

There are several precautions that can help private companies protect against viruses. These steps include scanning all floppy disks for viruses, especially those coming from employees' homes or in the mail. Many viruses are brought in when employees take work home on floppy diskettes. Companies may provide employees with virus protection software for their home workstations. Finally, once a PC is determined to be free from viruses, reconfigure the PC so that it will not boot from a floppy diskette.

Several vendors offer antivirus products. A study and comparison of antivirus products is provided in Phillips (1995a, 1995b). For additional details on viruses, see Ludwig (1990).

Security Ratings Of Computer Systems

Background

During the last decade, there has been an increasing focus on evaluating the security levels of computing systems. These efforts have provided detailed procedures to define and establish the security ratings. The two primary efforts in this area have been in the United States and Europe. In the United Kingdom, the Department of Trade and Industry developed a proposal called the *Green Book* for commercial IT (information technology) security products. In Germany, the German Information Security Agency published the first version of its criteria in 1989 (ZSIEC). At the same time, France developed a criterion, the so-called *Blue-White-Red Book* (SCSSI). In view of these countries' efforts, the European community developed the *Information Technology Security Evaluation Criteria* (ITSEC) described later in this section.

In 1985, the U.S. Department of Defense published *Trusted Computer System Evaluation Criteria* (TCSEC) as the DOD Standard 5200.28-STD, library number S225,711, December 1985, also known as the *Orange Book*. The National Computer Security Center (NCSC) has been in the business of defining the security requirements and evaluating vendor products against the TCSEC. As the government levies requirements on vendor products to be conformant to certain levels of TCSEC, more and more vendors and individuals need to learn about the Orange Book and its implications. By establishing these requirements, the government has helped both the industry and the government itself in procuring secure systems and helping vendors design and sell security as part of their product portfolio.

This section provides an overview of the requirements and the rating scale for TCSEC. This description includes information from Chokhani (1992) and Russell (1991, 103–161); both are good references on this topic.

The *Orange Book* specifies the TCSEC, which provides a basis for evaluation of a given system. The evaluated system is called the Trusted Computing Base (TCB). The TCSEC levies several requirements on the TCB. Based on the level of support by the TCB for these requirements, the TCB may be rated in a specific division and class, as described later. The NCSC spends government resources in evaluating vendor products, while the vendors invest in designing, developing, and documenting their support of the specified security requirements.

Trusted Computer System Evaluation Criteria (TCSEC)

As shown in Figure 3.5, the TCSEC requirements can be divided in the following categories: security policy, accountability, assurance, and documentation.

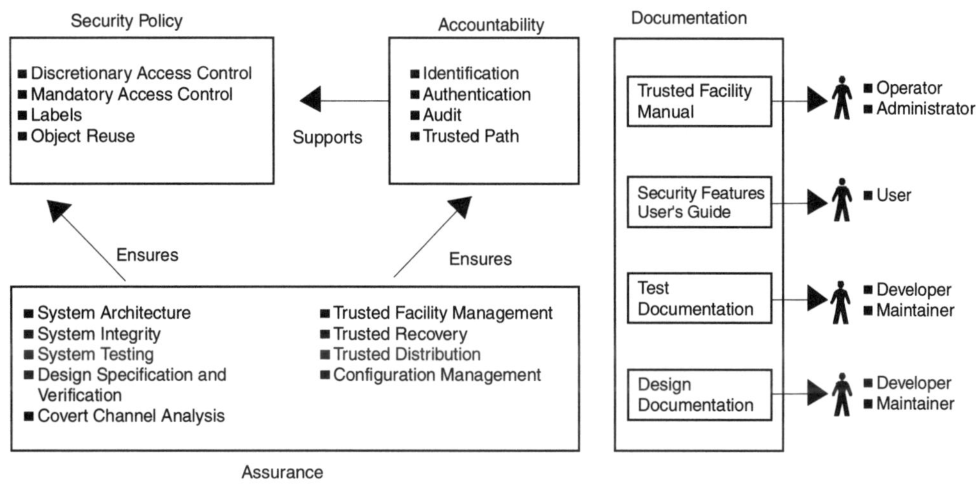

Figure 3.5: TCSEC Overview

Source: Santosh Chokhani, "Trusted Products Evaluation," Communications of the ACM, Figure 1. page 66 July 1992 Vol 35 No 7. Copyright ©1995, Association for Computing Machinery, Inc (ACM) . Reprinted by permission.

Security Policy

The requirements in this area consist of four topics: discretionary access control, mandatory access control, sensitivity labels, and object reuse.

Discretionary Access Control

Discretionary access control (DAC) specifies that users can deny or permit access to specific information that they own such as files. For example, the owner of a salary file may decide which users or user groups can access this file. The owner may also specify whether the user or the user group can read, write, or delete the file.

Mandatory Access Control

While DAC allows the owners to determine who may access the files, in *mandatory access control* (MAC) such access is controlled by the system.

A system that supports MAC assigns each subject (such as users, programs) and object (such as files, directories, devices, windows) a sensitivity label. A user's sensitivity label specifies the level of trust associated with that user; it is often called the user's clearance level. A file's sensitivity label specifies the level of trust that a user must have in order to be able to access the file. Mandatory access control along with sensitivity labels provides a multilevel security in the TCB (Trusted Computer Base).

Sensitivity Labels

Sensitivity labels consist of two parts, a classification and a category, as shown in Figure 3.6. The classification is a single, hierarchical list of the levels of security. For example, in the so-called military security model, there are four distinct levels:

- TOP SECRET
- SECRET
- CONFIDENTIAL
- UNCLASSIFIED

Each level is more trusted than those under it. For example, the SECRET classification is more trusted than CONFIDENTIAL. In a commercial environment, there may be the following classification:

- CEO ONLY
- EXECUTIVES ONLY
- COMPANY CONFIDENTIAL
- PUBLIC

The categories are nonhierarchical and represent the type of information under the classification. For example, there may be a file on employee information with three categories:

- Payroll
- Salary projection
- Biodata

Decision to access a file is based on the labels of the subject and the object. Consider the read and write rules for the Employee Pay File and the users shown in Figure 3.6.

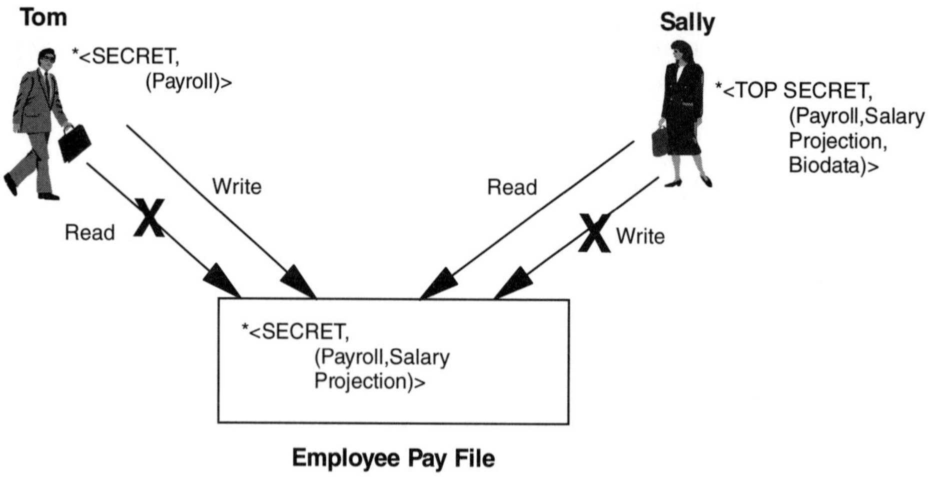

Figure 3.6: Mandatory Access Control

Read

To *read* a file, the subject's sensitivity level must be equal to or higher than that of the object. Furthermore, the list of categories that the subject may be allowed to read must include all the categories of the object.

For the employee pay file shown in Figure 3.6, the sensitivity level is Secret and the categories consist of Payroll and Salary projections. So Sally can read the file, since her sensitivity level is Top Secret (higher than that of the Employee Record file) and her authorized categories include Payroll and Salary Projection.

Now suppose Sally's sensitivity level was Confidential. Then she could not read the Employee Pay file since her level is not high enough. But if Sally's level was Secret, she could read the file since her level is equal to that of the file. If Sally's level was Secret but her authorized category was Payroll only, then she could not read the file. This is because the file contains another category not authorized for Sally, namely the Salary Projection. For the same reason, Tom cannot read the file as depicted in Figure 3.6.

Write

To *write* to an object, the subject's sensitivity level must be equal to or less than that of the object. In addition, the user's authorized categories must all be included in the categories of the object.

Consider Tom's sensitivity label as shown in Figure 3.6. Tom has the sensitivity level of Secret and he is allowed to access the category Payroll. Tom can write to the employee pay file. This is true since Tom has the level of Secret, which is equal to the level of the file. Tom is also allowed access to the payroll category, which is included in the categories of the Employee Pay file.

Now consider if Tom had the sensitivity level of Confidential. He would still be allowed to write, since his sensitivity level is less than that of the Employee Pay file. What if Tom's sensitivity level was Top Secret? Then he would not be allowed to write to Employee Pay file. This seems odd at first hand. Why would a person with Top Secret clearance not be allowed to write to Secret level files? The reason has to do with the concept of "downgrading information." If Tom has Top Secret clearance, and he is allowed to write to Employee Pay file with Secret level, then Tom may read some information from a Top Secret level file and write to a Secret level file. This may result in others with Secret level clearance being able to read Top Secret level information. This is the reason that Sally cannot write to the Employee Pay file.

Object Reuse

This capability ensures that the contents of the storage medium are cleared before it is assigned to a user. In this way, there is no intentional or unintentional data scavenging off the storage elements, such as disk sectors or memory pages, while these elements are assigned to different users.

Accountability

In order to support the security policy, the TCB should support the following features: identification, authentication, audit, and trusted path.

Identification allows the users to identify themselves to the TCB, and *authentication* permits the TCB to authenticate the identity of the user. *Audit* provides for recording security-sensitive information in a secure log for later use. Details of identification and authentication were presented in Chapter 2, and audit was described earlier in this chapter.

The *trusted path* requirement is to assure the TCB and the user that no other user or program is masquerading as the system. For example, a Trojan horse could emulate the logon sequence and steal a user password.

Assurance

Requirements in this area ensure that the TCB is designed to minimize errors and operates without circumventing the security features and controls described under Security Policy and Accountability.

System Architecture

These requirements address the system architecture for both the system development phase and the system operations phase. Examples for the system development phase include layering, data abstraction, and information hiding. For the operations phase, there is a requirement to isolate the TCB from the user processes, thereby improving the system security. An additional requirement for operations phase is the isolation of TCB's security critical kernels from the nonsecurity critical kernels.

System Integrity

TCSEC requirements for system integrity pertain to ensuring the correct operation of the system hardware, which is typically accomplished by running diagnostic software at frequent intervals.

System Testing

TCSEC requires that appropriate testing has been performed on the security features of the system.

Design Specification and Verification

This element of TCSEC ensures that the system design and specifications are correct and consistent with respect to the stated security policy.

Covert Channel Analysis

Covert channel analysis relates to analyzing methods that can be used to obtain information in violation of the MAC policy. For example, a user with Secret level may find out the existence of a Top Secret file. This is a piece of information that should not be available to the Secret level user. TCSEC requires that such channels be eliminated or audited for violation of MAC policy. The topic of covert channels is addressed in detail in Chapter 5.

Trusted Facility Management

Trusted facility management specifies separation of the roles of system operators and security administrators. It improves security by reducing the scope and probability of exposure.

Trusted Recovery

Trusted recovery provides for proper operation of security functions after the system has recovered from a failure or a crash.

Trusted Distribution

TCSEC also specifies requirements for hardware and software distribution. It ensures that the TCB hardware or software does not go through unauthorized modifications during transmission from the vendor to the customer computers.

Configuration Management

This requirement specifies use of suitable configuration management for the hardware, software, and the firmware.

Rating Scale

The TCSEC has grouped these requirements in three divisions: Division C, Division B, and Division A (most secure). Within each division, TCSEC provides one or more hierarchical classes. Figure 3.7 shows a summary of these divisions and classes. Each division is discussed more thoroughly below.

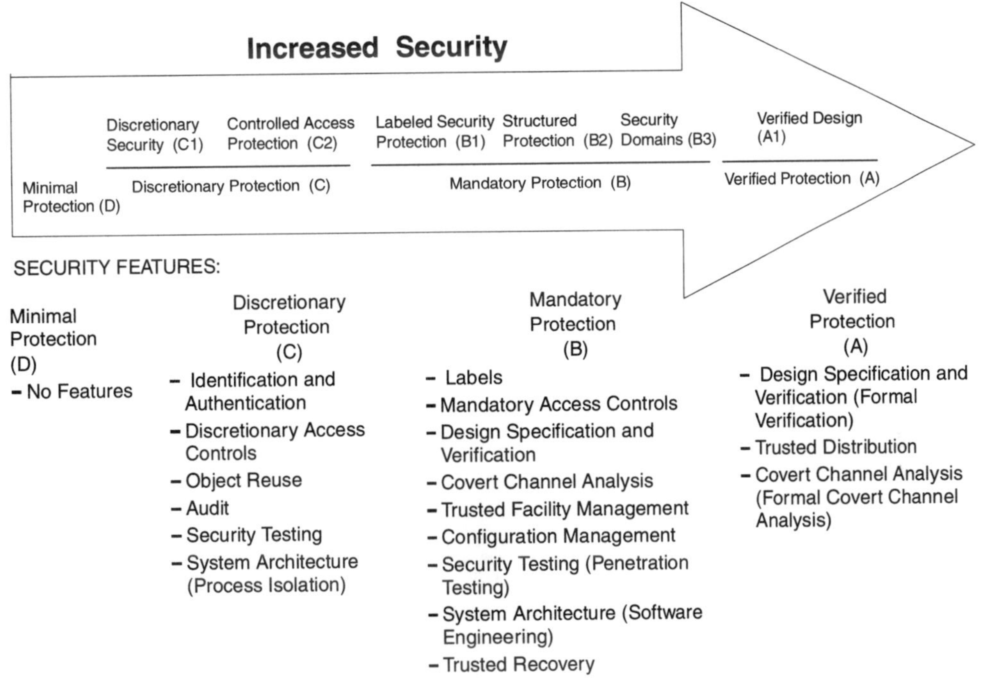

Figure 3.7: TCSEC Rating Scale

Source: Santosh Chokhani, "Trusted Products Evaluation," Communications of the ACM, July 1992 Vol. 35 no. 7. Figure 2 p. 68 Copyright ©1995, Association for Computing Machine, Inc. (ACM) . Reprinted by permission.

Division D—Minimal Protection

Division D includes no security features and provides minimal protection.

Division C—Discretionary Protection

In terms of security policy, Division C supports discretionary access control and object reuse. In the context of assurance, this division supports identification, authentication, and audit. Division C consists of two classes, C1 and C2, where C2 is a higher level security than C1.

Class C1

Class C1 provides for DAC, identification, and authentication. Some or all of these features may be provided for individuals or groups. For this class, there is no need to provide identification, authentication, or access control on the individual level; it can be provided at group level. As such, there is no requirement for security policy or accountability on an individual basis. Consequently, this class is not considered sufficient to protect systems that process sensitive information.

Class C2

Class C2 requires identification, authentication, and access control on an individual basis. Auditing is required on an individual basis. Object reuse is introduced in this class. C2 is considered as the minimum class for systems that process sensitive information.

Division B—Mandatory Protection

Division B requires multilevel security through the use of MAC and sensitivity labels that were described earlier. Several assurance requirements are also added, as shown in Figure 3.7. Security can be added to an existing system to achieve class B1 or C1 rating. For B2 or higher, it has been observed (Chokhani 1992, 69) that one must design the system with security in mind using sound system and software engineering practices.

Class B1

Class B1 is class C2 with MAC and sensitivity labels. The requirements for class B1 are such that security can be added as an afterthought to a given computer system.

Class B2

In class B2, the emphasis is on assurance requirements such as isolation of security-critical kernels, creation of a formal security policy, separation of the roles of system operator and security administrator, trusted path, and covert channel analysis. It also includes additional security policy and accountability requirements.

Class B3

In addition to class B2 requirements, class B3 also requires simplification of the TCB and real-time monitoring including alerts for security-based audit results.

Division A—Verified Protection

Division A adds the requirement for verification of the security controls using a formal model of the security policies.

Class A1

For class A1, the formal top-level specifications are verified against the formal security policy model. Formal or informal techniques are to be used to show consistency between the specifications and the security model. Formal techniques are required for covert channel analysis.

Information Technology Security Evaluation Criteria (ITSEC)

Information Technology Security Evaluation Criteria (ITSEC) have been developed by the European Community and published for use in evaluating the security levels for information systems. This brief overview of ITSEC is based on Version 1.2 published in June 1991 (ITSEC 1991).

The ITSEC requirements are described in the context of a Target of Evaluation (TOE). ITSEC first specifies the definitions and descriptions of security requirements. It recommends the following headings to describe and evaluate the security functions of a TOE:

- Identification and authentication
- Access control
- Accountability
- Audit
- Object reuse
- Accuracy
- Reliability of service
- Data exchange

The evaluation rating awarded to a TOE can be one of the seven levels, E0 through E6, with E0 being the least secure. The intended correspondence between the ITSEC ratings and the TCSEC ratings are as shown in Table 3.2.

ITSEC		TCSEC
EO	$\longleftrightarrow$	D
F-C1, E1	$\longleftrightarrow$	C1
F-C2, E2	$\longleftrightarrow$	C2
F-B1, E3	$\longleftrightarrow$	B1
F-B2, E4	$\longleftrightarrow$	B2
F-B3, E5	$\longleftrightarrow$	B3
F-B3, E6	$\longleftrightarrow$	A1

Table 3.2: Intended Correspondence between ITSEC and TCSEC Ratings

Source: Information Technology Security Evaluation Criteria (ITSEC) Version 1.2. June 1991. p 14.

ITSEC provides details on example functionality classes and how they relate to TCSEC. For Table 3.2, example class F-C2 is derived from the requirements for TCSEC class C2. It specifies a more refined DAC than class C1. Complete details on this topic can be found in ITSEC (1991).

Summary

In this chapter, we have described various aspects of evaluating and improving the security of workstations. Next to password security, workstation security is perhaps the most important security consideration in a network. The chapter began with a review of access, audit, and monitoring of the workstation. Another area of concern is the various forms of malicious software. Computer viruses continue to be a source for denial-of-service attacks. We have discussed the topic of malicious software with a focus on viruses. Finally, we presented an overview of the U.S. Department of Defense publication on the criteria for rating computer systems. These specifications can also be used to improve the security of a system. For example, the sensitivity labels can be used for selected files and users to control read and write accesses. We also included a brief overview of the European Community's ITSEC criteria for evaluating the security of computer systems.

Distributed Security Services

"What have you got to lose?"
"Everything I have!"

In a client/server network, there may be application programs that are distributed between a server and one or more clients. In order to exchange data securely, these *distributed applications* require access to a variety of security services, which include data confidentiality, data integrity, authentication, and non-repudiation. In this chapter, we present details on these services and the means to access them.

By providing an overview of the generic application program interface (API) to access security services, we will be led directly to the issues of data confidentiality and data integrity. These topics will be discussed in more detail, including an overview of the commonly used encryption technologies, and a section on one-way hash functions and the digital signature schemes. Finally, the security services provided by the Open Software Foundation's (OSF's) Distributed Computing Environment (DCE) will also be discussed.

Security API

Consider the client/server network shown in Figure 4.1. The application client at workstation C uses the services at the application server S. This is accomplished through a distributed application program that consists of a client code (residing at the workstation C) and a server code (residing at the server S). The data between the client workstation C and the application server S is exchanged through some network protocol which is not relevant to this discussion. It is conceivable that at times the data may include some sensitive information (such as the credit card number) that must be kept secret. In addition, the server may require authentication of the client before providing services to the client. The distributed application accesses these services through a security API.

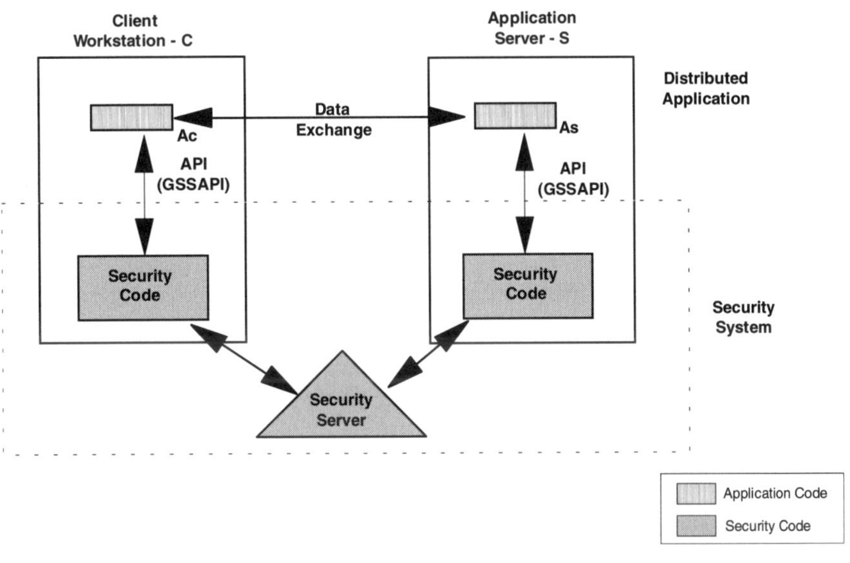

Figure 4.1: Distributed Applications and Security Services

In order to access the security services, the distributed application component Ac in the client workstation issues API calls to the security system. The security code at the client workstation C, shown in Figure 4.1, provides the security services to Ac. A similar exchange takes place at the server side. Suppose that the client code Ac has to transmit a packet of confidential data to the server code As. So Ac calls the encryption service through the security API. The security code at the client workstation encrypts the packet and returns the encrypted packet to Ac. Ac transmits this encrypted packet to As. On receipt of the encrypted packet, As calls the security code at the server S to decrypt this packet. The security code at server S decrypts the packet and delivers the decrypted packet to As.

While providing the security services, it is conceivable that the security code at the client workstation and application server may exchange information with the security server.

Requirements for a Security API

A security services API should satisfy the following requirements:

Mechanism independence: The API should allow access to different types of security systems (such as Kerberos or public key authentication) and not restrict the access from the application to a specific security system.

- The API should provide confidentiality through one or more encryption schemes.

- The API should provide data integrity through one or more message integrity algorithms.

Protocol independence: The API should be independent of the underlying communication protocol.

There are some other desirable features for a security API. For example, nonrepudiation service is required in order to transact secure commerce over the Internet (see Chapter 6).

Generic Security Service API (GSSAPI)

Background

For a long time, the security community had suffered for lack of a generic security services API. During the 1980s, Kerberos and the Data Encryption Standard (DES) were some of the common security services available in the industry. The API for Kerberos security services was specific to Kerberos and could not be conveniently used for another security scheme. In the absence of such a generic API, application programmers had little choice in providing callable security services for their applications.

It was not until the early 1990s that a viable security API was introduced. In 1992, J. Linn proposed a generic security API to the Internet Engineering Task Force (IETF). IETF approved it in 1993 and documented it as RFC 1508 (Linn 1993b) and RFC 1509 (Wray 1993). Since its approval, the *Generic Security Service Application Program Interface* (GSSAPI) has quickly gained acceptance. GSSAPI is currently implemented by several vendors and endorsed by some of the leading consortia.

In order to describe the GSSAPI, we first introduce a few definitions. The GSSAPI uses the term *security credentials* or simply *credentials*. Credentials relate to the information sent by the security server to a client or an application server. Credentials include the shared secrets between the clients (or servers) and the security server. This information is often encrypted using the client or server's password or session key. For example, in Chapter 2 under Kerberos, credentials are exchanged between a client and a server using their shared encryption key. Next, the term *security context* refers to a connection that is established after two given clients have authenticated each other's credentials.

GSSAPI Calls

The use of GSSAPI is sketched in Figure 4.1. The application program in the client workstation accesses the security services through GSSAPI. The client code of the underlying security system provides the requested services and returns the results to the application program at the client workstation. The application program at the client workstation communicates directly with the application program at the server.

CREDENTIAL MANAGEMENT

GSS_Acquire_cred	acquire credentials for use
GSS_Release_cred	release credentials after use
GSS_Inquire_cred	display information about credentials

CONTEXT_LEVEL CALLS

GSS_Init_sec-context	initiate outbound security context
GSS_Accept_sec_context	accept inbound security context
GSS_Delete_sec_context	flush context when no longer needed
GSS_process_context_token	process received control token on context
GSS-context_time	indicate validity time remaining on context

PER-MESSAGE CALL

GSS_Sign	apply signature, receive as token separate from message
GSS-Verifiy	validate signature token along with message
GSS_Seal	sign, optionally encrypt, encapsulate
GSS_Unseal	decapsulate, decrypt if needed, validate signature

SUPPORT CALLS

GSS_Display-status	translate status codes to printable form
GSS_Indicate_mechs	indicate mech_types supported on local system
GSS_Compare_name	compare two names for equality
GSS_Display_name	translate name to printable form
GSS_Import_name	convert printable name to normalized form
GSS_Release_name	free storage of normalized-form name
GSS_Release_buffer	free storage of printable name
GSS_Release_oid_set	free storage of OID set object

Table 4.1: GSSAPI Calls

Source: J. Linn, "Generic Security Service Application Program Interface," RFC 1508. September 1993. pp 15–16.

GSSAPI consists of several API calls, as shown in Table 4.1. In order to exchange data securely, the application client and application server execute a variety of GSSAPI calls that are grouped as follows:

- Authentication and creation of credentials

- Establishment of security context

- Protection of data using data integrity

- Protection of data using data confidentiality

- Removal of security context and credentials

In the following, we present an overview of these exchanges; additional details can be found in Linn (1993b).

Authentication and Creation of Credentials

GSSAPI does not specify the calls to create credentials for authenticating users and leaves it up to the underlying security mechanism. Credentials are often generated and distributed by an authentication server. For example, the client may log on the Kerberos security server. In response, the client receives the security credentials. GSSAPI specifies an API call, GSS_ACQUIRE_CRED, to acquire credentials in order to establish security context.

Establishment of Security Context

Once the application client and application server have obtained their credentials, a security context can be established.

The application client issues the GSS_INIT_SEC_CONTEXT API call; the call includes a parameter to specify the name of the security context. As a result of the call, a message (called *token*) is sent to the application server. The application server sends this token to GSS_ACCEPT_SEC_CONTEXT, and a security context is established between the application client and the application server.

The contents of the security context are dependent on the underlying security mechanism. The application client and the application server should have agreed a priori to support a particular mechanism. However, the GSSAPI calls are independent of the underlying security mechanisms.

Protection of Data Using Data Integrity

GSSAPI provides calls to protect data for transmission over the network using data integrity and data confidentiality.

First, the purpose of GSS_SIGN and GSS_VERIFY calls is to provide data integrity including authentication of the data origin. To begin with, the GSS_SIGN call leads to creation of a digital signature by the underlying security system. The digital signature includes the output of a one-way hash function for data integrity, such as those described later in this chapter. So, the application client issues GSS_SIGN, obtains a digital signature from the security system, and sends the data and the signature to the application server. At the application server, the GSS_VERIFY call is issued to process the digital signature along with the associated token. By using the same message integrity algorithm as in the client workstation, the security code at the application server checks whether the data has been tampered with during transmission.

Similarly, the application server can issue GSS_SIGN to protect data for transmission to the application client, and the GSS_VERIFY at the client workstation can verify whether the data was altered during transmission.

Protection of Data Using Data Confidentiality

GSSAPI also provides a pair of API calls for data encryption services. The GSS_SEAL and GSS_UNSEAL calls support caller-requested *confidentiality*. In addition, these calls also provide the *data integrity* and *data origin authentication* services of GSS_SIGN and GSS_VERIFY. The application client can issue GSS_SEAL call to the security code and include the data to be signed. The client can also select the option to encrypt the data. The security code returns signed and optionally encrypted data to the application client; the application client sends this data to the application server. The application server issues the GSS_UNSEAL call along with the received data. The security code at the application server verifies the data for integrity (GSS_VERIFY function), decrypts the data if required, and returns the resulting data to the application server. This completes the exchange for data protection using GSS_SEAL and GSS_UNSEAL. Conversely, the application server can sign and optionally encrypt data using GSS_SEAL, and the application client can use GSS_UNSEAL to verify and decrypt it if required.

It is important to note that the security code at the client workstation and at the server must support the same data integrity and encryption mechanisms. For example, if the security code at the client workstation uses a public key scheme to encrypt (or decrypt) the data, then the security code at the server must be able to decrypt (or encrypt) the data using the same public key scheme. Similar restrictions also apply to the data integrity services.

Removal of Security Context and Credentials

At the completion of the data interchange between the application client and the application server, the security context is deleted. The exchange to delete security context can be initiated by the application client or the application server but is more likely to be initiated by the application client. When the application client issues GSS_DELETE_SEC_CONTEXT, the security context is removed for the client program and a token is returned to the client program. The client program sends a token to the application server program. The application server uses GSS_PROCESS_CONTEXT_TOKEN to process the token and delete the security context. Conversely, the application server can initiate GSS_DELETE_SEC_CONTEXT and the application client processes the GSS_PROCESS_CONTEXT_TOKEN.

In addition, the application client or the server can issue a GSS_RELEASE_CRED call to release the buffers containing the security credentials.

Finally, note that there is no direct communication between the security code at the application client and that at the application server. Security codes at the client workstation and at the server communicate with each other through the applications executing at the client workstation and the server, as shown in Figure 4.1.

GSSAPI Usage

GSSAPI has been implemented by several vendors and consortia. IBM implemented GSSAPI in Network Security Program Secured Logon Coordinator (NetSP SLC) and made it available in December 1993 (IBMSLC 1994). Some implementations of Kerberos also include support for GSSAPI calls.

Encryption Schemes

"Security refers to protection against unwanted disclosure, modification, or destruction of data in a system and also to the safeguarding of systems themselves."

Computers at Risk. National Academy Press. 1991. page 2 David D. Clark, Chairman System Security Study Committee, National Research Council.

Background

The idea of *encryption* dates back to 2000 B.C. when Egyptians used to carve funeral messages in modified hieroglyphs. However, these messages were not meant to be secret but instead to increase their mystery. During the battles in early times, the generals would send secret messages to the home front. These messages were encrypted so that if the enemy captured the messenger, the secret message would not be revealed. In the sixteenth century, Mary, Queen of Scots, lost her life because the encrypted message she sent from prison was intercepted and deciphered. Encryption was also used, analyzed, and broken extensively during World War II.

In the period between 1790 and 1800, an amateur cryptologist invented an interesting encryption scheme that was ahead of its time. This inventor was a well-known writer, an architect, an agriculturalist, and a statesman. He created a machine that consisted of 36 wheels strung together over a common shaft. Each wheel could move freely and had 36 slots on the periphery. On each slot, an alphanumeric character was printed, jumbled, and disarranged. There were nuts at the ends of the shaft. When the nuts were tightened, the wheels would clamp together. To encrypt a word, the wheels were aligned so the letters on wheels would form the original text of the word. At that point, the nuts were tightened so the wheels would clamp together. Then the wheels were turned so any of the other 35 letter combinations along the wheels were read and sent as encrypted text. The receiver also had an identical set of wheels. The receiver would turn all the wheels until the letters on the wheels formed the received encrypted text. At that time, the nuts were tightened so the wheels were clamped. Then the clamped wheels were scanned until the line of characters was found that made sense. The inventor became President, filed the papers, and never suggested it for use to people in his administration. It was rediscovered among his papers in the Library of Congress in 1922, as described in IBMDATAS (1977). He was Thomas Jefferson.

Data confidentiality requires that given information must be protected from disclosure to unauthorized recipients. In the modern age of computers and networking, there is the need to protect the contents of electronic mail (*E-mail*) and files during transmission over the network. There may be secrets that are important for national security (weapon deployment), law enforcement (identities of undercover agents), competitive advantage (product plans, new technologies), commerce (credit card numbers), or personal privacy (credit history). Additionally, security data such as passwords and encryption keys must be protected during transmission over the network. Finally, sensitive information should be stored as encrypted text. For example, in UNIX system, passwords are stored only after several iterations of DES encryption (see Chapter 2).

Next, we discuss the concepts in encryption including a description of some of the common encryption schemes.

Concepts

Encryption is the process of transforming data into an unintelligible form in such a way that the original data can be obtained only by using the decryption process and the encryption key. The original data is called *cleartext* or *plaintext*, and the encrypted data is called *ciphertext, codetext,* or *cipher,* as shown in Figure 4.2.

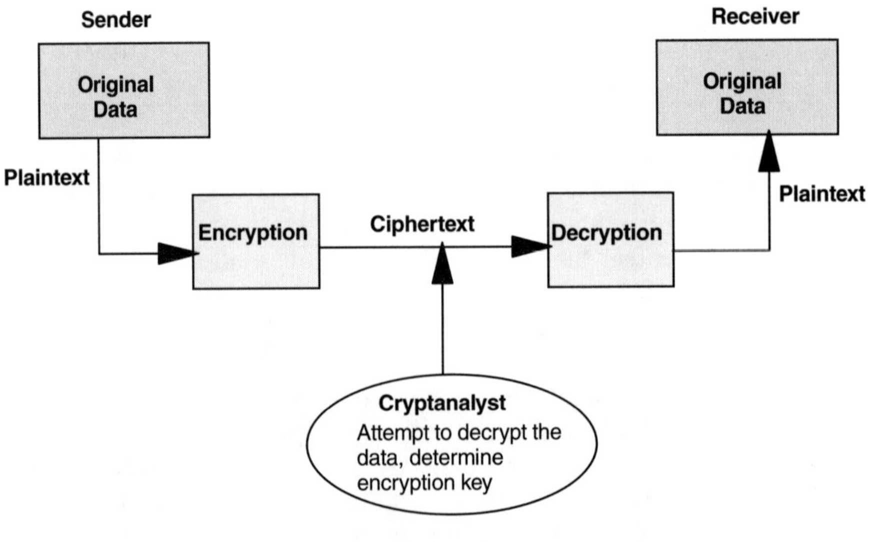

Figure 4.2: Encryption Process

Cryptography is the study of encryption and decryption. It comes from the Greek word *kryptos* meaning *hidden,* and *graphia* meaning *writing. Cryptanalysis* is the process of decrypting a ciphertext without the availability of the encryption key. Cryptanalysis is used by an intruder to break the ciphertext into plaintext and to determine the (secret) encryption key.

There are two basic techniques commonly used in building an encryption scheme. A given plaintext set of characters can be modified by either transposing or substituting the characters in the text, as explained below.

Transposition

A given text can be transposed in several ways. Consider the word *PRIVATE*. This word can be transposed to *VRIPTEA*, as shown in Figure 4.3a. In order to decrypt this word, the recipient will attempt different positions of the letters until an intelligible word is found.

The above simple *transposition* approach can be the target of a brute force attack where the attacking program attempts each permutation of the encrypted text while looking for a meaningful text.

A more secure approach is to use the transposition matrix. Consider the sentence *FIRE THE MISSILE AT FOUR*. Assume that we decide to use a transposition matrix of five columns. Then this sentence can be written along the rows of a five-column matrix, as shown in Figure 4.3b. Now the complete matrix is written out one column at a time and transmitted as the encrypted text. The receiver recreates the matrix leading to derivation of the plaintext message.

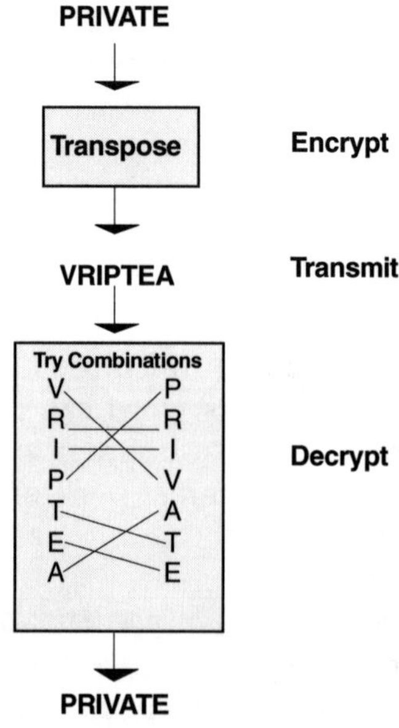

Figure 4.3a: Transposition

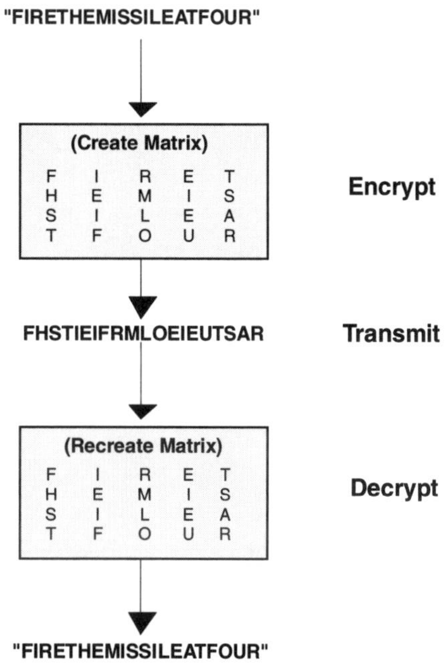

Figure 4.3b: Transposition Using Matrix Approach

Substitution

A given text can also be encrypted by substituting each letter with another letter.

A common approach for *substitution* is to replace letters by other letters in the alphabet. For example, the sender may decide to substitute each letter by another letter located three letters away in the alphabet, as shown in Figure 4.4. Then for the word *PRIVATE*, the transformed text is *SULYDWH*. The receiver performs the reverse process to decrypt the word and obtains the word *PRIVATE*. The famous Caesar substitution approach is based on this scheme.

Original Character	Substitution Character
A	D
B	E
C	F
W	Z
X	A
Y	B
Z	C

Substitution Matrix

Example

Encrypt		Transmit		Decrypt	
P	→ S	→	S	→	P
R	→ U	→	U	→	R
I	→ L	→	L	→	I
V	→ Y	→	Y	→	V
A	→ D	→	D	→	A
T	→ W	→	W	→	T
E	→ H	→	H	→	E

Figure 4.4: A Substitution Scheme

Next, we review some of the common encryption schemes. The public key encryption scheme is not included here; it was described in Chapter 2.

Data Encryption Standard (DES)

IBM developed an encryption scheme in the 1970s that was later modified and adopted by the National Bureau of Standards in 1977 as the *Data Encryption Standard* (DES). An outline of the DES algorithm is presented here; details can be found in Schneier (1994) and Stallings (1995).

The DES algorithm encrypts using the input of a 64-bit plaintext block and a 56-bit encryption key; the output is a 64-bit ciphertext. (The decryption process is described later.) First, the

64-bit plaintext is processed through an initial permutation using a permutation table. The permuted bit string goes through a sequence of 16 iterations of substitutions and transpositions, as shown in Figure 4.5. At the end of the sixteenth iteration, the resulting bit string is inverse permuted and the output is delivered as the ciphertext.

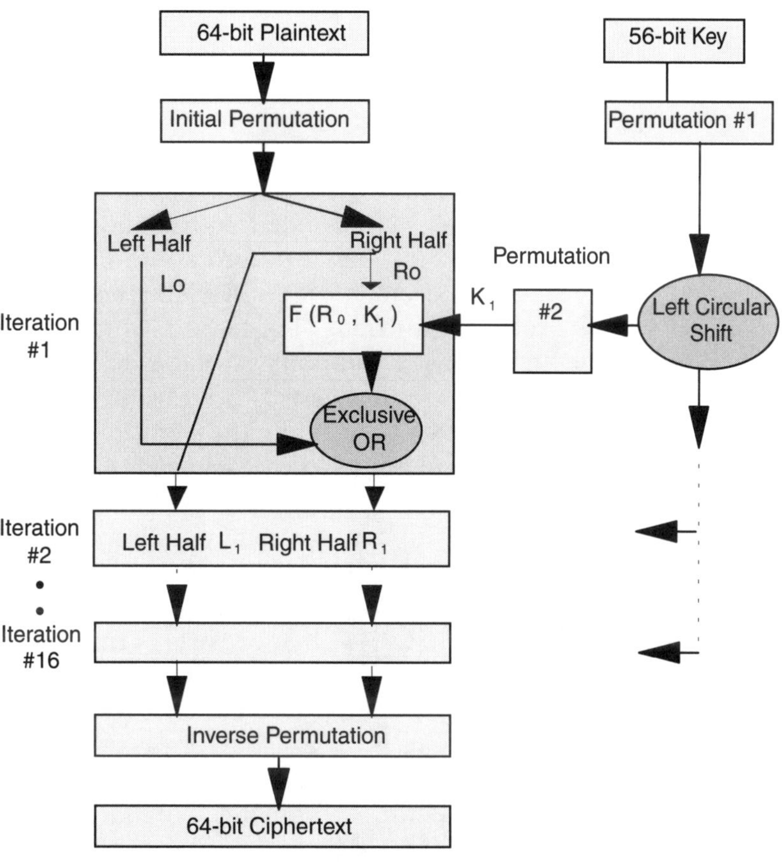

Figure 4.5: Overview of DES Algorithm

At each of the 16 iterations, the following operations take place. The 64-bit string is divided into two parts of 32 bits each, labeled L (left) and R (right). After the first iteration, each of the subsequent iterations obtains its L from the R of the previous iteration. At each iteration, R is obtained by performing an XOR (exclusive OR) operation on previous L and a complex function of previous R and the key K. So,

$$L_i = R_{i-1}$$

$$R_i = L_{i-1} \oplus F(R_{i-1}, K_i)$$

where $\oplus$ stands for the exclusive OR operation.

The encryption key is handled as follows. To begin with, the key is passed through a permutation function. Next, a subkey of 48 bits is generated through a left circular shift followed by a permutation function. This 48-bit key, K_1, is used as input for the first of the 16 iterations. At the same time, the resulting key after the left circular shift is used as input to generate the key for the next iteration. While the same circular shift and permutation function are used in each iteration, the resulting key is different for each iteration. This is true because the input value of the key is different for each iteration due to the left circular shift before each iterations.

The function $F(R_{i-1}, K_i)$ consists of the following steps. First the R input from the previous iteration is expanded from 32 bits to 48 bits by using a table to select the 16 bits of R to be duplicated. (This is the E-Table for password encryption in AIX systems, described in Chapter 2). Next, an XOR (exclusive OR) operation is performed on this expanded right half bit string with the 48-bit subkey, K_i. The resulting 48-bit string is divided into 8 blocks of 6 bits each. Each 6-bit string goes through a substitution function that results in a 4-bit string. This reduction to 4 bits is achieved by using 8 matrices, each with 4 rows and 15 columns. Each entry in the matrix has a 4-

bit value. The row and the column in each matrix are selected using the 6-bit input as follows. The first and last bits of the 6-bit string are used to form a 2-bit number. This 2-bit number is used to select the row, while the middle 4 bits of the 6-bit string are used to select the column. For the selected row and the column, the 4-bit entry from the matrix is used as the output of the substitution function. The 8 matrices correspond to the 8 substitution functions or *S*-boxes. The matrices can be found in Schneier (1994) and Stallings (1995).

The process for DES decryption is similar to that for encryption. The ciphertext is used as input to the DES algorithm. The keys are used in the reverse order; so K_{16} is used for the first iteration, K_{15} for the second iteration, and so on.

Modes of Operation

DES can operate in one of four modes, as described next.

Electronic Codebook Mode (ECB)

The ECB mode depicts the basic method for block encryption. Here, each 64-bit block is enciphered independently. If a message is longer than 64 bits, then it is divided into two or more 64-bit blocks. The last block is padded if necessary. It is called *Electronic Codebook Mode* because for a given block of text and a given encryption key, the same block of ciphertext is produced. So if the same 64-bit block appears more than once in a message, then in ECB mode, DES will produce the same ciphertext.

Sometimes messages have standard format, such as always beginning with some predefined fields. Given that the same ciphertext would be created for a given 64-bit block, this can give a cryptanalyst additional information in breaking the encryption scheme.

Cipher Block Chaining Mode (CBC)

In this mode, if the same 64-bit plaintext block is repeated, it produces a different ciphertext. The approach is to XOR (exclusive OR) the first 64-bit block of plaintext with an initialization vector. The resulting bit string is used as input to the DES algorithm. Every subsequent 64-bit plaintext block is first XORed with the enciphered text of the preceding 64-bit block, and the resulting 64-bit block is used as input to the DES algorithm. In this way, the same 64-bit blocks in the plaintext result in different enciphered texts. The initialization vector is provided to the receiver as well as the sender.

Feedback Modes

DES can operate in feedback modes that can handle variable-length plaintext. In these modes, DES operates as a *stream cipher* algorithm. A stream cipher algorithm encrypts an 8-bit character at a time. In a real-time environment, as new characters arrive, these characters are encrypted and transmitted. As such, the stream cipher eliminates the need to require the padding of the plaintext for complete 64-bit blocks. Furthermore, the ciphertext is the same size as the plaintext.

The stream cipher can work either in *Cipher Feedback Mode* (CFB) or in *Output Feedback Mode* (OFB). In CFB, the input to encryption function is a 64-bit shift register. To begin with, the shift register is set to an initialization vector. The leftmost 8 bits of the output of the encryption function are XORed with the plaintext character. The resulting output is transmitted as ciphertext. In addition, the shift register is shifted left by 8 bits, and the rightmost 8 bits are substituted by the ciphertext.

The OFB mode is similar to CFB except for the feedback to the shift register. In OFB mode, the high-order 8 bits of the output of the encryption function are inserted as the low-order 8-bits of the shift register. While in CFB mode, as described earlier, the final 8-bit output of the XOR function is inserted in the low-order 8 bits of the shift register.

DES Usage

DES technology has been implemented in several commercial products and is the most commonly used encryption algorithm of choice. Several companies offer DES-based products, including IBM, Motorola, General Electric, and Digital Equipment Corporation. DES has also been implemented in hardware chips to provide high-performance encryption for bulk data and voice. Although the government agencies cannot use DES to protect extremely sensitive information, DES is used by the U.S. Department of Energy, the Department of Justice, and the Department of the Treasury. DES is also commonly used in the banking industry, although some of the banks are considering more secure schemes such as IDEA and Triple-DES, described below

Triple-DES

Due to concerns about the strength of a 56-bit DES, such as the brute force attack described later, a triple-DES scheme is being used in some environments. *Triple-DES* performs three iterations of encryption or decryption of the plaintext. It can use the same 56-bit key for each iteration. However, it is possible for each iteration to use a different 56-bit key. A common technique for Triple-DES is to use the encrypt-decrypt-encrypt (EDE) mode. In EDE mode, as shown in Figure 4.6, two 56-bit encryption keys are used. In the first step, the plaintext is encrypted using the first key. In the second step, the output from the first step is decrypted using the second key. Finally, in the third step, the output from the second step is encrypted using the first key. The resulting ciphertext is sent to the receiver. The receiver performs exactly the reverse process. It first decrypts using the first key, then encrypts the result using the second key, and finally decrypts this result with the first key. This mode is also called DES-EDE and is used in Privacy-Enhanced Mail (PEM) on the Internet (see Chapter 6). DES-EDE requires two independent keys of 56 bits each, or a total key length of 112 bits.

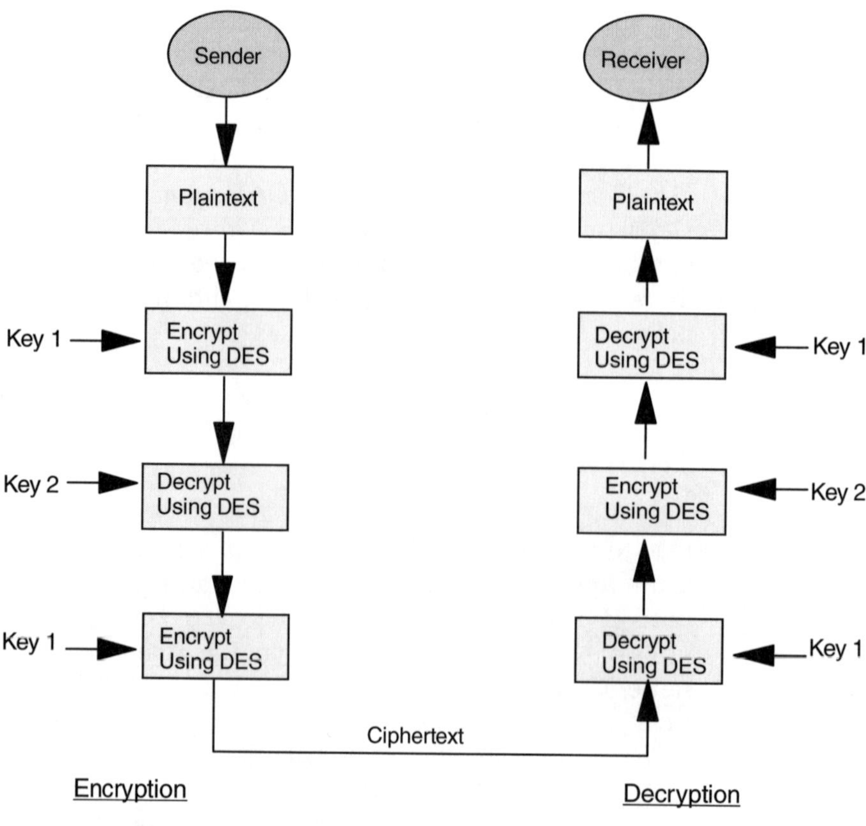

Figure 4.6: Triple-DES Overview

Triple-DES is a convenient approach for existing DES implementations to enhance the strength of their encryption algorithms. While it requires secret distribution of 112 bits of encryption keys (instead of 56 bits for single-DES), the same DES code can be used for implementing Triple-DES.

Commercial Data Masking Facility (CDMF)

CDMF was designed by IBM. It uses the data encryption algorithm of DES as the basis, but weakens the cryptographic operations by defining a key generation method that produces 40-bit keys instead of the 56-bit DES keys. According to Johnson (1994), products implementing the CDMF algorithm in an appropriate manner, in general, may be freely exported from the United States. IBM has implemented the CDMF algorithm and offers products using this encryption technique. Details of CDMF can be found in Johnson (1994).

International Data Encryption Algorithm (IDEA)

IDEA was invented in 1991 by James Massey and Xuejia Lai of the Swiss Federal Institute of Technology. IDEA uses 128-bit keys to encrypt 64-bit data blocks. As stated earlier, DES also uses 64-bit data blocks, but 56-bit keys. The additional key length adds to the strength of the IDEA algorithm. It uses 8 iterations, compared to the 16 iterations for DES shown in Figure 4.5. But each IDEA iteration works as if it were a double DES iteration.

RC2 and RC4

RC2 and RC4 are proprietary cryptographic algorithms developed by Ron Rivest. Rivest is a cryptographer at MIT and also works for RSA Data Security, Inc. RC2 is a variable-key-size 8-byte block cipher algorithm using symmetric keys, and RC4 is a symmetric stream cipher algorithm.

RSA Data Security, Inc. claims that these algorithms are as fast as or faster than DES (RSA 1993). The reference also states that these algorithms have been given special status by the U.S. government for export. As a result, the approval process is more simple for getting export permission from the U.S. government. To qualify for quick approval, the products must limit the RC2 and RC4 key lengths to 40 bits; 56 bits is allowed for foreign subsidiaries and overseas offices of U.S. companies, according to RSA Data Security, Inc.

RC2 and RC4 have been used in several products including Lotus Notes®, Apple's® Open Collaboration Environment (AOCE), Secure Sockets Layer (SSL), and Secure HyperText Transfer Protocol (S-HTTP).

The key sizes for some of the common encryption technologies are summarized in Table 4.2.

Encryption Algorithm	Key Size
DES	56 bits
Triple-DES	112 bits
CDMF	40 bits
IDEA	128 bits
RC2	variable
RC4	variable
RSA Public Key	variable

Table 4.2: Key Sizes for Encryption Schemes

Brute Force Attack

A straightforward approach to attacking an encryption algorithm is to use the brute force attack. In brute force attack, each possible key combination is attempted. So, for a 56-bit DES, all 2^{56} combinations of 56 bits are exercised. Such an attack is always possible. Strategies to resist brute force attacks include making it too time-consuming or too expensive to mount such an attack.

Schneier (1995, 25) analyzes the amount of time required to launch a brute force attack. The analysis assumes that the attacker has $1 million available to build specialized hardware. He estimates that in 1995, a hardware brute-force attack would take 0.2 second for 40-bit keys, 3.6 hours for 56-bit keys, 10^{13} years for 112 bits, and 10^{18} years for a 128-bit key. In the year 2000 with a $1 million equipment, it is expected to take 0.02 second for 40-bit keys, 21 minutes for 56-bit keys, 10^{12} years for 112-bit keys, and 10^{17} years for a 128-bit scheme. As stated earlier, Triple-DES EDE mode uses 112-bit keys, and IDEA uses 128-bit keys.

Export Implications

There is no restriction in selling DES-based products to companies located, owned, and controlled in the United States, as stated in Russell (1991, 197–198). These products can be exported only with an appropriate license. The U.S. government closely regulates the sale and export of cryptographic products developed in the United States. Products using encryption schemes with 40-bit (or less) keys may be allowed for export to selected countries after a government license for export is obtained. Examples include RSA's RC2 and RC4 algorithms using up to 40-bit encryption keys.

Encryption algorithms are receiving renewed attention given the growth in Internet usage. Invention of new algorithms and analysis of existing algorithms are expected to continue for the foreseeable future. Given the space, this section has only presented an overview of the encryption algorithms. Complete details of encryption algorithms can be found in cryptography books such as Schneier (1994). Other related references on this topic include Schatz (1995), Simmons (1994), Barlow (1993), and Stallings (1995).

Data Integrity

"Integrity: An Unimpaired Condition"

Webster's New Collegiate Dictionary. G & C Merriam Company. 1977.

Data integrity pertains to protection of information from modification by unauthorized users. A network security scheme must provide the services to protect information against the threat of unauthorized modifications. This threat exists while the information is saved in a local system storage as well as when it is transmitted over the network. In both cases, an intruder may modify some secret information that is not protected.

Data integrity is not the same as data confidentiality. *Data confidentiality* implies that confidential data is not disclosed to an unauthorized user. Data integrity requires that no unauthorized user can modify the data. However, data integrity does not prevent unauthorized disclosure of confidential data. Consider a company's income report. The information in the income report is company-confidential until the company announces its income to the press. So this report should be stored and transmitted as encrypted text until it is time to release the company income report. After the income report is made public, anyone can read the income report and there is no need to keep it confidential. However, if someone modifies the income report, it can mislead the readers.

Now consider the previous day's stock prices. They are public knowledge. Suppose someone modifies the previous day's stock prices while they are being transmitted to a newspaper, thereby misleading some readers into buying or selling stocks the next day. So while stock prices are public information, this information should be protected from unauthorized modifications. As such, it is critical to use data integrity services to protect this information. However, there is no need to encrypt the information on stock prices.

Protection of data from changes by unauthorized users can be accomplished in two steps. The first step is for the sender to perform a *one-way hash* function on the data. The result of this function, called a *message digest*, is appended to the data. Upon receiving the data, the receiver needs to verify that the data has not been modified. So the receiver performs the same one-way hash function on the received data as that performed by the sender. Next, the receiver compares its own results of the one-way hash function with the message digest appended to the data, as shown in Figure 4.7. A mismatch in the results implies that the data has been modified, in which case the receiver should reject the data.

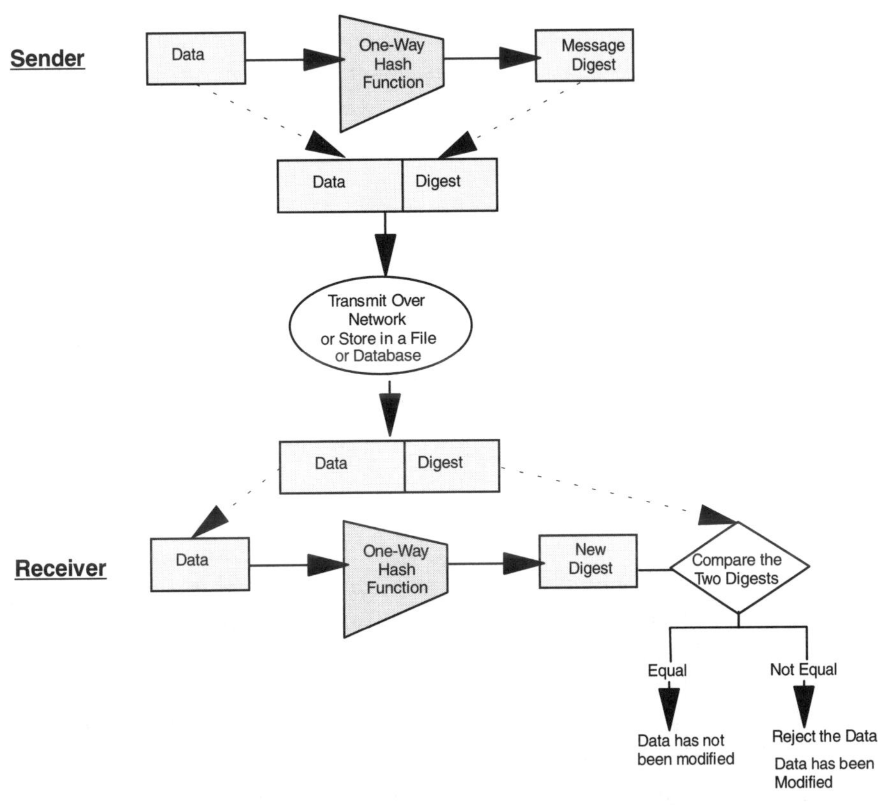

Figure 4.7: Data Integrity Using One-Way Hash Function

The second step is to encrypt the message digest. Consider an intruder that intercepts the data during transmission. The intruder modifies the data, performs the hash function on the modified data, removes the original message digest, appends the new message digest to the data, and sends it to the receiver. The receiver accepts the data since the one-way hash function yields the same message digest as that appended by the intruder. So in order to prevent such an attack, the message digest should be encrypted. An encrypted message digest cannot be modified by the intruder without the secret encryption key. Encryption of message digest is accomplished through *digital signature*, which is described later in this section.

One-Way Hash Functions

One-way hash functions have been used for a long time in the computer industry. During the 1970s, data transmission took place over analog links which were prone to introducing errors during transmission. So, there was a requirement to detect changes to messages during transmission. In order to detect any errors during transmission, the link layer protocols included a *checksum*. In simplified terms, a checksum is obtained by performing certain operations on the protected data. The checksum is appended to the message. The receiver performs the same operations, obtains a new checksum, and compares it with the checksum appended with the message. If the receiver detects that the message was modified during transmission, a negative acknowledgement is transmitted to the sender. This acknowledgement implies that the sender should resend the message.

A one-way hash function has many names: *message digest, check sum, contraction function, data integrity check, message authentication code, message integrity check*, and *data authentication code*. The purpose of a one-way hash function is to provide the means for the receiver to detect whether the message has been modified by unauthorized means. The hash function should produce a *fingerprint* of the message, as described next.

Let us call H the one-way hash function and M the data message to be protected. Then we apply the function H on a data block M and obtain a message digest d. So,

$$d = H(M)$$

Next, we list the requirements to be satisfied by one-way hash functions.

1. The one-way hash function H can be applied to a data block M of arbitrary size.

2. The resulting message digest, d, is of fixed size. The message digest size is usually 128 bits or 160 bits.

3. The one-way hash function H is easy to implement in both hardware and software.

4. Given the message digest d, it is very hard to find the original message M. This requirement is to protect the secret data when the one-way hash function is applied to the data. In such cases, the secret data itself is not sent; instead only the message digest is sent. For example, in authentication systems such as Kerberos, the password is not sent to the security server. Instead, a one-way hash such as the message digest is transmitted to the security server. If the intruder can recreate the password from the message digest, then the intruder can misuse the password.

5. Given the message M, it is very hard to find a data block N such that $H(N) = H(M)$. This implies that a hacker cannot forge an original message M with a substitute message N without requiring a change in the message digest. This requirement addresses the following threat.

When the message digest is encrypted, the hacker has no convenient way to modify the message digest. In such cases, the hacker would like to substitute the data block with another data block without having to decrypt and modify the encrypted message digest. So it should be hard for a hacker to substitute a message block with another message block without requiring a change to the message digest.

> 6. It is very hard to find any two data blocks x and y such that $H(x) = H(y)$. This requirement is to address the *Birthday Attack*, described later in this section.

Several one-way hash functions have been designed and implemented. Some of the common hash functions are briefly reviewed below; additional details can be found in Stallings (1995), Schneier (1994), and Tsudik (1992).

Message Digest Algorithms: MD5, MD4, and MD2

Message Digest 5 (MD5) is a one-way hash function designed by Rivest after some cryptanalytic attacks were discovered against Rivest's previous MD4 algorithm.

MD5 handles data blocks of arbitrary lengths as input and produces a message digest of 128 bits. Complete details are documented in RFC 1321 (Rivest 1992a). In the RFC, Rivest conjectures that MD5 is as strong as possible for a 128-bit hash. MD5 is used in Pretty Good Privacy (PGP) and Privacy-Enhanced Mail (PEM) as a one-way hash function. PGP and PEM provide secured E-mail over the Internet (see Chapter 6).

MD4 was a precursor to MD5; it is documented in RFC 1320 (Rivest 1992b). MD2 is a simplified one-way hash function and produces 128-bit hash. MD2 was also designed by Rivest. It is believed to be less secure and slower than MD4 and MD5.

Secure Hash Algorithm (SHA)

SHA was developed by National Institute of Standards and Technology (NIST) and published as a federal standard in 1993. SHA is also a one-way hash function, but it provides a message digest of 160 bits. This algorithm uses concepts similar to those in MD4. However, it is considered to be more secure, given the larger size of the message digest. Furthermore, there are no known cryptanalytic attacks on this algorithm, other than the brute force attack. Given the 160-bit message digest size, a brute force attack will take a very long time, as described below.

Brute Force Attack

One-way hash functions can be subject to brute force attack. Here, the message digest d is given, and the attacker finds the message M such that $H(M) = d$. The attacker can succeed by attempting message after message, until a message yields the desired message digest. According to Schneier (1995), using $1 million in equipment, a hardware brute force attack in 1995 will take 38 days for a 64-bit message digest and 10^{18} years for a 128-bit message digest. In the year 2000, it is projected to take 4 days for a 64-bit message digest and 10^{17} years for a 128-bit message digest.

Birthday Attack

Now consider a brute force attack to find any two message blocks that hash to the same value. This attack takes less time that the previous attack. Here the objective is to find any two messages that would hash to the same message digest. For example, how many people have to be in a room so there is a 50 percent chance that one of them has same birthday as yours? The answer is 183. Now how many people have to be in the room so there is a 50 percent chance that two of them have the same birthday? The answer is only 23. (For details on how this number is derived, consult a book on probability or see Stallings (1995, 202)).

If the intruder can create two messages that hash to the same value, then the attacker can substitute a valid message with an incriminating message for the same message digest, as follows. Once the attacker has obtained two messages that hash to the same value, the attacker can have the sender sign an innocuous message. Next the attacker takes the message digest of the innocuous message and appends it to an incriminating message that would yield the same message digest. The incriminating message would be assumed valid by the receiver, since it has the correct message digest.

According to Schneier (1995, 61), with $1 million in equipment, a hardware brute force attack in 1995 to find two messages that hash to the same message digest is estimated to take 19 days for 64-bit message digest, 38 days for 128-bit message digest, and 7000 years for a 160-bit message digest. For the year 2000, Schneier estimates 2 days for 64-bit message digest, 4 days for 128-bit message digest, and 700 years for 160-bit message digest.

Digital Signature

Digital signature provides proof of authenticity and origination of data. Digital signature is different from encryption, since encryption provides confidentiality. There is a variety of options between confidentiality, data integrity, one-way hash functions, and digital signatures, as shown in Figure 4.8. For example, Pretty Good Privacy (PGP) and Privacy-Enhanced Mail (PEM) offer the use of encryption and digital signature. The following description uses public key scheme, described in Chapter 2.

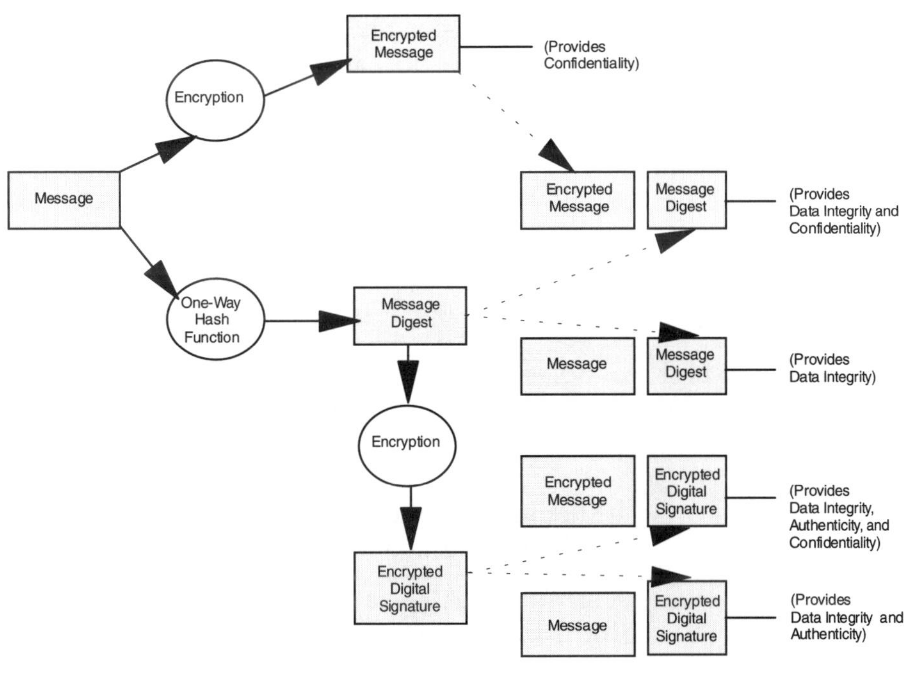

Figure 4.8: Data Integrity and Confidentiality

Digital signature addresses two types of attacks or problems. Consider an order for a stereo from Mary. The legitimate process is that Mary fills in the form and sends it to a merchant. Now an intruder X assumes the identity of Mary and sends the order as if it came from Mary. While Mary may be the one pay-ing for the stereo, X gets the stereo. This attack is similar to the credit card fraud, where the attack succeeds because the attacker has all the requisite information on the credit card. The digital signature addresses this attack by requiring the use of Mary's private key, which only Mary is expected to know. In this way, an intruder cannot assume Mary's identity without obtaining her private key.

The second problem relates to nonrepudiation (defined in Chapter 1). Now consider that John places an order for purchase of a large number of shares of a company to a stockbroker. The share price drops, and John denies he ever ordered the stocks. Now the broker must prove that John had indeed sent the purchase order for the shares. With the digital signature, the broker has received the message along with a message digest. In particular, the message digest is encrypted using John's private key. Since only John should know his private key, no one else could have sent this message to the broker.

In both examples, the digital signature establishes the authenticity of the originator of the data. A digital signature scheme should support the following characteristics.

- It should be able to verify the author, the date, and the time of the signature.

- It should be able to authenticate the contents of the document at the time of the signature. (This requirement is to ensure that the message contents have not been modified since the time it was signed.)

- It should use a signature scheme that can be verified by third parties to resolve disputes.

A digital signature is achieved through the use of a one-way hash function and the public key scheme, described in Chapter 2. Consider as an example that Alice needs to send a message to Dave. Additionally, Dave must ensure that the message indeed came from Alice. Dave must also verify that the message has not been modified since the time Alice signed it. To begin with, Alice performs the following steps as the sender.

1. Alice writes the message.

2. Alice adds the time, the day, and her name to the message.

3. Alice generates a message digest using a one-way hash function, such as MD5 described earlier.

4. Alice encrypts the message digest using her private key. (This step is also referred to as Alice *signing* the message digest.)

5. Alice appends the encrypted message digest to the message and sends it to Dave.

Dave executes the following steps as the receiver.

1. Dave separates the message from the message digest.

2. Dave finds Alice's name from the text of the message.

3. Dave finds Alice's public key from a key server or some yellow pages.

4. Dave decrypts the message digest from step 1 by using Alice's public key.

5. Dave applies the same one-way hash function on the message as that used by Alice and compares the resulting message digest with that obtained in step 4.

6. If the two message digests match, then Dave is satisfied that the message came from Alice and that it was not modified since the time she signed the message. If the two message digests do not match, then Dave

concludes that either it was not Alice that sent the message or the message was modified since the time it was signed by Alice. Nevertheless, a mismatch of the message digests should result in rejection of the message and a request for retransmission.

Consider the two problems outlined earlier that are addressed by digital signature. First, Dave knows that Alice sent the message, since Dave could decrypt the message digest using Alice's public key. Since only Alice knows her private key, no one else could have encrypted this message digest. Second, Alice cannot deny that she sent this message. This is true since only Alice could have known her private key that was used to sign this message.

Digital Signature Standard (DSS)

The *Digital Signature Standard* (DSS) is a draft Federal Information Processing Standard published by the National Institute of Standards and Technology. The DSS uses Secure Hash Algorithm outlined earlier in this section and describes a new digital signature approach. The DSS was originally published in 1991 and revised in 1993.

Digital Signature Usage

Digital signature is used in X.509 certificates, as described in Chapter 2. Digital signature is also used in PGP and PEM, as described in Chapter 6.

OSF DCE Security Services

This section presents an overview of security services provided by Open Software Foundation's (OSF's) *Distributed Computing Environment*. OSF, a nonprofit company, was founded in 1988. OSF membership includes system vendors, independent software vendors, end users, government agencies, research centers, and universities. OSF has developed vendor-neutral computing environments for use by the industry. Since its inception, OSF has developed an open UNIX system (OSF/1), a graphical user interface (MOTIF), and a Distributed Computing Environment (DCE). OSF DCE provides an integrated set of system services for heterogeneous computing environments.

Distributed Computing Environment (DCE)

OSF DCE, or simply DCE, was first introduced in 1992. DCE addresses the important requirement of interoperable system services among diverse computing systems. End users and companies require the ability to mix and match hardware and software from various vendors. The goal for DCE is to provide a comprehensive set of basic system services for the development and use of applications in a distributed environment.

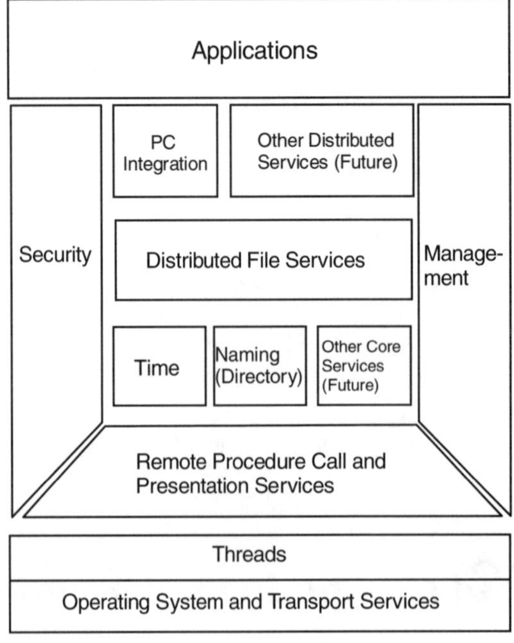

Figure 4.9: Architecture of OSF's Distributed Computing Environment

Permission to reprint this copyrighted OSF illustration has been granted by the copyright owner, Open Software Foundation, Inc.

DCE consists of several components, as depicted in Figure 4.9. OSF solicited and received technology submissions from vendors for these components and made selections based on the rationale described in OSF (1990).

Remote Procedure Call

Remote Procedure Call (RPC) is used for communication among the components of a distributed application. By using the RPC, a program can call another program independent of the location of the program. RPC extends the local procedure calls to a distributed environment. OSF DCE uses NCS 2.0 RPC that was submitted jointly by Digital Equipment Corporation and Hewlett-Packard.

Naming (Directory)

Naming or *directory* component provides storage and access to information about the objects in the network, such as computers, people, and files. This service is provided independent of the location and system. OSF selected Digital Equipment Corporation's DECdns as the cell naming service and Siemens DIR-X X.500 as the directory service. The cell directory service is used for local naming within a cell, while X.500 is used for global naming service across the network.

Time Service

Time service provides synchronization of time across the computing systems in the network. Time synchronization helps applications ensure the order of events, compute the time interval between events, and schedule events at specific times. DCE uses DECdts, Digital Equipment Corporation's Distributed Time Synchronization Service.

Distributed File System

The *distributed file system* extends the local file system model to the distributed network, thereby allowing users to access files across the network. OSF has chosen the Andrew File System (AFS) from Transarc Corporation for the distributed file service.

Other Components

Other components of DCE include *security, Personal Computer Integration, management,* and *threads.*

Personal Computer Integration extends the MS-DOS environment by providing access to resources such as file and print over the network. The management component is to provide complete management services for all the DCE components and is planned for the future by OSF. The threads component allows parallel processing of multiple execution sequences. Details are beyond the scope of this book and can be found in Rosenberry (1992).

DCE Security

The security component of DCE is designed to prevent unauthorized access to resources in the distributed environment. OSF evaluated three technology submissions for security and selected MIT's Kerberos Version 5 augmented by other Hewlett-Packard security components.

In the following, we present the requirements for DCE security services followed by a description of DCE security. Additional details on this topic can be found in OSF (1990), Lockhart (1994), and Rosenberry (1992).

DCE Security Requirements

1. Users should be authenticated based on the password. A typed password is the means to authenticate the users. The authentication is performed securely, without exposing the password during transmission.

2. Users should be required to log on only once in order to access any service in the network. Once the user has been authenticated, he or she should be allowed access to all the services in the DCE network. This requirement is similar to the single logon topic discussed in Chapter 2.

3. The security scheme should provide access rights to users at the operation level. It should be possible to selectively allow or reject access to individual operations.

DCE Security Components

DCE security uses the concept of *cells,* where each cell has its own security service. A cell is the basic unit of operation and administration in DCE. The term *principal* is normally used to refer to either users or servers.

DCE security consists of three elements; authentication, authorization, and access control. DCE security also provides secret key encryption using DES.

Authentication

DCE authentication of principals is based on Kerberos Version 5. As explained in Chapter 2, the user logs on by entering the ID and the password. The Kerberos system authenticates a principal and provides the user with an encrypted data structure called a *ticket.* Later, the principal uses this ticket to prove its identity to other principals.

During the logon process, the principal also obtains a *Privilege Attribute Certificate* (PAC) from the security server. To begin with, the DCE logon sends a request to the security server for a *privilege service ticket.* On receiving the privilege service ticket from the security server, the DCE logon code sends a request to the privilege server for the PAC. The privilege server creates the PAC and sends to the user; the PAC is used as part of the authorization process. The privilege server is part of the security server.

Authenticated RPC

DCE security uses encryption to exchange secret keys between the client and the application server. The application server obtains a *shared key* as part of the ticket sent to the server by the client. Now the client can use this shared key to encrypt portions of the RPC calls destined for the server. On receiving the calls, the server can decrypt the calls using the shared key. This method of authentication is called authenticated RPC.

Authorization

Authorization identifies the type of principal, which in turn determines the rights and privileges for that principal. Authorization takes place after the authentication process is completed.

The security server creates the PAC using information from the DCE security registry. The DCE security registry contains entries for the principals, accounts, groups, and organizations. The password associated with the principal is used during the authentication process. When a PAC is created, it contains the identities of all the groups to which the principal belongs.

A *group* is simply a named collection of principals that are allowed to do the same things. When a change is made for the access rights of a group, it applies to all the principals in the group. A *principal* can belong to one or more groups. An *organization* is a named collection of the principals to provide administrative convenience. For example, a decision to change the minimum size of the password can be applied across an organization. A principal belongs to only one organization.

Access Control

DCE access control is described in Chapter 5.

Summary

Distributed applications require access to security services through an application program interface (API). A key requirement for a security API is its independence from the underlying security scheme. The Generic Security Service API (GSSAPI) satisfies this requirement and has gained acceptance in the industry over the last few years.

Data confidentiality is achieved by the sender encrypting the message and the receiver decrypting it. Several key encryption algorithms are presented. Data integrity is accomplished by calculating a message digest for the message using a one-way hash function, optionally encrypting the message digest using the sender's private key, and then appending the message digest with the message. Finally, OSF DCE provides distributed system services for heterogeneous computing environments. DCE security is based on MIT's Kerberos Version 5. We concluded the chapter with a discussion of OSF DCE and its security services.

Access Control

In a typical client/server network, there are several resources distributed across the network. In order to secure these resources, the first step is to authenticate each user or application. However, it is quite conceivable that users may be assigned different levels of authority and corresponding degrees of access to the resources. For example, while the security administrator may be allowed to read and write the password file, no other user is normally allowed to read or write on the file. This process of enforcing different levels of access to network resources is accomplished through a collection of mechanisms that are generally called *access control*.

There are three main topics that must be addressed in discussing access control. First, a general review of access control concepts is necessary in order to more fully understand the intricacies of access control. Second, the issue of covert channels must be described. *Covert channels* result from misuse of legitimate communication channels through covert means. Third, we must complete the OSF/DCE review (Chapter 4) by outlining the access control in DCE.

Concepts and Approaches

An access control mechanism is based on three types of information.

1. **Subjects:** A *subject* is capable of accessing an object. Examples of a subject include an individual user, a user group, a terminal, a host, or an application.

2. **Objects:** An *object* is an entity to which access can be controlled. Examples of objects can be as detailed as the individual data fields or as aggregate as groups of programs, records, files, or entire databases.

3. **Access Rights:** *Access rights* define the ways in which a subject can access the object. Access rights are specified for each pair of subjects and objects. Examples of access rights include read, write, and execute. The right to read or write an object is straightforward. The right to execute pertains to searching a file or executing the file if it is a program. The access rights for the users are specified based on the security policy for the network. Sometimes the term *user permissions* is used in describing the access rights for the subjects.

So, access control enforces the access rights when a subject requests to access an object. Access control has also been defined as comprising the mechanisms that enforce mediation on subject requests for access to objects as specified in the security policy.

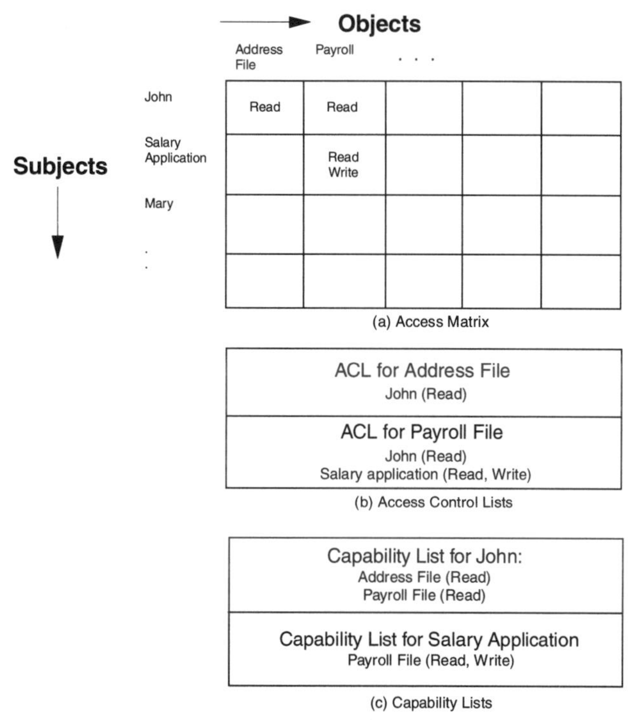

Figure 5.1: Access Control Mechanism

The *access matrix*, shown in Figure 5.1a, contains information to specify the *access control lists* and the *capability lists*. For each object, there is an *access control list* (ACL), which is pronounced *ackle*. An ACL for a given object defines the access rights for each subject. Figure 5.1b shows the access control list for two objects. Access control lists are the most common form of access control in use today. Most PCs, servers, and hosts have ACLs to provide access control services.

Each subject may have a capability list. A *capability list* for a subject specifies the rights to access each object. Figure 5.1c shows the capability list for John, based on the access matrix of Figure 5.1a.

Secure Xenix ACLs

According to Amoroso (1994, 258), XENIX is a secure UNIX-based implementation that was targeted for the IBM PC/AT workstation. The semantics for XENIX ACLs follow the traditional semantics for ACLs. A XENIX ACL consists of the following pair associated with each object:

<principal identifier, access privilege>

The *principal identifier* portion specifies the principal user and the group. Thus, Tom.Group3 identifies the principal Tom belonging to Group3. A XENIX user may be a member of several groups, but the user must specify which group the user should belong to at logon time.

The *access privilege* portion of XENIX ACL specifies the access rights. So,

<Tom.Group3,R>

implies that Tom, member of group 3, is allowed to Read from the object.

XENIX also allows the use of a *DON'T CARE* wild card using the ∗ notation. As an illustration, <Sally.∗, W> specifies that any user with the name Sally in any user group is authorized to write to this object. In addition, XENIX provides support for specific exclusion of users to access the object. This capability allows for the use of wild card specifications when all but a few users are allowed to have access.

Access Control Mechanisms

So, access control is commonly provided through access control lists or capability lists. Access control can also be implemented through the use of *sensitivity labels*, described in Chapter 3. Access to resources can also be managed by implementing network controls, such as filters, routers, and bridges, that can inhibit access to resources. For example, Internet firewalls can filter the IP packets based on their source and destination addresses. To summarize, the following mechanisms are used for access control:

- Access control lists

- Capability lists

- Sensitivity labels

- Network controls or technical incompatibilities

Access Control Design

Access control is often implemented as part of the process to access resources. For example, when a user or program calls for opening a file, the file system initiates the open sequence, as shown in Figure 5.2. During this sequence, the access control mechanism is called. The access control mechanism checks the access rights of the calling user (or application) against those authorized for the user. This is accomplished through the use of access control lists or some other access control scheme. If the user is within his or her access rights, the process to open the file continues. If the user is attempting access outside the authorized rights, the access is denied and an error message is generated.

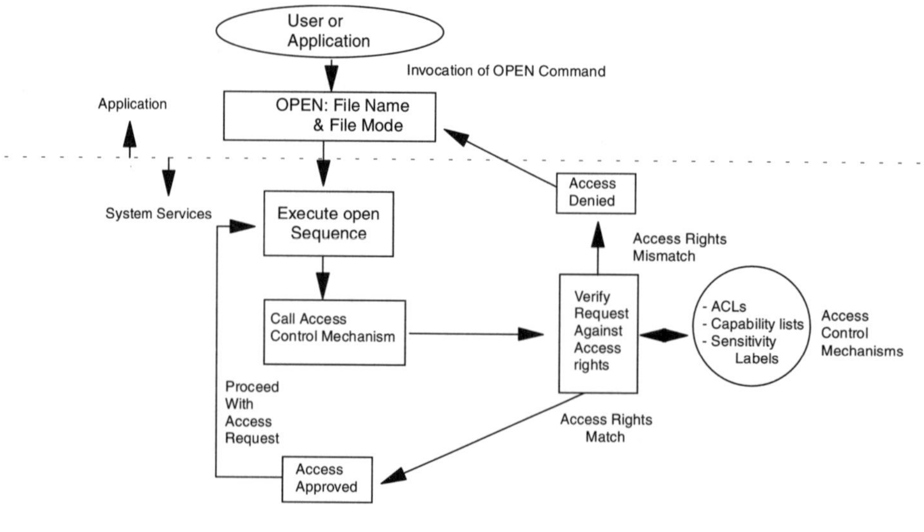

Figure 5.2: Access Control Design

Access control can be classified based on whether the access rights are assigned by the owner of the resource or by a system administrator. This classification leads to the two well-known approaches for access control, namely Discretionary Access Control and the Mandatory Access Control.

Discretionary Access Control

A *Discretionary Access Control* (DAC) consists of the procedures and mechanisms that perform access control at the discretion of the individual user. Thus the owner of the data specifies the rules for accessing the data. As such, the access rights for each user are established by the owners of the data. DAC is often implemented using the access control lists or capability lists.

The DAC approach provides flexibility and ease of data access to users, so security becomes less of an impediment to the benefits of general data sharing among users. A common risk with DAC is that some resources may be inadequately protected if the owner forgets to implement adequate protection or is unaware of the available protection mechanisms. DAC policies may also be circumvented, since they are not consistently applied across a given network. So the security policy for such an environment must consider the vulnerabilities of the resources to attacks to corrupt or steal data. Since DAC parameters can be easily changed, resources protected by DAC may be susceptible to Trojan horse attacks.

Mandatory Access Control

In contrast to DAC, *Mandatory Access Control* (MAC) does not allow individual users to define the access rights and their enforcement. Instead, a designated system administrator defines the access rights for users and user groups. A MAC scheme is attractive for implementation of consistent security policy across the network. MAC is often implemented using sensitivity labels, as described in Chapter 3.

MAC makes it easier to enforce strong security policies consistently across all users and resources. As such, MAC is commonly used when there is sensitive data to be protected across the environment. Critics may argue that MAC mechanisms are less flexible and interfere in open data sharing among users. A typical environment may require a mix of DAC and MAC mechanisms, thereby protecting the sensitive data (using MAC) as well as providing flexibility to users for sharing their information (using DAC).

UNIX Permissions Mechanism

Permissions in UNIX systems are defined through a 3-bit string, 1 bit each for read, write, and execute. These permissions can be viewed as tags that are assigned to files or directories. Consider a file CARPRICES that has the following three 3-bit strings for permissions.

$$(rwx)\ (rwx)\ (rwx)$$

Here, the file CARPRICES can be accessed by the owner of the file (first string), the designated user group (second string), and all other users (third string). Every one can read, write or execute the file. If a permission is to be denied, then that is reflected by a "-". Now consider the following three 3-bit permission strings:

$$(r-x)\ (r-x)\ (r-x)$$

Based on these permissions, we conclude that no one is allowed to write on the file. It should be noted that the execute permission for directories, if allowed, implies that the user can search the directory. For this permission scheme, the DAC mechanism is commonly used for access control.

Superuser Issues

In UNIX, a *setuid* (contraction for set user identification) program temporarily grants permissions to users. Users can invoke a setuid program to accomplish a task for which a normal user would not have proper authorization. For illustration, suppose that a normal user wishes to change the password. The normal user begins by executing a setuid program. The program begins with the normal user permissions until it reaches the point at which to change the password file. At that time, the user permissions are (temporarily) upgraded by the program, and the password is changed. After the password is changed, the user permissions are downgraded to his or her normal permissions.

A common attack on UNIX systems has been to find and compromise setuid programs to obtain superuser (or root) access. So setuid programs should be adequately protected through suitable access control mechanisms.

In the above, we have reviewed the concepts and mechanisms for access control. Additional information on access control can be found in Wichers (1990), Strack (1990), Carson (1990), Amoroso (1994), Russell (1991), and Salamone (1993).

Covert Channels

"Covert channel: A secret way to convey information."

Client/server networks consist of mechanisms that provide information transfer and resource sharing among their users. These mechanisms include channels for information exchange among the users. The network design permits the use of such channels for legitimate transfer of information. These channels are called *overt channels*.

A problem arises when a channel is used for illegitimate transfer of information by avoiding the normal security control mechanisms. For example, a disgruntled employee encodes the file name in such a way that the name communicates some company confidential information. If the file name (not the file) is accessible to external users, then an unauthorized user can receive information encoded in the file name. In this example, the channel for communicatig the file names has been misused to transfer some secret information, although the channel was originally not designed to transfer such information. Such channels are called *covert channels,* as shown in Figure 5.3.

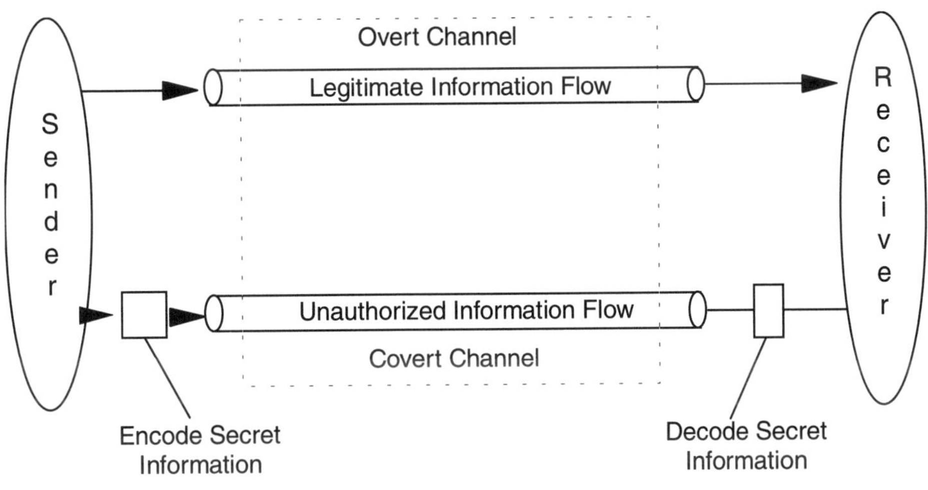

Figure 5.3: Overt and Covert Channels

In concept, covert channels are used to transfer confidential information to unauthorized recipients. A *covert channel* is defined as a communication channel that allows two processes to transfer unauthorized information without violating access control and other security mechanisms. The problem is worse because the covert channels are often available 24 hours a day, 7 days a week. The information over the channel may be delivered in real time or delivered at a later time by storing it in a record on a disk. Furthermore, covert channels are not easy to detect and certain types of channels are even difficult to eliminate after detection. In some cases, one can only reduce the bandwidth of a given covert channel, as described later in this section.

Covert channels are often described in terms of a *high user* and a *low user*. A high user is one with a higher level of security clearance, while a low user has a lower level of security clearance. Then the covert channel is described as one where a high user can transfer information to a low user. Clearly, such a data transfer is not authorized and should be preventable through the enforcement of MAC. Covert channels are often created to bypass the MAC mechanisms, particularly when MAC is incorrectly implemented.

Conditions for Covert Channels

Covert channels result from the following possible conditions.

1. Oversight during implementation of network design may lead to eventual misuse of a channel. For example, the network administrator may not have correctly implemented the design of the file naming convention, thereby leading to the misuse of a file name as a covert channel.

   During the design phase, a channel may have been designed for normal and legitimate use, without realizing its potential use as a covert channel. For example, consider the design where a high user and a low user are permitted to list all the active users on the system at a given time. A high user can encode secret information in the user names or in the way the list is displayed to the user. The low user can decode the secret information from the list of the users.

   Covert channels resulting from implementation oversights are usually cheaper to eliminate than those due to basic network design.

2. An incorrect implementation or operation of the access control mechanism may also expose some channels for use as a covert channel. If MAC is

enforced in a system but the implementation is incorrect, then the existence of covert channels is possible. If a network does not implement MAC, then the potential ways to exploit overt channels increase to the point that the existence of covert channels may be unavoidable.

3. The existence of a shared resource between the sender and the receiver, through which the information can be covertly transferred.

4. The ability to implant and hide a Trojan horse in the code that transfers information over the covert channel. The Trojan horse program encodes the confidential information for delivery to the unauthorized user. In order to accomplish this information transfer, the sender and the receiver of the covert channel have to a priori devise and agree on a scheme for encoding and decoding the information.

Types Of Covert Channels

In broad terms, there are two types of covert channels: covert storage channels and covert timing channels. A *covert storage channel* uses some storage mechanism to communicate information to the unauthorized user. A *covert timing channel* uses the sequence of events over time to communicate the unauthorized information. In the following, we illustrate the two types of channels through examples.

Covert Storage Channels: Examples

1. **Disk Space:** A covert channel can be created by sharing information about the amount of available disk space. Assume that every process can inquire about and receive information on the available disk space. Then a *low-end process* (with a lower level clearance) and a *high-end process* (with a higher level clearance) can allocate the disk space as well as determine the free disk space. So the high-end process can allocate the amount of disk space that corresponds to the encoded information. The low-end process inquires about the amount of available disk space before and after the high-end process has allocated disk space, thereby obtaining the information that the high-end process intended the low-end process to obtain.

2. **Print Spacing:** A covert channel is obtained by manipulating the amount of space between certain words in a text. Again, assume that the high-end process can write on some shared resource which is also accessible to the low-end process. The resource may contain general information such as system availability over the next holiday weekend. By manipulating the number of spaces between the words of a sentence, or the spaces between the sentences, the high-end process can transfer secret information to the low-end process.

3. **File Naming:** A covert channel can be created through encoded file names, as described earlier in this section.

Covert Timing Channels: Examples

1. **CPU Utilization:** A covert channel is possible if every user is permitted access to the amount of its CPU utilization. At certain times when no other processes are interfering, a high-end process can change the CPU utilization at predetermined time intervals. The low-end process can record such utilization and decode it to obtain the unauthorized information. For example, if a high CPU utilization (predefined by the two processes) at certain times is agreed to be a "1", and a low CPU utilization a "0", then binary data can be transferred from a high-end process to a low-end process. In this way, the CPU utilization may be manipulated by the high-end process and interpreted by the low-end process as shown in Figure 5.4.

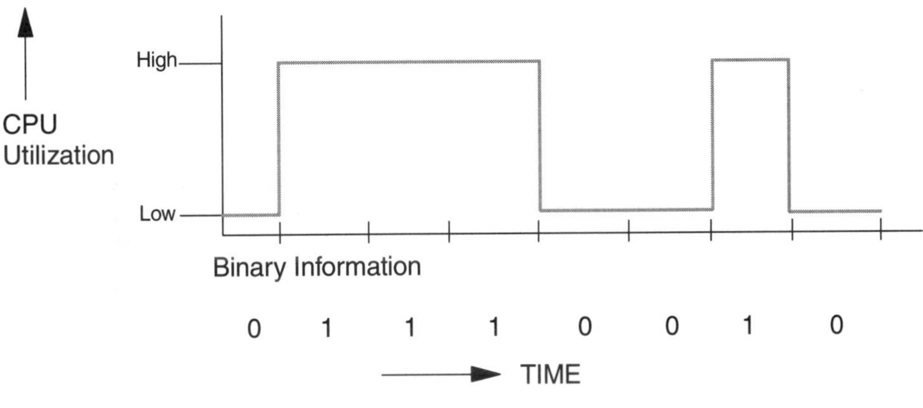

Figure 5.4: Covert Timing Channel Using CPU Utilization

2. **Resource Availability:** A covert channel may exist if a given resource is accessible by both the high-end and the low-end processes. This is true whether the

access rights are for read, write, or execute operation. Consider an example where a file or a database is accessible to a high-end process and a low-end process. The high-end process allocates the resource at a predetermined time. If the low-end process attempts an access to the same resource, the resource is busy and therefore unavailable. A *busy resource* may imply a "1", and a *free resource* may imply a "0". Both processes have agreed a priori to attempt this action at particular time intervals. In this way, the high-end process can covertly transfer information to the low-end process by manipulating the availability of a shared resource.

Bursty Covert Channels

The bandwidth of a covert channel depends on the duration of channel availability for covert operation and the channel data transfer rate. Certain channels allow a relatively constant leakage rate, such as a few bits over a long time span. On the other hand, some channels may display a high bandwidth over short time intervals, interspersed with little or no leakage. Such channels are called *bursty covert channels*.

Bursty covert channels can potentially cause more damage than channels with relatively constant leakage at low data rates. For example, consider a bursty channel allowing 300 kilobytes of burst once a month. Such a single burst may consist of transferring approximately 120 pages of text every month (assuming 50 lines/page and 50 characters/line). Now consider a covert channel with constant leakage rate of, say, 1 bit/second. This rate yields 3600 bits/hour or 324 kilobytes/ month. So a short burst of 300 kilobytes/month may inflict a loss that is equivalent to that of a 1 bit/second constant leakage rate.

Covert Channel Elimination

Covert channels are required to be addressed for B2 and higher (security) level systems, as described in Chapter 3. Analysis of covert channels consists of several steps:

1. Identify the covert channels.

2. Determine the security level of the data that can be transferred over the identified covert channels.

3. Determine the amount of data that can be transferred over each covert channel, or calculate the bandwidth of the covert channel.

4. Use the above information to create a cost-benefit analysis. This analysis computes the cost to eliminate the channel (or reduce its bandwidth) versus the benefits resulting from preventing the loss of data through the channel.

Steps 1 and 3 are described next. Step 2 pertains to the classification of data in the computer system. Step 4 requires analysis of system design to eliminate the channel or reduce the bandwidth of the channel. These actions depend on the specific covert channel; the details are beyond the scope of this book.

Detection of Covert Channels

A comprehensive approach for covert channel detection is to analyze all types of information flows in the system. This approach can be tedious and expensive. To begin with, the system specifications are analyzed to break down the system design to the level of specific information flows. Next, examine each information flow for any possible communication from a high user to a low user (with lower level clearance). Any information flow from a high user to a low user is considered a covert channel. However, it should be noted that such an approach leaves room for error due to differences between the design and implementation.

As in a typical software system, the best remedy is a sound system design from the beginning. In this way, the system resources and their information flows are confined to different levels of users and processes. Thus, any information flow from a high user to a low user is a violation of the design. Formal techniques can be developed to verify the system specifications for any violation of the design principles.

Resource Matrix Approach

Richard Kemmerer (1983) has proposed a resource matrix approach to identify the covert channels in a computer system. This approach, called *Shared Resource Matrix Methodology*, is based on analyzing all the shared resources in the system. A *shared resource* is any object or collection of objects that may be referenced or modified by more than one process. Next, the attributes of each shared resource are identified. For example, the first process may be able to determine only whether a file is locked, while the second process may only access the size of the file.

Each row of the matrix represents an attribute of a shared resource. Each column of the matrix represents a primitive operation that can be performed on any of these resources. Examples of these primitive operations include Write File, Read File, Lock File, and File Locked. An entry in the matrix represents the effect of the operation (the column) on the resource (the row). So an entry of M indicates that the operation modifies the resource, R denotes that the operation simply references the resource, and a blank entry implies that the operation does not apply to this resource.

Given the shared resource matrix, each of the operations can be associated with one or more processes or users that use the operation. Then a covert storage channel exists if the following criteria are met.

1. A high user and a low user have access to the same attribute of a shared resource.

2. A means for the high user to force the change to this attribute.

3. A means for the low user to detect changes to the attribute.

4. A mechanism for initiating communication between the high user and the low user and for sequencing the events correctly.

A covert timing channel exists if the following criteria are met.

1. A high user and a low user have access to the same attribute of a shared resource.

2. A shared reference to the time value by the high user and the low user.

3. A means for modulating the low user's response time in detecting changes to the shared attribute.

4. A mechanism for initiating communication between the high user and low user and for sequencing the events.

Covert Channel Bandwidth Determination

The bandwidth of a covert channel is estimated by analyzing the channel behavior. The basic parameters for obtaining the bandwidth are as follows.

- The number of times the shared resource can be modified by the high user

- The number of times the low user can sense the changes

- The amount of interference by other processes

Other factors that affect the channel bandwidth include noise and parallelism. The noise effect includes the interference due to the existence of other activities over the channel. The parallelism effect pertains to simultaneous use of more than one resource or more than one channel path (driver-receiver pairs) to transfer the information.

Covert channels have been addressed by several authors and continue to be a favorite research topic. For more information, refer to Kemmerer (1983), Russell (1991), Shaffer (1994), Loepere (1985), Girling (1987), Kang (1995), Browne (1995).

OSF DCE Access Control

OSF introduced a *Distributed Computing Environment* (DCE) that provides interoperable distributed services among heterogeneous computing systems. An overview of the components of DCE was presented in Chapter 4. Here we discuss the access control provided in DCE services.

Objects

DCE uses various types of objects in the context of access control. An *object* is a resource such as a hardware device, a single item of data, a whole file or database, or even an entire computer system such as a server.

Objects can be either *simple objects* or *container objects*. Container objects, as the name implies, can contain other objects. A container object can contain simple objects and some other container objects, as shown in Figure 5.5. For example, a file system directory is a container object, and an individual directory entry is a simple object contained in it.

DCE Access Control Lists

A DCE access control list (ACL) is a list of access control entries to protect an object. Each entry in the ACL specifies a set of permissions or rights for users or groups to perform specified operations on the protected object.

DCE provides several types of ACLs. Suppose we want to protect an object with an ACL. In order to do so, we register this object in the cell directory, and the associated ACL is made accessible. In addition, the Cell Directory Service creates an ACL to protect each entry in the directory. So there may be two types of ACLs associated with the same object; one ACL is to protect the directory entry for the object, and the other ACL is to protect the object itself.

In addition, default ACLs are defined for initial creation of objects. So DCE security provides three types of ACLs: *object ACLs, initial object creation ACLs,* and *initial container creation ACLs.* Note that only the container objects have the initial object creation ACL as well as the initial container creation ACL. These ACLs are not used to control access; their role is simply to provide default values when new objects are created within the container object.

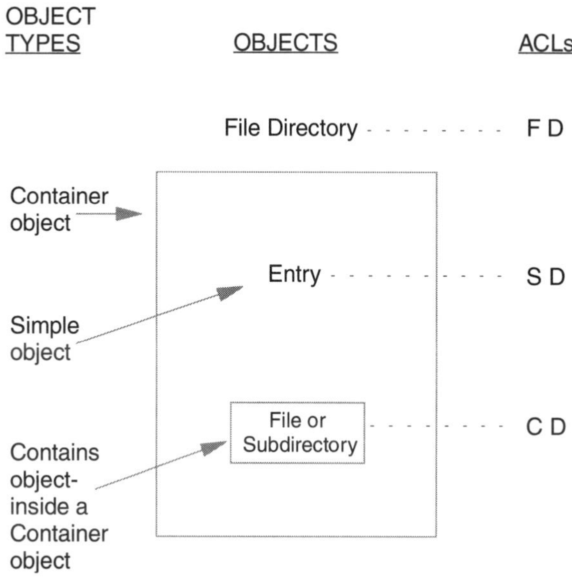

Figure 5.5: DCE Objects and ACLs

An example is shown in Figure 5.5. The container object is the file directory. The file directory object has three ACLs, one each for the file directory (FD), default for a simple object (SD), and default for a container object (CD). So, if a new simple object such as a directory entry is created, the default values for its initial object creation ACL will come from SD. If a new container object such as a file or a subdirectory is created within the file directory, then its ACL default values will come from CD.

Access Control List APIs

OSF DCE security supplies a set of application programming interfaces (APIs) to access and modify the ACLs. These API calls begin with *sec_acl*. The API calls are made by the clients and executed by an OSF-supplied editor. The editor provides a command line mode as well as an interactive user interface mode for editing the ACLs.

The ACL APIs refer to the ACLs as follows:

- *sec_acl_type*: Collectively to all of the following ACLs

- *sec_acl_type_object*: Object ACL

- *sec_acl_type_default_object*: initial object creation ACL

- *sec_acl_type_default_container*: initial container creation ACL

Access Control Resource Manager

The OSF DCE provides a reference implementation for *Access Control Resource Manager* (ACRM) to manages the ACLs. The reference implementation consists of four major components described below.

1. *sec_acl* API: Described earlier in this section.

2. *acl_edit* Editor: The ACL editor works at three levels: the entire ACL, the individual entries of ACL, or the permission bits within an entry. At the ACL level, it can list the contents, remove or replace all entries,

and assign the modified ACL to its object. At the entry level, it can add or delete a single entry. At the permission level, it can display, test, or change permissions.

3. *rdacl* Interfaces: The rdacl interfaces are supplied by OSF so that the ACRM writers will know the required implementation for interfacing with the client-side calls to the ACRM. Each ACRM needs to implement the code behind rdacl interfaces for functions such as reading privilege attribute certificate, listing and returning ACLs for an object, replacing ACLs, and testing access to an object.

4. *sec_acl_mgr* Interfaces: The *sec_acl_mgr* interfaces are specified in the DCE documentation and the source code is supplied as part of the Registry Resource Manager. These interfaces include functions such as to configure the ACL manager, returning the types of ACLs and printable ACL strings. The DCE approach is for each server writer to develop its ACL manager code using the source code as reference. In addition, the server writer needs to provide some form of storage medium for storing the ACLs, such as a file or a database.

DCE has been implemented by several vendors, such as IBM's AIX implementation IBMAIX (1994). Additional details can be found in Lockhart (1994), Rosenberry (1992), and OSF (1990).

Summary

This chapter addressed the topic of access control including covert channels. First, two common ways to provide access control are described and compared. Discretionary Access Control allows the resource owner to assign the access rights. Mandatory Access Control permits the system administrator to assign the access rights. Next, we addressed the topic of covert channels. Covert channels are created by exploiting the vulnerabilities of the design or implementation of the information flow among the network users or processes. Detection and analysis of covert channels require an in-depth study of shared resources and their attributes among high users and low users. Theoretically, every piece of stored information can be a potential covert channel. However, it is quite cumbersome to transfer meaningful data using covert channels. It is noteworthy that the Orange Book reserves covert channel analysis for high levels of security (B2 systems and above). Finally, we discussed the implementation of access control services by DCE.

Internet Security

> *"Internet theft: Online bandits will steal $10 billion worth of corporate information this year. Catching them won't be easy."*
>
> *Information Week Front Page. August 25, 1995.*

Internet is a collection of tens of thousands of interconnected IP networks, and it is growing at an extraordinary rate. According to survey data collected by Network Wizards, there were 1.776 million hosts and 26,000 domains on the Internet in July 1993. By July 1995, there were 6.642 million hosts and 120,000 domains, an increase of approximately 400 percent within 2 years.[1] The security-related incidents on the Internet have also been growing. According to InfoSec (1994), the number of incidents on the Internet has also grown from approximately 200 in

---

1. Data produced by Network Wizards and available on the Internet at http://www.nw.com/. Reprinted with their permission.

1990 to approximately 1300 in 1993, an increase of approximately 600 percent in 3 years.

This chapter addresses various aspects of security on the Internet. First, we need to review some of the TCP/IP protocols and the related security issues. Then we proceed to discuss security schemes for three primary areas of Internet usage. Specifically, we describe security mechanisms for electronic mail (E-mail), the World Wide Web, and electronic commerce.

TCP/IP

TCP/IP represents a collection of networking protocols and applications. Originally, TCP/IP was developed under the auspices of the U.S. Defense Advanced Research Projects Agency and was deployed in ARPANET in 1983. TCP/IP is also one of the most pervasive networking protocols in nearly all kinds of data networks.

The term TCP/IP is a combination of *TCP* which stands for *Transport Control Protocol*, and *IP*, for *Internet Protocol*. This description of TCP/IP protocols is necessarily brief; details on TCP/IP can be found in several books, including Comer (1991) and IBMTCP (1990).

The protocols of TCP/IP can be divided into four hierarchical layers, as shown in Figure 6.1. Starting from the lowest layer, the network interface layer provides the device drivers that interface to the communication hardware. TCP/IP does not specify any particular protocol for this layer but permits the use of almost all network interfaces such as Token Ring, Ethernet, and X.25.

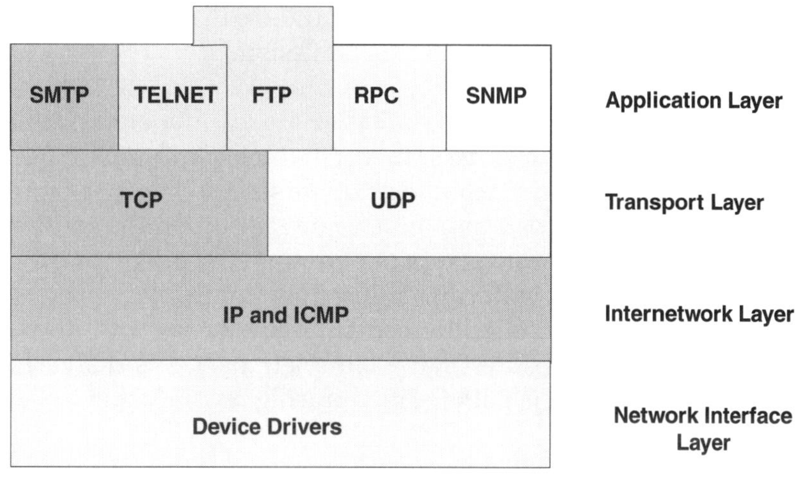

Figure 6.1: TCP/IP Layers

The internetwork layer consists of Internet Protocol (IP) and *Internet Control Message Protocol* (ICMP). While the physical addresses are used for communications over the network interface layer, only IP addresses are used at the internetwork or higher layers. Next, the transport layer consists of connection-oriented (TCP) or connectionless (UDP) protocols. The applications layer consists of various applications or higher level protocols that use TCP/IP. The higher level application protocols include TELNET and FTP (File Transfer Protocol).

Internet Protocol (IP)

The Internet Protocol (IP) multiplexes packets from higher layers. Each IP packet consists of a 32-bit-each source address and destination address and a checksum for the header. IP does not guarantee that a packet will be delivered or delivered only once. It also does not guarantee that no errors are introduced in the packet during transmission.

Every packet is a stand-alone unit of transmission. A long packet may be split into two or more smaller packets for transmission. Each packet traverses one hop at a time. The packet is forwarded by a given node based on the routing information. A congested node may reroute the packet or drop it. So IP does not provide reliability, flow control, or error recovery. These issues are addressed by a higher layer protocol such as TCP. TCP ensures that a complete packet is delivered and that the packet is not modified during transmission.

Finally, IP does not guarantee that the source address is indeed the address of the node that originated the packet. In fact, a host can send a packet with any source address. Many operating systems ensure that the packet carries the correct source address, but there is no guarantee that the source address is valid. As a result, an intruding host can use the source address of a legitimate host and spoof on behalf of the legitimate host. This vulnerability led to the IP Spoofing Attack described in Chapter 7.

IP Addressing

Each IP address is 32 bits long. The 32 bits are assigned based on the network classes, as shown in Table 6.1. The network class is identified by the leftmost 1 to 4 bits. A class A network allows more than 16 million hosts, while a class C network permits no more than 254 hosts. (Host addresses of all 0's and all 1's are reserved.) The most popular class is class B, where a network can have up to approximately 65,000 hosts. However, there can be only 16,634 networks in this class, given the 14 bit network address. As such, this class is running out of network addresses, and design of a new addressing scheme is under way. The class D addresses are reserved for broadcasting.

Network Class	High Order Bits	Network Address	Host Address
A	0 1 bit	0-127 7 bits	0-16,777,214 24 bits
B	10 2 bits	0-16364 14 bits	0-65,534 16 bits
C	110 3 bits	0-2,097,152 21 bits	0-254 8 bits
D	1110 4 bits	multicast address 28 bits	

Table 6.1: IP Address Format

Generally, the IP addresses are indicated in a dotted format. The 4 bytes are written out as x.y.z.w, where each of the four numbers represents 8 bits of the 32-bit address. For example, the dotted address

$$128.5.7.9$$

translates to

$$10000000\ 00000101\ 00000111\ 00001001.$$

The two leftmost bits specify the network class. As shown in Table 6.1, a 10 in those bits means it is a class B network. The network address is 5, taken from the low-order 14 bits of the two high-order bytes. The host address is hexadecimal 79 based on the two low-order bytes of the address fields.

Internet Control Message Protocol (ICMP)

IP is used for datagram services for a set of interconnected networks. The connecting host between two networks is called a *gateway*. ICMP provides a mechanism for a gateway to report an error condition to the originating source. ICMP is considered an integral part of IP and must be implemented by every IP module. ICMP has the limited purpose of reporting error conditions. Although in certain cases some possible actions are suggested, ICMP is not to make IP more reliable. For a fragmented packet, ICMP reports errors on only fragment zero. ICMP can report errors on any IP datagrams except ICMP packets, to avoid infinite repetitions. It is up to the originating host to relate the errors to individual applications and to take corrective action.

User Datagram Protocol (UDP)

UDP is a connectionless protocol. It provides no reliability, flow control, or error recovery. UDP simply serves as the multiplexer/demultiplexer to deliver IP datagrams to and from the applications. UDP avoids the overhead that is required to set up a TCP connection. Given the little overhead for using UDP, it is attractive for inquiry/response applications when the number of messages exchanged is small.

An application in TCP/IP is uniquely identified by a pair:

$$socket = <IP\ Address, port\ number>.$$

This pair is also called a *socket address*. The IP address identifies the host in the network. The port number is a 16-bit field that identifies which higher level application or protocol should receive the IP packet, as shown in Figure 6.2. A higher level TCP/IP application such as TELNET and FTP is accessed through a fixed port number in all TCP/IP implementations. For example, the port number for FTP is 20 for data and 21 for control, TELNET is 23, SMTP is 25, and Domain Name Server is 53.

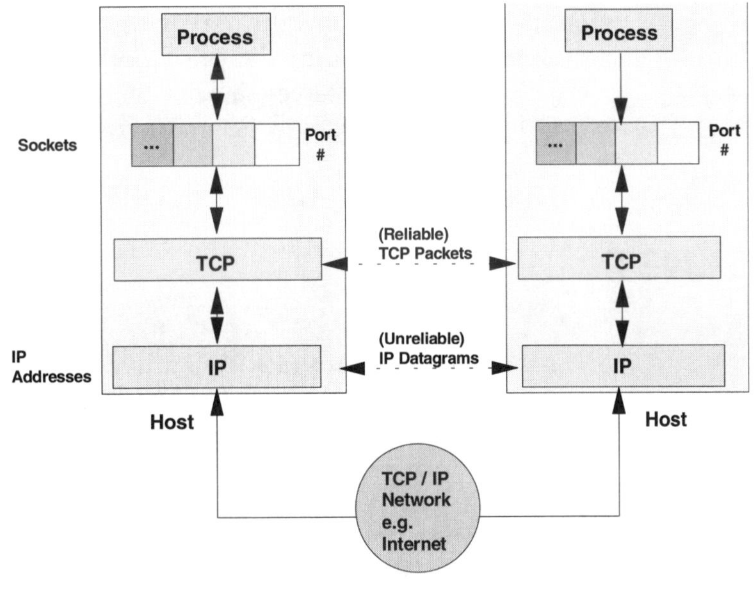

Figure 6.2: TCP Connection

Transport Control Protocol (TCP)

TCP provides a reliable virtual connection to user processes. TCP retransmits lost or damaged packets. Fragmented packets are assembled in proper sequence for delivery at the destination node. As such, TCP provides reliability, flow control, and multiplexing. Every TCP message uses a virtual circuit. A *virtual circuit* consists of the host address and *port number* for the source host and the destination host.

$$\langle localhost, localport, remotehost, remoteport \rangle.$$

This 4-tuple uniquely defines a virtual circuit. A server listens to a particular port number. Any packet arriving at that port number is received by the server as a service request. Client processes rarely require a specific port number, although they can do so. They receive packets on whatever port numbers their local host chooses to assign them.

TELNET

TELNET protocol provides a standard interface for a client to access services in a remote host. The key part of the protocol is that the client appears to the remote host as if it were a locally connected terminal. Figure 6.3 illustrates how TELNET works. There is a TELNET client in the client host and a TELNET server in the remote host where the server resides. When the user invokes TELNET, a TELNET client in the user's host sends a request for connection to a TELNET server at the remote host. Once the connection is established, the TELNET client transfers the keystrokes to the TELNET server. The TELNET server forwards the information from the TELNET client to the local operating host and vice versa. The TELNET client also receives keystrokes from the TELNET server and displays them to the user.

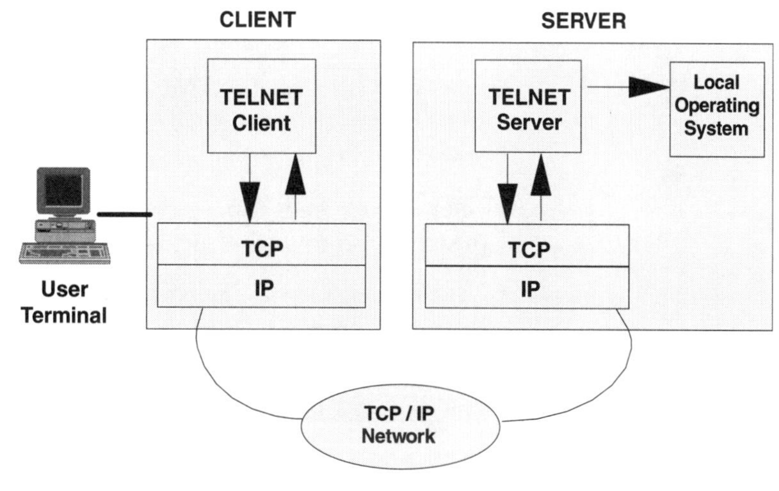

Figure 6.3: TELNET Client and Server in TCP/IP Network

TELNET provides two sets of functions. First, TELNET defines an imaginary *network virtual terminal* (NVT). Each TELNET client and server program maps into NVT. Second, TELNET allows each client and server to negotiate several options. For example, TELNET allows the option to use a 7-bit ASCII or an 8-bit EBCDIC character set. Clients and servers negotiate these options by exchanging verbs such as *DO, DON'T, WILL, WON'T*.

File Transfer Protocol (FTP)

FTP is used to transfer files from one TCP/IP host to another. FTP uses TCP protocol in order to ensure end-to-end reliable data transfer. The file transfer can take place in either direction. The client may send a file to the server, or the client may request a file from the server. A file transfer using FTP is accomplished as follows:

- User enters *ftp* along with the name of the host where the FTP server resides. FTP server prompts user to enter the ID and a password.

- User enters the ID and password. FTP server uses this information to authenticate the user.

- User can enter the *GET* subcommand to copy a file from the remote host to the local file system.

- User can also enter the *PUT* subcommand to copy a file from the local file system to the remote host.

These subcommands include the name of the file at the source host and the new name of the file at the destination host.

- To end the transfer, user enters the QUIT command.

FTP is one of the most commonly used application protocols in TCP/IP networks. Most of FTP usage comes from *anonymous FTP*. In anonymous FTP, any user can copy files from the FTP server. In this case, the user ID is *anonymous*. The password is often required to be the user's electronic mail address in the form *user@host*. Anonymous FTP allows sites to provide open file access to users on the Internet. As such, the FTP server offers direct access to Internet users. However, the site must protect the rest of its private network from intruders by installing a firewall or some other security gateway.

Domain Name System

Domain Name System allows the use of symbolic names instead of IP addresses. For example, instead of entering

$$telnet\ 128.5.7.13,$$

one could enter

$$telnet\ xyz.com,$$

where *xyz* is the name of a company.

The highest level of the domain name hierarchy provides the domain name; some examples are listed in Table 6.2.

Domain Name	Domain
edu	Educational institution
gov	Government institution
com	Commercial organization
mil	Military groups

Table 6.2: Domain Name Hierarchy

For example, the symbolic user address

$$avahuja\ @\ eos.ncsu.edu$$

identifies the user A. V. Ahuja at the *eos* subdomain within NCSU (North Carolina State University), which is an educational institution.

Finally, we briefly define some other TCP/IP protocols. A *Name Server* provides the translation from symbolic names to the *dotted* IP address. For each leaf of the domain name hierarchy tree, a name server is installed. *SMTP* (Simple Message Transfer Protocol) provides message exchange between TCP/IP hosts but has no support for document translation. *Remote Procedure Call* (RPC) allows programs to call subroutines that are executed at a remote host.

Internet Security Issues

The growth of Internet has led to several security concerns and exposures. Next, we outline some of the important security issues for the Internet.

1. **Authentication:** Internet requires two types of authentication. First, each user needs to be authenticated for logging to a TCP/IP application, such as TELNET and FTP. TCP/IP applications require the user to enter an ID and a password for authentication. Unless otherwise protected, a typical TELNET client and server code exchange the ID and password in cleartext.

   Second, many messages, transactions, and E-mail over the Internet may require authentication of the source. For example, a memo from the president of a company must authenticate the source of the memo before the employees take actions.

2. **Confidentiality:** Internet requires that any secret or private information be encrypted. Encryption is

required to protect sensitive information included in E-mail, FTP, and electronic commerce over the Internet.

3. **Data Integrity:** For certain types of data, Internet users may require assurance that the data has not been altered during transmission over the Internet. Data integrity may be required to protect FTP or E-mail files for transmission over the Internet.

4. **Nonrepudiation:** Nonrepudiation provides proof of the origin of data or delivery of data. It protects against the sender falsely denying sending the data or the recipient falsely denying receiving the data. This requirement must be satisfied in order to transact secure commerce over the Internet.

5. **Internet Access:** In order to attach to the Internet, private company networks may require a gateway to intercept and examine messages from and to the Internet. An Internet gateway intercepts each message from the Internet and authenticates the source of the message. In addition, these gateways filter the packets based on IP addressing and port numbers. These Internet gateways are called *firewalls*.

Security Services for TCP/IP Applications

To address the above requirements, a TCP/IP application protocol can be treated as an application accessing security services. Then the TCP/IP protocols, such as TELNET or FTP, can authenticate the clients, securely transmit the passwords, and provide encryption and data integrity services. The security services may be accessed using GSSAPI, described in Chapter 4. This approach is outlined in Figure 6.4.

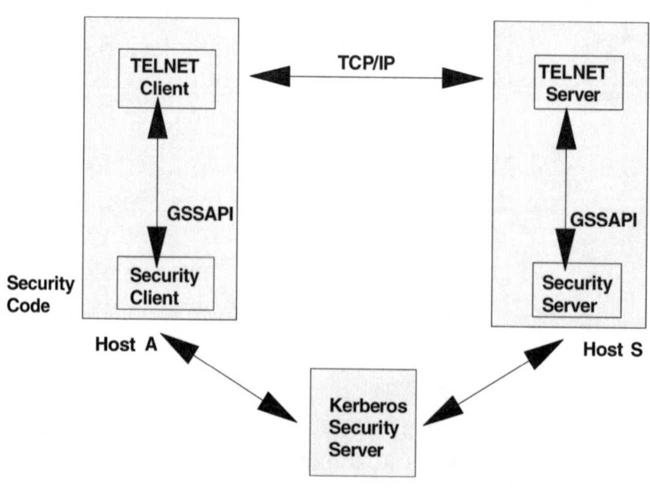

Figure 6.4: Secured TELNET

For example, consider that a user requires to access TELNET protocol, as shown in Figure 6.4. We assume that the network implementation includes GSSAPI to access security services, along with Kerberos as the underlying security scheme.

1. The user at host A logs on the security server and obtains Kerberos credentials. The password is not transmitted over the network. This is the only user logon required for access to various applications, including TELNET. (In order to achieve this single logon, each participating TCP/IP application must implement GSSAPI calls for security services. See Chapter 2 for details.)

2. The user wishes to establish a TELNET session with a server at host S. So the user enters the TELNET command along with the host name S.

3. The underlying security client code sends the user credentials to the server host S.

4. Assume that the server at host S has already been authenticated to the security server. Then the server accepts the user credentials and a TELNET session is established between the TELNET client and the server.

In the remainder of the chapter, we describe the security schemes for E-mail, the World Wide Web, and electronic commerce over the Internet.

E-Mail Security

E-Mail

Electronic mail (*E-mail*) is one of the most commonly used applications on the Internet. E-mail is primarily used to exchange messages over the Internet.

There is a standard format for E-mail on the Internet. An E-mail message consists of two parts, a message header and the message data, separated by a blank line. The *To:* line specifies the E-mail address of the intended recipient of the mail. The *From:* line identifies the E-mail address of the sender. The

Reply-To: line, if present, contains the E-mail address for replies. If this line is not present, the return address is taken from the *From:* line. The *cc:* line is used to specify E-mail addresses of secondary recipients of the message.

The E-mail address consists of two components, *local-port @ domain-name.* The *local-port* is the address of a mailbox. The *domain-name* is the name of the domain where the mailbox is located. For example, my E-mail address is

vahuja @ vnet.ibm.com.

The local name server at the sender's domain must have access to the appropriate name server that can determine the IP address of the intended destination of E-mail.

E-Mail Security

E-mail security requirements include those described earlier: authentication, confidentiality, data integrity, and nonrepudiation. In addition, E-mail security requires anonymity. This requirement provides the capability to send a message such that the recipient of the message cannot determine the identity of the sender.

Privacy-Enhanced Mail (PEM)

PEM was developed by the Internet community to add security to text messages. It was started as a project by the Internet Architecture Board in 1985; the final documents were published in 1993.

PEM provides confidentiality, data origin authentication, message integrity, nonrepudiation of origin, and key management. Every PEM message includes authentication, data integrity, and nonrepudiation. Data integrity and origin authentication are provided by including encrypted digital signatures. However, message confidentiality is an optional feature.

PEM is described in four Internet RFCs (requests for comments). RFC 1421 (Linn 1993a) describes message encryption and authentication procedures. RFC 1422 (Kent 1993a) addresses certificate-based key management. This document provides the key management architecture and infrastructure using public-key certificates. It provides keying information to message originators and recipients. RFC 1423 (Balenson 1993) describes the encryption and message integrity algorithms, including key management. Finally, RFC 1424 (Kaliski 1993) describes three types of services to support PEM: key certification, *certificate-revocation list* (CRL) storage, and CRL retrieval.

PEM allows use of several algorithms for data encryption, key management, and data integrity. Key management is used to encrypt data encryption keys and *message integrity check* (MIC) values. PEM does not require the use of a specific algorithm. Several algorithms are specified in RFC 1423 for each of these functions.

Encryption Algorithms

Data encryption algorithms:

- DES in CBC (Cipher Block Chaining) mode

Key management algorithms:

- DES in ECB (Electronic Codebook) mode
- DES in EDE (Encrypt-Decrypt-Encrypt) Triple-DES mode
- RSA

Message integrity check (MIC) algorithms:

- RSA and MD2 Message Digest Algorithms
- RSA and MD5 Message Digest Algorithms

PEM uses 56-bit keys for DES encryption. For Triple-DES, PEM uses two DES keys for a total key length of 112 bits. The size of RSA keys is not specified. For key management, PEM allows use of DES as well as RSA. However, while DES is often used for data encryption, RSA should be used to encrypt the DES keys for transmission.

Message Types

A PEM message is always signed, but encryption is optional. PEM specifies three types of messages:

- MIC-CLEAR
- MIC-ONLY
- ENCRYPTED

A *MIC-CLEAR* and *MIC-ONLY* message provides data integrity and authentication, but no encryption. A MIC-CLEAR message provides data integrity and authentication. A MIC-ONLY message has the same attributes as the MIC-CLEAR message. In addition, a MIC-ONLY message includes an encoding step. So for human-readable form, a MIC-ONLY message must be first transformed using PEM software. An *ENCRYPTED* message has all the features of a MIC-CLEAR message plus encryption.

Message Transmission

There are four steps required to send a PEM message:

1. Canonicalization
2. Message integrity and digital signature
3. Optional encryption
4. Optional transmission encoding.

A MIC-CLEAR message follows steps 1 and 2; a MIC-ONLY message follows steps 1,2, and 4; and an ENCRYPTED message follows steps 1 through 4.

The *canonicalization* step transforms the message text into a standard format. Many word processors and operating systems generate text messages with different formats and representations. For example, there is a different representation for new lines in various operating systems. In MS-DOS, it is a carriage return and a line feed, while Macintosh only uses a line feed. An additional consideration is that in case of PEM, the format of a message cannot be changed after it is encrypted. The reason is that such a message will not decrypt correctly at the other end. So PEM converts every message to a standard format before applying the message integrity algorithms.

For message integrity and digital signature, PEM allows use of the algorithms listed earlier. In order to avoid spoofing attacks (where someone can modify the message in transit and recompute the MIC), the MIC is signed by the sender. To allow the receiver to verify the MIC value and the identity of the sender, an X.509 certificate of the sender is attached to the message. A PEM message is always signed.

Next, if the user has opted for data encryption (message type is ENCRYPTED), the message text is encrypted.

Finally, a PEM message is encoded for transmission, if it is type MIC-ONLY or ENCRYPTED. PEM supports the transformation of a message from 8-bit characters to 6-bit encoding.

Upon receiving the PEM message, the receiver first checks the message type. If the message type is either MIC-ONLY or ENCRYPTED, then the message is decoded by inverting the 6-bit encoding into 8-bit text. The next step is to decrypt the message if the message type is ENCRYPTED. Next, the data integrity of the message is verified. Finally, the message canonical format is converted to a format that is suitable for the receiving end.

Certification Hierarchy

PEM has a well-defined *certification hierarchy*. At the root of the hierarchy tree is the *Internet Policy Registration Authority* (IPRA). IPRA establishes the goals and policies for all certificate generation activity under this hierarchy. Under IPRA, there are *Policy Certification Authorities* (PCAs). Each PCA publishes its policies for registration of users and organizations. This publication will be in the form of an informational Internet RFC. Each PCA will be registered with the IPRA. Below the PCA, there will be *Certification Authorities* (CAs) that will certify users and subordinate organizations.

Certificate Usage

PEM uses *X.509 certificates*, described in Chapter 2. The MIC is encoded by the sender using his or her private key. The sender also attaches his or her X.509 certificate. The certificate itself is signed by a certification authority (CA). The receiver first decodes the certificate using the CA's public key. (The receiver obtains the CA's public key starting with IPRA as the root of the certification path.) In this way, the receiver is assured that the certificate was issued by a valid CA and it is not a bogus certificate. Now the receiver checks whether the certificate has been revoked. Assuming the certificate is valid, the receiver obtains the public key of the sender from the certificate. Next, the receiver uses this public key to decode the MIC. A successful verification of the MIC authenticates the source of the message and also establishes that the message was not altered during transmission.

As stated earlier, a complete description of PEM is provided in RFCs 1421 through 1424 (Linn 1993a, Kent 1993a, Balenson 1993, and Kaliski 1993). In addition, (Schneier 1995 and Kent 1993b) are good references for reviewing this topic.

Pretty Good Privacy (PGP)

PGP is also an electronic mail security scheme. It is easy to use, freely available on the Internet, and works on several workstation operating systems. PGP uses public key cryptography.

PGP Version 1 was designed and developed by Philip Zimmerman in 1991. PGP Version 2.0 was developed by several people outside the United States to avoid the patent and export laws. PGP Versions 2.5 and 2.6 were released by the Massachusetts Institute of Technology, which holds the PGP patent. With the release of Version 2.6, MIT made an announcement that it was being released with the cooperation of RSA Data Security Inc. This means that Version 2.6 is noninfringing on all the parties, so it can be legally used for personal and noncommercial use. Version 2.6 is the current freeware version of PGP. ViaCrypt sells PGP Version 2.7 for commercial use.

PGP provides confidentiality, data origin authentication, message integrity, and nonrepudiation of origin. PGP is designed to automatically provide authentication, data integrity, and confidentiality for all messages. However, it is possible to send a message without confidentiality. PGP also allows a message to be sent without providing for authentication or integrity. Authentication and integrity go together, and both are achieved by performing a one-way hash on the message and encrypting the results prior to transmission.

Encryption Algorithms

PGP Version 2 uses the following algorithms.

> **Data Encryption Algorithm:** IDEA in Cipher Block Chaining (CBC) mode

> **Key Management Algorithm:** RSA

> **Message Integrity Check and Digital Signature Algorithms:** MD5 and RSA

PGP's RSA keys can be one of three lengths: casual grade (384 bits), commercial grade (512 bits), and military grade (1024 bits).   The 384-bit keys should be used only for testing and encrypting the message text. For key management and digital signatures, 1024-bit keys are recommended. The 512-bit keys should be used if security is not a major concern.

Message Transmission

There are four steps required to send a PGP message: *signature* (optional), *compression, encryption* (optional), and *transmission encoding* (optional).

PGP signature allows the receiver to authenticate the origin as well as to verify that the message has not been altered during transmission. PGP first executes MD5 algorithm to compute the one-way hash function of the message. The resulting hash value is encrypted using the sender's private key. The digital signature, including the hash value, can be sent with the message. Alternatively, the digital signature can be stored and sent separately from the message. An important benefit of detached signatures is that the sender (or the receiver) can keep a separate log of all the signatures sent (or received).

Next, PGP applies the compression algorithm to the message. This compression results in reduction of message size and removal of any redundancies in the message.

Encryption is an optional feature in PGP. PGP uses IDEA for encrypting the message text. As described in Chapter 4, IDEA provides 128-bit secret key encryption. In order to transmit the 128-bit encryption key, it is encrypted using the RSA algorithm and receiver's public key. If the message is destined for more than one receiver, then PGP encrypts a copy of the secret key with the public key of each receiver.

PGP also supports conversion of an 8-bit binary stream of ciphertext to printable ASCII characters. PGP uses the same algorithm as that used in PEM. This conversion is required since many electronic mail systems permit the use of only ASCII characters.

The receiver begins processing the message by first checking whether it was encoded. An encoded message is decoded back into 8-bit character text. Next, PGP determines if the message was encrypted. If so, the receiver first decrypts the secret key by using the receiver's private key. Next, the secret key is used to decipher the ciphertext. Finally, PGP checks whether the message is signed. If so, PGP first decrypts the hash value using the sender's public key. Then it verifies the integrity of the data as well as authenticates the origin of data.

Certificate Usage

For certificate origination and acceptance, PGP uses a different approach than that used by PEM. This is perhaps the main area of distinction between PEM and PGP.

PEM uses a hierarchical structure for certificate authorization. PGP key certification is based on the notion that trust is a social concept. Mary will get her key signed from someone she knows. Tom will accept Mary's key if it is signed by someone whom Tom trusts. So, Tom and Mary can accept each other's keys if they are signed by a common friend.

For many connections, it may not be necessary to establish full authenticity of the other party. Suppose Tom starts a dialog over the Internet with someone he does not know. The person on the other end uses some anonymous name. Depending on the type of dialog, the two can communicate with each other without requiring a strong authentication. This is analogous to Tom meeting a person on the subway and following up by casual correspondence with that person.

So with PGP's approach, a given PGP user cannot verify the validity of every other user. With PEM, there is a single hierarchy of certification authority, which lends to easy verification of others' certificates. Additional details on PGP may be found in Schneier (1995) and Zimmerman (1995).

World Wide Web Security

"I just ordered us a pizza online."
"How do I download it?"
Newsweek, December 24, 1994. p 94.

World Wide Web

For a long time, Internet was deficient in two areas, usability and security. The World Wide Web started to address the usability problem. The Web clients (or browsers) and servers also offer some of the security services including authentication, confidentiality, data integrity, and nonrepudiation.

The Web is a fast-growing segment on the Internet. According to Dunlap (1995), there are 10 million to 15 million Web users and 100,000 Web sites. Every day, an estimated 50 to 100 Web sites go on line, according to Hwang (1995).

The *World Wide Web* is also known as *W3*, *WWW*, or the *Web*. The Web is the most user-friendly service on the Internet. It is a distributed hypermedia system. No one controls the Web, just as no one *controls* the Internet. The Web was invented at CERN (Center for Nuclear Research), a European center for research in high-energy physics located in Switzerland. They saw the need for a simple stateless hypertext protocol between clients and servers. The protocol should be lightweight, so as to retrieve multimedia objects over the Internet. CERN developed a *HyperText Transfer Protocol* (HTTP). HTTP is the common language used between the Web clients and servers on the Internet. Major contributions in client research were made at the

National Center for Supercomputing Applications (NCSA). *Mosaic*, a Web browser (client portion of the Web client/server), was developed at NCSA. Mosaic is free and runs on Windows, Macintosh, and many types of UNIX systems. Several vendors market the Web browsers. These browsers are enormously popular since they offer a highly useable graphical interface to access a variety of Internet resources.

The Web can be viewed as a collection of HTTP servers on the Internet. It is used by businesses to provide information about their products and services. The information for the business is stored in the form of a home page at a Web server. Once retrieved, the home page is displayed at the Web client. The Web client also presents options to obtain additional information on highlighted topics.

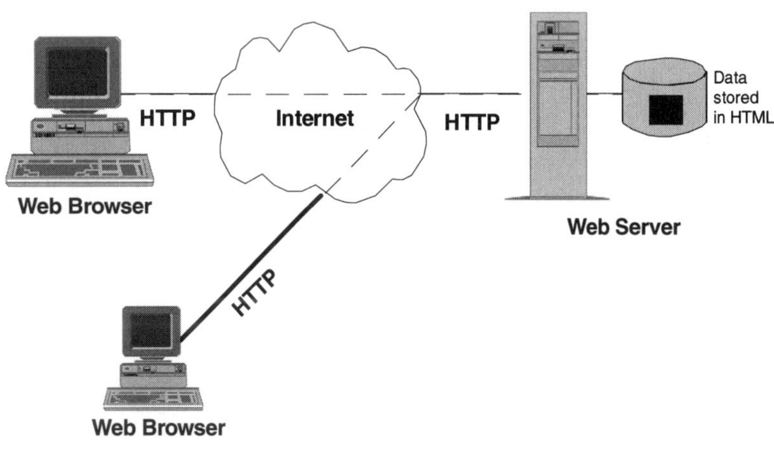

Figure 6.5: Web Browsers and Servers

Figure 6.5 depicts Web connections. It is a typical client/server network, where the client is called the *Web client, Web browser,* or simply a *browser.* The server is called the *Web server.* So when a user clicks on a hypermedia link, a TCP/IP connection is established between the client and the server. Once connected, the client sends a request to the server. The server processes the request, sends the response to the server, and closes the connection.

HyperText Transfer Protocol (HTTP)

Consider an exchange that begins with a user bringing up a Web browser. The user enters a *Uniform Resource Locator* (URL) address and clicks to proceed with the connection. (A URL is the address of a file located in a host and accessible through the Internet.) So in effect, the Web client is instructed to retrieve a file (called a *home page*) from the Web server. First, the client establishes a TCP/IP connection to the host name specified in the URL address. After the connection is made, the client sends a request along with the object of the request. The request is sent in the form of an HTTP command to the server. A typical command is *GET* (to retrieve a home page from the server) along with a Universal Resource Identifier (URL without the host name). The server responds with the requested data and closes the connection. Both the client and the server can provide additional information during this exchange.

The Web home pages are created by writing the text in a tag language called *Hypertext Mark-Up Language* (HTML). An HTML file may include graphics, video references, file transfers, and sound systems. An HTML document can easily link to other HTML documents. A simple example of an HTML page is given next. The HTML page starts with <html> and ends with </html>. Simple text requires no additional tags. The bold letters start with <b> and end with </b>.

<html>
This book treats the topic of security for networks including Internet security.
<b> Chapter 6 is on Internet Security. </b>
</html>

This overview of the Web is necessarily brief. Additional details on the Web including HTML can be found in other references including Mathiesen (1995), Ford (1995), LeVitus (1996a and 1996b).

Web Security Requirements

Security requirements for the Web include provision for an authenticated secure pipe between the Web client and server. Similarly to E-mail, the Web requires users to authenticate the data origin, provide encryption, and ensure integrity of data between the client and the server.

Shortly after the introduction of Web clients and servers, some of the vendors and Internet forums started investigating security for the Web. The two notable offerings are the Secure Sockets Layer and SecSure HyperText Transfer Protocol.

Secure Sockets Layer

Netscape developed a security protocol for communications between the Web browsers and servers. *Secure Sockets Layer* (SSL) provides privacy on the Internet. At the time of writing, SSL description is available in Hickman (1995), an Internet draft dated June 1995.

SSL provides authentication, encryption, and message integrity. It is designed to authenticate the server and optionally the client. SSL uses TCP as the underlying transport protocol for reliable data transmission and reception. Since SSL resides at the socket level, it is independent of the higher level application. As such, it can provide security services to higher level protocols such as TELNET, FTP, and HTTP.

SSL consists of two protocols, *SSL Record Protocol* and *SSL Handshake Protocol*. The SSL Record protocol is described later. The SSL handshake protocol is used to negotiate security parameters for an SSL connection. This description of SSL uses Wayner (1996) and Hickman (1995).

SSL Handshake Protocol

In the SSL Handshake Protocol, the client and server exchange a series of message to negotiate security enhancements. The SSL Handshake Protocol consists of six phases, described next.

The first phase is the *Hello* phase; it is used to agree on a set of algorithms for privacy and authentication. In addition, this phase discovers any existing session ID from a previous session. The client begins by sending the CLIENT-HELLO message to the server. It includes three types of information: the type of encryption scheme that the client can handle, the session ID left over from a previous broken session (if any), and a random data to challenge the server. If the server recognizes the old session ID, then the session is restarted. If it is a new session, then the server sends an X.509 certificate to the client. The certificate includes the server's public key that is signed by the private key of a certificate authority (CA). The client will use the CA's public key to decipher the server's public key. The server's public key, in turn, is used to read the server's certificate. The following messages are exchanged in this phase:

CLIENT-HELLO
SERVER-HELLO

The second phase is the *key exchange* phase. In this phase, information on keys is exchanged between the client and the server. At the end of the phase, both sides have a shared *master key.* SSL Version 3 supports three key exchange algorithms: RSA, Diffie-Hellman, and Fortezza-KEA. The key is sent as encrypted text using the server's public key. For export versions, only a part of the key is sent as ciphertext. The following messages are exchanged in this phase:

CLIENT-MASTER-KEY
CLIENT-DH-KEY

The third phase is the *session key production* phase; it provides for exchange of the actual key used to communicate during the current session. The following message is exchanged in this phase. It is sent by the client and establishes one or two session keys with the server.

CLIENT-SESSION-KEY

The fourth phase is the *server verify* phase. This phase is used only when the RSA key exchange algorithm is used. It verifies the master key and the subsequent session keys obtained by the server. Upon receiving the master key and subsequent session keys from the client, the server decrypts the keys using its own private key. Next, the server sends a confirmation to the client by responding to the random challenge sent to it by the client in the CLIENT-HELLO message. The client decrypts the response to random challenge, and if everything matches, a trusted session is established between the client and the server. The following message is exchanged during this phase:

SERVER-VERIFY

The fifth phase is the *client authentication* phase. If client authentication is required, then the server requests the client for a certificate. The client responds with a CLIENT-CERTIFI-CATE. At the time of writing, SSL supports only X.509 certificates (described in Chapter 2). The following messages are exchanged during this phase:

REQUEST-CERTIFICATE
CLIENT-CERTIFICATE

The sixth and final phase is the *finished phase*. In this phase, both the client and the server exchange their respective finished messages. The client indicates completion of authentication by sending the session ID as encrypted text. The server sends a SERVER-FINISHED message. This message includes the session ID encrypted with the master key. A trusted session is now established between the client and the server. The following messages are exchanged in this phase:

CLIENT-FINISHED
SERVER-FINISHED

SSL Record Protocol

The *SSL Record Protocol* specifies encapsulation of all transmitted and received data. The data portion of SSL record has three components:

- MAC-DATA
- ACTUAL-DATA
- PADDING-DATA

The MAC-DATA is the *message authentication code*. For MD2 and MD5, this field is 128 bits long. The ACTUAL-DATA is the application data (payload) to be transmitted. The PADDING-DATA is the data required to pad the message when a block cipher is used. When the SSL record is sent as cleartext, the MAC-DATA and PADDING-DATA fields are not included. The MAC-DATA is computed by applying the hash function on

MAC-DATA = HASH(SECRET, ACTUAL-DATA, PADDING-DATA, SEQUENCE-NUMBER).

The contents of the SECRET field depend on the party that is sending the message and the type of encryption. The SEQUENCE-NUMBER is a counter maintained by the client and the server. For each transmission direction, two counters are maintained; one counter is kept by the sender and the other by the receiver. The counter is incremented by 1 every time a sender transmits a message. Each sequence number is a 32-bit unsigned number.

Encryption Algorithms

As part of the negotiations between the client and the server, the sender can identify the encryption algorithm it supports. SSL Version 2 and Version 3 support:

- RC4 128 bits and MD5

- RC4 128 bits (export 40 bits) and MD5

- RC2 128 bits CBC (Cipher Block Chaining) and MD5

- RC2 128 bits (export 40 bits) and MD5

- IDEA 128 bits CBC (Cipher Block Chaining) and MD5

- DES 64 bits CBC and MD5

- DES 192 bits EDE3 CBC (Triple-DES using Encrypt-Decrypt-Encrypt with Cipher Block Chaining) and MD5

MD5 is used as the hash function for computing the MAC.

There are constraints on the size of the encryption key for exporting software products. The export regulations will permit a key size of up to 40 bits, although certain exceptions may be permitted (see Chapter 4). SSL recommends the use of at least 128 bits for the key length with RC2 and RC4 for domestic use in the United States. For export purposes, only 40 bits of the key are kept secret; the remaining 88 bits are sent in the clear.

Secure HyperText Transfer Protocol (S-HTTP)

Secure HyperText Transfer Protocol (S-HTTP) was developed by Enterprise Integration Technologies (EIT). This description of S-HTTP is based on the Internet Draft (Rescorla 1995). S-HTTP provides flexible security services for HTTP transactions. S-HTTP-aware clients can communicate with S-HTTP-oblivious servers and vice versa, although such transactions would obviously not utilize the security features of S-HTTP.

Through a process of negotiations between the client and the server, a variety of security enhancements and the associated algorithms are provided. For example, the user can select whether the request and the reply are signed, encrypted, or both. Any message may be signed, authenticated, encrypted, or any combination of these, including no protection. Key management mechanisms include manually shared secrets such as passwords, public key exchange, and Kerberos ticket distribution. If digital signature support is selected, then the appropriate certificate should be attached. S-HTTP supports X.509 certificates and certificate chains, such as the one used in PEM.

The negotiations between the client and the server are conducted by exchanging formatted data. This data includes various security options that the originator would accept. The lines in the data should conform to the following rules:

<Line> := <Field> ':' <Key-val>(';',<Key-val>)*
<Key-val> := <Key> '=' <Value>(',' <Value>)*
<Key> := <Mode>'-'<Action>
<Mode> := 'orig' | 'recv'
<Action> := 'optional' | 'required' | 'refused'

The *<Mode>* value indicates whether the action is for a message originated at this agent or for a message received by this agent. The *agent* is the source of this formatted data.

The *<Action>* parameter specifies the action to be performed. The *recv-optional:* value implies that the receiver will process the security feature if the other party also uses it but will also process messages without this feature. The *recv-required:* value means that the receiver will not process messages without this feature. The *recv-refused:* specifies that the receiver will not process messages with this security feature. In addition, for information originating at this agent, corresponding action values are specified. For example, *orig-required:* indicates that the agent will always generate this security feature.

The negotiation headers include options to select a variety of algorithms for each header line. There is a header line for each of the following items.

SHTTP-Privacy-Domains

This header specifies the class of encryption algorithms as well as the packaging of data. The two values defined for this header are PEM and PKCS-7.[1]

For example,

> *SHTTP-Privacy-Domains: orig-required=pem;*
> *recv-optional=pem, pkcs-7*

implies that the agent always generates PEM-compliant messages but can read PEM or PKCS-7 messages.

---

1. PKCS-7 is a cryptographic message encapsulation format similar to PEM. PKCS-7 is defined by RSA and uses OSI's Abstract Syntax Notation (ASN.1).

SHTTP-Certificate-Types

This specifies the acceptable certificate format. Currently, S-HTTP permits the value of *'X.509'* for X.509 certificates.

SHTTP-Key-Exchange-Algorithms

This line indicates the algorithms to be used for key exchange. The permitted values are *'RSA'*, *'Outband'*, *'Inband'*, and *'Krb'*. RSA is used if enveloping of data uses RSA. Outband is specified if there will be some external arrangement. Inband and Krb are used when keys are specified directly between the client and the server.

SHTTP-Signature-Algorithms

It specifies the algorithm for digital signature. The two supported algorithms are *'RSA'* and *'NIST-DSS'*.

SHTTP-Message-Digest-Algorithms

This line identifies the algorithm for providing data integrity using the hash functions. The supported algorithms are *'RSA-MD2'*, *'RSA-MD5'*, and *'NIST-SHS'*.

SHTTP-Symmetric-Content-Algorithms

This line specifies the symmetric-key block cipher algorithm used to encrypt the data. The symmetric encryption algorithms for S-HTTP are listed below.

- **DES-CBC:** DES in Cipher Block Chaining (CBC) mode.
- **DES-EDE-CBC:** Two-key Triple-DES using EDE in outer CBC mode.

- **DES-EDE3-CBC:** Three-key Triple-DES using EDE in outer CBC mode.

- **DESX-CBC:** RSA's DESX in CBC mode.

- **IDEA-CFB:** IDEA in Cipher Feedback Mode.

- **RC2-CBC:** RC2 in CBC mode.

- **RC4**

- **CDMF:** IBM's CDMF in CBC mode.

SHTTP-Symmetric-Header-Algorithms

This line provides a list of the symmetric-key encryption used to encrypt the headers.

- **DES-ECB:** DES in Electronic Codebook (ECB) mode.

- **DES-EDE-ECB:** Two-key Triple-DES using EDE in ECB mode.

- **DES-EDE3-ECB:** Three-key Triple-DES using EDE in ECB mode.

- **DESX-ECB:** DESX (RSA's) in ECB mode.

- **IDEA-ECB:** IDEA in ECB mode.

- **RC2-ECB:** RC2 in ECB mode.

- **CDMF-ECB:** IBM's CDMF in ECB mode.

SHTTP-Privacy-Enhancements

This header line specifies the security enhancements associated with the messages. The possible values are *'sign'*, *'encrypt'*, and *'auth'*. These values respectively indicate whether the messages are signed, encrypted, or authenticated.

There are other header lines pertaining to specifying the various keys and their symbolic names. See Rescorla (1995) and Wayner (1996) for additional details on S-HTTP.

S-HTTP and SSL

S-HTTP and SSL use different approaches to provide security services for Web users. SSL executes a negotiation protocol to establish a secure socket level connection. The SSL security services are transparent to the user and the application.

S-HTTP protocols are integrated with HTTP. Here, the security services are negotiated through the headers and the attributes attached to the page. S-HTTP services are available only to HTTP connections, and the application (HTTP) is well aware of S-HTTP services.

Given that S-HTTP is at the application layer and SSL is at the sockets layer, it is conceivable to devise a combined approach for S-HTTP and SSL.

Secure Commerce

A typical shopping trip of the future:

log on,
download some electronic cash in the hard drive,
go shopping on the electronic malls,
find bargains,
negotiate prices,
make purchases,
log off.

In July 1995, the U.S. Congress was told by experts that electronic commerce is on the verge of happening. According to Maddox (1995), the Holiday Inn Worldwide in Atlanta was the first in its industry to offer secure on-line reservations on the Internet, in June 1995. Its Web site gets about 7000 visitors a week, with about three-quarters checking the availability of rooms. The number of Web sites is growing rapidly, and so is the commerce on the Internet. According to a Forrester Research report quoted in Press (1994), the total U.S. retail sales in 1993 were $1.5 trillion. Of that, $200 million was on-line shopping on the Internet, CompuServe, and other on-line services. By 1998, they project the on-line sales to grow to $4.8 billion.

Commerce on the Internet is emerging in various forms. It ranges from universities admitting students over the Internet to tracking mail packages on line. This section presents an overview of electronic commerce on the Internet and the related security issues and technologies.

Commerce on the Internet

For transacting business on the Internet, there are some unique opportunities and security issues to be addressed. First, we outline some of the unusual marketing avenues available to the businesses.

- Capability to quickly update the product advertisements on home pages. For example, shops can update their catalogs with new products almost instantly, compared to the long cycle of printing and distributing the catalogs.

- Special sales to handle open seats or vacancies for near-term events or services. For example, an airline can offer a special discount for that day's flight from New York to London, since there have been some last-minute cancellations. Similarly, hotels can offer special discounts if the rooms are vacant for a very near date. Broadway may offer a special presentation of a play at short notice.

- Capability to track events in real time. For example, one can track and transact stocks and shares across the world. Other examples include determining the arrivals, departures, and delays of airlines, trains, and buses.

- Access to on-line commercial services. Examples of on-line services include banking, insurance, and travel, as well as advertising merchandise over the Internet.

Despite all these benefits, the path to pervasive and profitable commerce on the Internet is fraught with some hurdles.

1. The Internet commerce needs to closely emulate our current way of transacting business. Today's real-world commerce consists of shopping and advertising, negotiating (e.g., car prices), ordering and billing, payments and settlements, and accounting.

2. The Internet commerce should be sufficiently flexible to handle errors, resolve disputes, and furnish legally acceptable documentation for all aspects of commercial transactions.

3. The Internet commerce must offer sufficient levels of usability and security to earn the trust and respect of existing customers. The Web is addressing the usability issues; we present the security issues later in this section.

4. The Internet commerce must provide smooth integration with the existing merchant systems. For example, there should be no impact to the existing order processing, inventory management, or payment processing system. Figure 6.6 depicts some of the components of an electronic commerce system and traditional merchant systems.

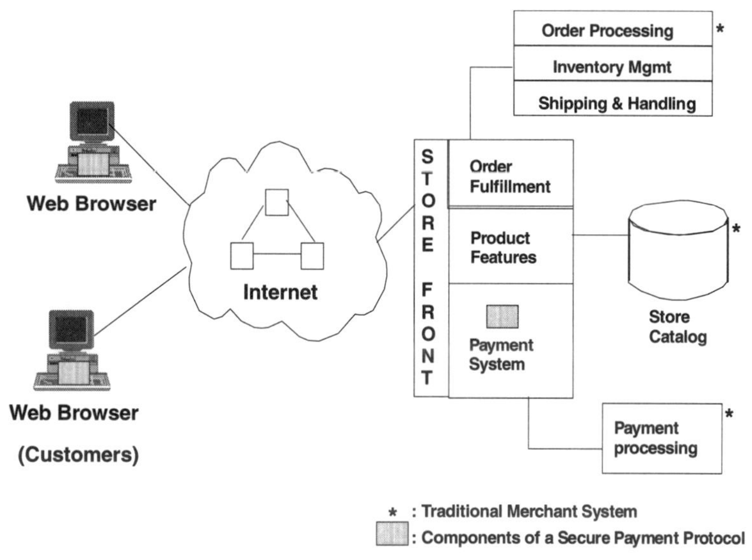

Figure 6.6: Web Browsers and Servers

Clearly, these hurdles may potentially result in slower migration to the electronic commerce business. It is expected that for some time, the current businesses will begin by using the Internet as a new advertising channel, followed by opening their shops and malls for sales and commercial transactions over the Internet.

Security Requirements

Security is the underpinning for attaining successful commerce on the Internet. Customers, businesses, banks, and credit card companies—everyone will demand strong security in order to make purchases or transmit payments on the Internet. Some of the important issues related to security for electronic commerce are listed below.

1. There must be a mechanism for affording secure transfer of payment information. The secure payment mechanism should be capable of handling different modes of payments, such as credit cards, electronic checks, debit cards, and digital cash.

   In addition, the secure payment mechanism must provide for a three-way distribution of private data. Consider an example in which John puts in an order to buy a TV set from the home page of a merchandise store. John is prompted to enter his credit card number and its expiration date. While the store must ensure that John has valid credit card with sufficient funds, it may be unnecessary to expose John's credit card information to the merchant. However, the issuing bank (of the credit card) must get this credit card information, validate it, and approve the purchase of the TV set. This example demonstrates the requirements for a three-way exchange of secure data to handle payments over the Internet.

2. There must be a mechanism to enforce nonrepudiation on the commercial transactions. For example, there must be a way to prove that the sender really sent the purchase order and the receiver really received it. This issue is partially addressed by authenticating the origin of each message.

3. There must be a mechanism for ensuring data integrity over the Internet. This requirement relates to the topic of transaction privacy. When Mary orders a special china set, she may require that there is no alteration in her purchase order or the amount of payment while this information is transmitted over the Internet. Furthermore, for privacy reasons, Mary may

require that no one other than the store can interpret the details of her order. These requirements are addressed by data integrity and confidentiality approaches described in Chapter 4.

4. There must be an infrastructure to establish trust among several parties. For example, anyone can initiate a transaction and claim he is John. There must be a way that John can prove his identity to the store. This requirement is addressed by John sending an X.509 certificate to the merchant. However, customers will need a legitimate authority that can issue the X.509 certificates. There will perhaps be more than one type of certificate, just as we have several credit cards for making payments and identification.

Secure Commerce Model

Based on the above requirements, we outline a model to support credit card–based secure commerce on the Internet. There are three parties involved in a credit card transaction: a Web browser, a Web server, and a gateway. The Web browser includes a secure payment application to handle the payment. The Web server provides merchant server functions. It is also linked to the merchant's order processing and related systems. Finally, there is a gateway to the finance network that links the merchant server to the bank that issued the credit card.

Consider the purchase of a video camera by Sally on the Web client. Sally provides her credit card number, the expiration date, and the amount of purchase. The electronic purchase order is created at the Web browser. The Web server obtains the details of the video camera and forwards this information to the merchant's order processing and fulfillment system. The credit card information along with the amount of purchase is forwarded to the gateway.

Finally, consider the security technologies required to support this hypothetical model. Assuming that each party has a public/private key pair, the payment information can be encrypted using Sally's private key. The message can also be signed using her private key. In addition, Sally should send her X.509 certificate to prove that indeed she is Sally. Therefore, the certificate itself is to be issued by someone whom the bank trusts as an approved CA. Furthermore, a three-way exchange protocol is required to ensure secure distribution of appropriate information among the three parties. Finally, we may optionally secure the order information, in addition to the payment information. This is achieved by using a Web security protocol, such as SSL or S-HTTP described earlier.

IBM's iKP

IBM Research Division has devised a family of protocols to securely transfer payments over the Internet. This work was presented at the USENIX Workshop on Electronic Commerce in July 1995 (Bellare 1995). The *iKP* scheme is also described in Wayner (1996). The most significant feature of this scheme is that it provides complete cryptographic protection of data including an audit trail to resolve disputes. The iKP scheme arbitrates payment information among three parties, compared to the two-party SSL and S-HTTP protocols. It is based on RSA public key scheme and can be extended for debit card or electronic check models of payment.

There are three parties involved directly in a payment transaction: the customer, the merchant, and the acquirer gateway (or *gateway*). The customer makes the payment and the merchant receives the payment. The acquirer gateway interfaces with the existing payment infrastructure and authorizes the transaction by using the existing infrastructure.

The iKP stands for i-Key-Protocol, $i = 1, 2,$ and 3. The value of i determines the number of parties that hold their public/private key pairs. So, *1KP* is the simplest protocol where only the acquirer gateway possesses the public/private key pair. For *2KP*, the acquirer gateway and the merchant server possess the public/private key pair. Finally, the *3KP* protocols require each of the three parties to possess the public/private key pairs. Clearly, 3KP protocol offers the highest level of security, while 1KP protocol offers the lowest level of security in this scheme.

In case of 1KP, the customer and the merchant are not required to possess the public/private key pair. However, the customer as well as the merchant must be capable of ensuring the authenticity of the gateway. In order to do that, the customer and the merchant are provided with the public key of the certification authority (CA) that issues the certificate to the acquirer gateway. So when the customer or the merchant receives an X.509 certificate from the acquirer gateway, they can use the CA's public key to decrypt the certificate. A successful decryption of the certificate also implies that the certificate was indeed issued by the appropriate CA. Since there would not be too many gateways, the credit card company may issue these certificates. In this 1KP scheme, the customers are authenticated by their credit card number and possibly the *PIN* (personal identification number). While this scheme is simple, it does not offer nonrepudiation of messages sent by the customer or the merchant. As such, this scheme does not provide the means to resolve disputes related to the authenticity of the payment.

For the 2KP protocol, the merchant and the gateway possess the public/private key pairs. So this protocol also provides nonrepudiation of messages originated by the merchant. It enables the customer and the gateway to ensure that they are dealing with a legitimate merchant.

The 3KP protocol provides nonrepudiation of messages from all three parties. Payment orders are authenticated by the digital signature, the credit card number, and (optionally) the PIN number. According to Bellare (1995), this makes the forging of payment orders computationally infeasible. Finally, note that each customer, merchant, and the gateway require a public/private key pair. So for this scheme, an infrastructure will be required to issue X.509 certificates to all the parties.

This description of electronic commerce is brief. Several papers and books have been published on this topic. Other references on this topic include Press (1994), Churbuck (1995), Maddox (1995), Wayner (1996), and Mathiesen (1995).

Summary

This chapter has covered a variety of security issues and technologies for Internet. Internet relies on TCP/IP protocol for providing end-to-end packet transmission. Therefore, the chapter began with an overview of some of the TCP/IP protocols, including their security issues. This leads to security issues for the three important applications on the Internet: E-mail, World Wide Web, and electronic commerce. We learned that for secure E-mail, PEM and PGP are the two important schemes on the Internet. Next, we discussed the World Wide Web, which is built on HTTP protocols along with HTML scripts for the Web pages. There are two commercially available security schemes for the Web, namely SSL and S-HTTP. While both of them provide security for Web connections, they operate at different levels. Finally, for the emerging electronic commerce, we discussed the benefits and concerns for secure transactions, including some of the secure payment protocols.

Internet Firewalls

The Internet is rapidly transforming from a source of academic and research exchange to a global facility for information access and commerce. Every day, more and more networks are attaching to the Internet. As the size of the Internet grows, so do the risks to private networks attached to the Internet. To protect private networks from eavesdropping, intrusion, and other attacks from the Internet, an adequate barrier is required. This barrier, called a *firewall*, should intercept all the traffic between a given private network and the Internet. It should not only protect the company resources from hackers on the Internet but also intercept any transmission of valuable company information from the private network to the Internet.

In order to describe the topic of firewalls, we must review the concepts and functions of firewalls. Next, we describe each component of a firewall, namely the filters, proxy servers, domain name service, and mail handling. The chapter concludes with a review of some of the emerging security services provided by firewalls, including confidentiality

Concepts

Firewalls

A *firewall* provides controlled access between a private network and the Internet. It intercepts each message between the private network and the Internet. Depending on the configuration, the firewall determines whether a data packet or a connection request should be permitted to pass through the firewall or be discarded. Figure 7.1 depicts the purpose of firewalls. In describing the firewalls, we will refer to two types of host systems. First, there are host systems on a secure, private, and trusted network. These host systems can access the Internet only through a firewall. The other host systems are those that reside on the Internet and can be accessed only through the untrusted Internet.

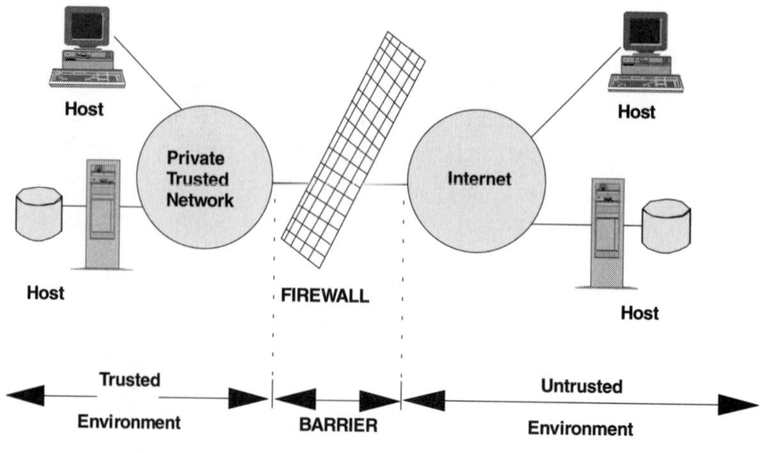

Figure 7.1: Firewall

Need for a Firewall

In the preceding chapters, several approaches to protecting networks were presented. In particular, we described several schemes to provide secure Internet services such as secure E-mail, secure Web clients/servers, and secure commerce on the Internet. Here we address the relationship of these Internet security schemes with firewalls.

A secure E-mail protects communications between two Internet users. A secure Web protects transactions and exchanges between two Web users. But none of these approaches protect other resources of a private network. A firewall is similar to locking the doors of a house or employing a doorman. The objective is to ensure that only the authorized people can enter the house, and no one from inside the house can walk away with the family jewels.

When a private network is attached to the Internet, there are three areas of potentials concerns or risks:

1. **Information:** Someone can steal or destroy the information that is stored on the private network.

2. **Resources:** Someone can damage or misuse the computer systems on the private network.

3. **Reputation:** Someone can damage the reputation of a business by demonstrating vulnerabilities in its network security.

There is an additional business need for firewalls. A company may desire to isolate the networks of different parts of its business. A university may require that the administrative network (where all student grades are stored) should be isolated from the students' computer network. Hospitals may want to keep the patient records network separate from its administrative network for legal and ethical aspects of patient privacy. Such an intracompany protection can be provided by a firewall. This concept of department-level firewalls is shown in Figure 7.2. One or more firewalls may be used to provide isolation and controlled access between different parts of a company, as shown in Figure 7.2.

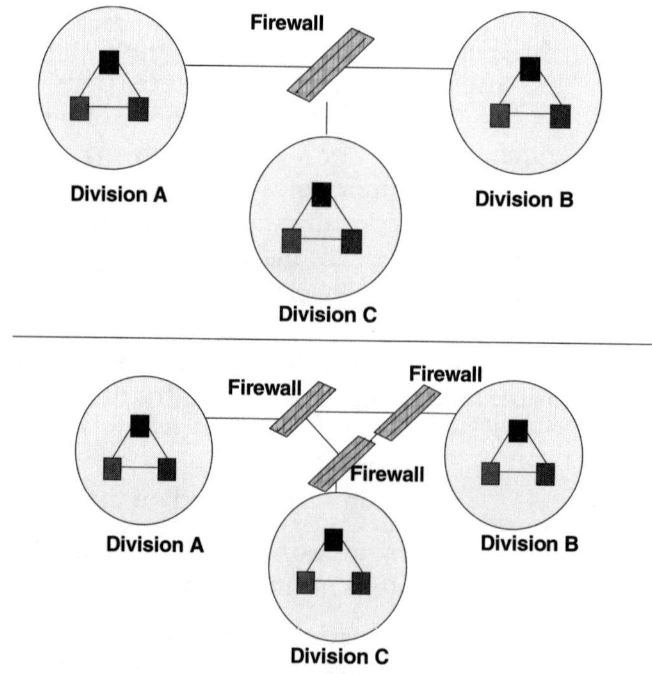

Figure 7.2: Firewall Usage for Intracompany Security

So a *firewall* is a software component that controls access between a private network and the Internet or among different parts of a given private network. A firewall should satisfy the following requirements.

1. Any packet that is not explicitly permitted should default to a denial.

This requirement implies that the administrator should explicitly specify the legitimate traffic that is to be allowed through the firewall. All other traffic, by default, should be rejected.

2. Wherever possible, keep outside users outside the private network.

This requirement states that the access from outside users into the private network should be restricted. If there is a need for Internet users to have open access to some files (such as a company's public files), then those files should be located outside the firewall and on the Internet side (see Figure 7.7 under Proxy Servers).

3. Enforce extensive logging, auditing, and alarm generation.

This requirement means that the firewall should be capable of logging and auditing the traffic passing through the firewall. The firewall should also generate alarms when it suspects that someone is attempting to break into the firewall.

Firewall Design

A firewall design consists of several components. These components, depicted in Figure 7.3, are divided in five groups: secure operating system, filters, gateways, domain name service, and E-mail handling. We review these components next, the details are presented later in this chapter.

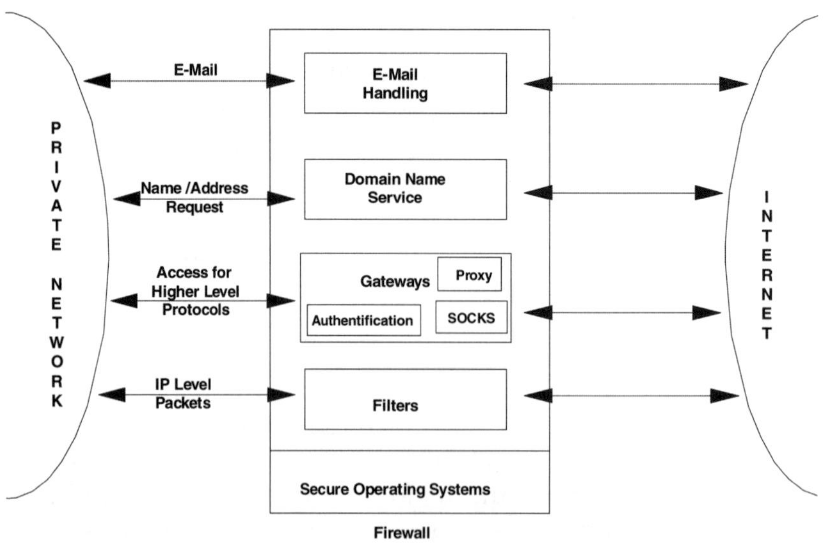

Figure 7.3: Components of a Firewall

First, the firewall itself must be in a secure environment by residing on a secure operating system. In Chapter 3, we presented the security classification schemes for operating systems. A secure operating system can protect the firewall code and files from attacks by intruders. Often, the firewall code is the only application permitted to execute on a given host system. Absence of other applications on the firewall system reduces the possibility of unauthorized attempts to penetrate the firewall.

The Internet community often uses the term bastion host to refer to a firewall host. A *bastion host* is a highly secure computer, since it is exposed to direct attacks from the hackers on the Internet. The term *bastion* comes from the heavily fortified projections on the exteriors of castles in medieval times.

Next, we introduce the concept of *filters*. The primary purpose of a firewall is to intercept the packets and permit only authorized traffic through the firewall. So, the firewall intercepts each packet that is transmitted between the private network and the Internet. The filter executes a set of rules that have been defined by the firewall administrator at configuration time. The rules are based on a variety of parameters including the IP addresses, the port numbers, and the type of application. The primary concern about the filters approach is that it is based on IP addresses, which in themselves are not secure. As a result, a given host can spoof another host by changing the IP source address. We provide details on filters later in this chapter.

An *application gateway* intercepts the traffic and authenticates users at the TCP/IP application level. The application gateway function is often provided by implementing a *proxy server*. A user on the private network logs on a proxy server, and the proxy server authenticates the user. After authentication, the user logs on the remote server on the Internet. Similarly, all the Internet communications to the private network are received by the proxy servers, analyzed, and forwarded appropriately. Since a proxy server operates at the application level, a separate proxy server may be required for each type of application. The proxy server authenticates each user, both from inside the private network and from the Internet. A strong authentication scheme is required to prevent unauthorized users from getting in or out of the private network.

The *SOCKS* server also provides gateway support through the firewall. A primary difference between the proxy server and SOCKS server is that proxy requires a change in the way the user accesses the Internet server without modifying the client software. SOCKS, on the other hand, requires modifications to the client software, but no change is required to the user procedures.

Firewalls may also include a domain name service and mail handling. The *domain name service* isolates the name service of the private network from that of the Internet. As a result, the internal IP addresses of the private network hosts are not exposed to the Internet users. The *mail handling* capability ensures that any E-mail exchange between the private network and the Internet is processed through the firewall.

Grades of Firewall Security

Depending on its components, several grades of firewall security can be obtained. As shown in Figure 7.4, there is *no security* in allowing open access between the Internet and the private network. Next, filters can be added to traditional router products to obtain a certain level of interception of unauthorized traffic. Next, the firewall can include the filters and the application gateways. A variety of proxy servers can be added along with different strengths of the authentication schemes. We can also improve the security for the private network by adding mail handling and name service functions to the firewall. Next, the firewall can reside on a secure operating system, thereby improving the underlying security for the firewall itself. A firewall can also provide data confidentiality and integrity, as we will describe later in this chapter. Finally, the company can deny any access to the Internet, thereby ensuring complete security (no access, no risks). While this is seemingly a theoretical option, for certain highly secure environments this may be the only prudent approach.

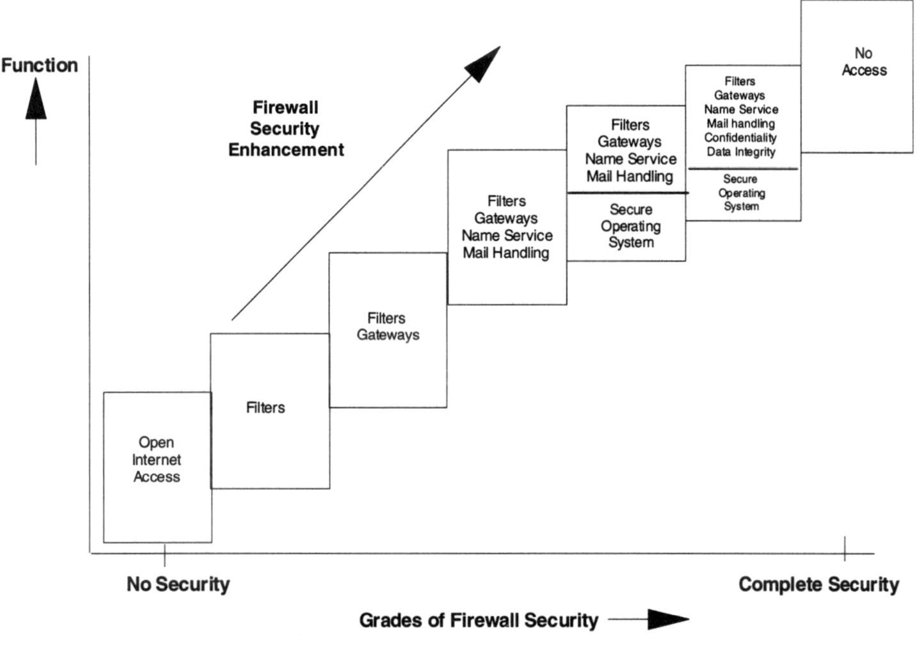

Figure 7.4: Grades of Security Provided by Firewalls

Risks Not Addressed By Firewalls

There are several types of security exposures to private networks that a firewall cannot address. We list some such exposures.

1. **Insider's Intrusion:** The firewall cannot protect the resources from attack by an internal user of the private network. The firewall is a gateway that simply intercepts the traffic between a private network and the Internet. In addition, an intracompany firewall

can intercept traffic among different parts of a company. In any case, an insider may steal critical company information or damage its resources without any awareness at the firewall. This threat can be addressed by implementing appropriate authentication and access control mechanisms, described earlier.

2. **Direct Internet Traffic:** A firewall is beneficial only if all the Internet traffic is handled through the firewall. The firewall cannot protect the resources of the private network from the traffic that takes place directly with the Internet, bypassing the firewall. For example, if a user on the private network exchanges data over a direct access (such as a dial connection) to the Internet, the firewall cannot intercept and examine that data. As such, it is important for the private network to ensure that all the traffic to and from the Internet is transmitted through the firewall.

3. **Virus Protection:** Typically, a firewall cannot protect a private network from external viruses. A virus may be transferred to the private network using File Transfer Protocol (FTP) or other means. In order to implement such protection, the firewall must implement the logic to detect viruses.

Packet Filters

There are several router products in the industry that route IP packets based on the destination address in the IP header. If the router knows how to send the packet to the destination address, it does so. If the router does not know how to send the packet for the given destination address, it returns the packet using an ICMP "destination unreachable" message to the source address.

The routers that are used in firewalls are called *screening routers* or *filters*. Upon receiving a packet, a filter determines whether the packet should be discarded or forwarded to the destination address. This decision is based on the filter rules that are specified by the firewall administrator.

Filter Rules

Filter rules are often defined at the firewall installation time, although rules can be modified, added, or deleted later. Each filter rule consists of two parts: the action field and the selection criteria. The action field specifies the action to be taken if the packet is selected by this rule. Two types of actions are allowed:

1. **BLOCK (or DENY):** This action implies that the selected packet should be rejected.

2. **PERMIT (or ALLOW):** This action specifies that the selected packet should be forwarded.

The selection criteria can be based on a variety of parameters. Some of the common parameters are listed below.

1. **Source and Destination Address:** The filter rule includes an address mask for selecting a packet based on its source address and destination address.

The address selection is accomplished by specifying two dotted-decimal addresses. The first address is the desired address, and the second is a mask to select the bits in the address field. For example, suppose we want to select any packet with a source address that begins with 157.4.5. Then we will have 157.4.5.0 as the defined source address and 255.255.255.0 as the address mask for selecting a packet. So, for this address mask, the first 3 bytes of the mask will select all of the 24 bits of the first 3 bytes of a packet's source address. Next, the selected 24 bits are compared against 157.4.5. If there is a match, the packet is selected. A similar process can be used for the destination address.

2. **Source and Destination Port:** The filter rule may apply to a specific port number of the source host or the destination host.

3. **Protocol:** A packet may also be selected based on the higher level protocol. For example, a packet may be selected if it is using TCP, UDP or ICMP protocols.

4. **Direction:** The packet can also be selected based on the direction of packet transmission with respect to the firewall. For example, an *inbound packet* is one coming from the Internet to the private network, and an *outbound packet* is one going in the opposite direction.

A typical firewall may allow up to 255 filter rules. The last rule specifies to discard (block/reject) all packets, as described later.

So, the filter component of the firewall works as follows. When a packet arrives at the filter component, it is tested against the first filter rule. If the first rule applies to the packet, then the specified action for that rule is carried out (the packet is rejected or forwarded). If this rule does not apply, then the second rule is checked, and so on. Note that at every rule, if the packet satisfies the selection criteria, then the action specified by that rule is performed. Suppose the packet is not selected by any of the rules, up to the last but one rule. The last rule, however, specifies to discard all packets. So, the last rule takes effect, and the packet is rejected. In short, the default action for packet filtering is to discard the packet, unless otherwise selected by a filter rule. This is a recommended security policy to prevent unauthorized packets getting into the private network. The above process is shown in Figure 7.5.

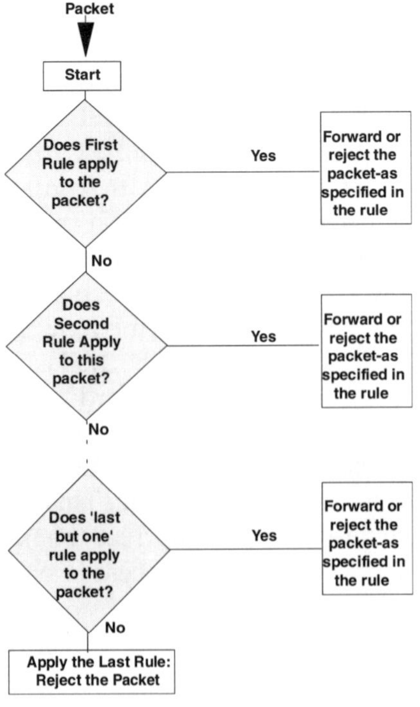

Figure 7.5: Processing a Packet through a Firewall Filter

Configuring Filters

A common concern pertaining to packet filtering relates to the complexity of configuring filter rules. The rules are complex and may require knowledge of the TCP/IP addressing scheme. As a result, administrators may commit a mistake in defining the filter rules. The industry direction is to make it simpler to specify the rules and not require intricate knowledge of TCP/IP. In addition, some utilities may be provided to check the syntax of the rules.

IP Spoofing Attack

On January 22, 1995, the Stanford Linear Accelerator Computing Center (SLAC) detected that some one was monitoring a host behind a firewall. It was discovered that the intruder's program was hiding in the operating system and was collecting the accounts (user IDs) and passwords. The next morning, the SLAC computer system was shut down and all external network access was cut off. The attacker had used the IP spoofing attack.

In this case, the *attacking host* sends a request to a target host by forging the source address with that of the *attacked host*. Now the target host is expected to send back a response to the connection request. So, the attacking host must prevent the attacked host from detecting the response and cancelling the connection, since it is a forged connection. To achieve that, the attacking host sends numerous connection requests to the attacked host. As a result, the true host is flooded with the connection requests, and in the process it misses the response for the forged connection. Next, the attacking host must respond to the connection response that was sent by the target machine. In addition, the response from the attacking host must include a sequence number. However, most of the installations use the Berkeley implementation of TCP, for which the sequence numbers can be reasonably predicted. So the attacking host predicts the sequence number and sends a response to the target host. As a result, the connection is made, and the attacking host can send various commands to the target host for subversion.

This attack may be thwarted by configuring the firewall appropriately, as described next.

Recommended Rules

1. As explained in the preceding attack, one of the weaknesses of the filters approach is that the source address in the IP header is not secured. As such, a host can change the source address of a packet to appear as if it is coming from another host. To prevent such an attack, the filter rules should discard any packet from the Internet that contains the source address of a host inside the private network. The reason is that a packet from the Internet with the source address of a host inside private network implies that the packet is fraudulent. Therefore, the filter rules should specify to discard the packet.

2. If some host on the Internet is known to be sending fraudulent packets, then block all traffic to and from that host. This can be done by adding a new filter rule, at the beginning of all the existing rules, that will discard a packet with a source address equal to that of the attacking host.

Proxy Server

Proxy servers intercept and examine traffic at the TCP/IP application layer. The user in the private network is required first to access the proxy server, before accessing an application server on the Internet. Most firewall proxy servers include TELNET and FTP. Since this service is at the application layer, separate proxy servers are required for each type of application. The proxy client, however, can be implemented in several ways, as described later.

The purpose of a proxy server is to intercept the user access to an Internet application, authenticate the user, ensure that the user is authorized to access the application, and then permit the user to access the server on the Internet. Similar service is also available for a user from the Internet to access an application server on the private network.

Figure 7.6 depicts the concept of a TELNET client and server using a proxy server. It shows that TELNET client A is residing in the private network. TELNET client A accesses the proxy server at the firewall for TELNET logon. Once the user at the TELNET client is authenticated by the proxy server, the proxy server verifies if the user can access TELNET over the Internet. If so, the user is permitted to send a TELNET request on the Internet. A procedure for using the proxy server is described next.

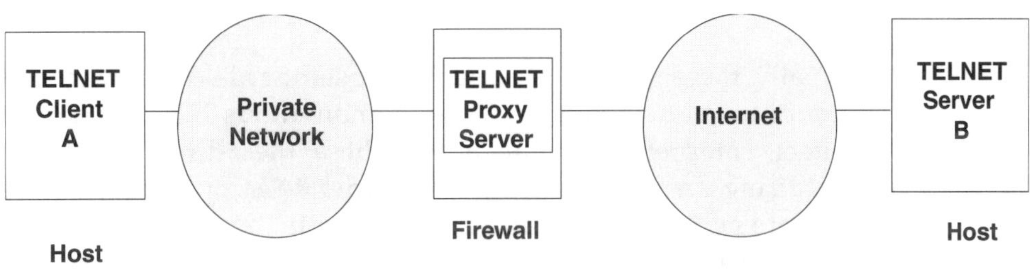

Figure 7.6: Firewall Proxy Server Example—TELNET

1. Client A on the private network sends a TELNET request to the firewall. (This is a new procedure for the user to follow but requires no modifications to the client software.)

2. The proxy server at the firewall prompts the user to enter the user ID and a password.

3. The user enters the ID and the password. The proxy server authenticates the user by verifying the user ID and the corresponding password (see Chapter 2 for details). If user authentication fails, the user request is rejected. If user authentication succeeds, proceed to step 4.

4. The user sends the TELNET request to TELNET server B on the host over the Internet.

5. Server B authenticates the user. If the user is successfully authenticated, proceed to step 6; otherwise reject the request.

6. For any traffic going from client A to server B, firewall code intercepts the traffic and replaces the source address of the IP packet with that of the firewall's address. As such, the internal addresses of hosts on the private network are not exposed to the hosts on the Internet.

Finally, there may be files, such as a standards document, that are to be made available through anonymous FTP support. In effect, Internet users can access these files directly without requiring any authentication. In order to support that, some private networks provide a server outside the firewall. Such an externalized server restricts Internet user access to only the local resources residing at the server. Clearly, the connection from the externalized server to the private network should be through the firewall, as shown in Figure 7.7.

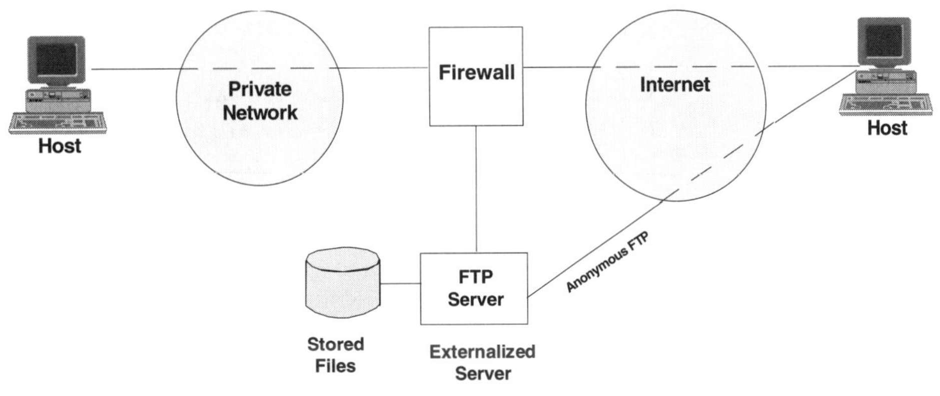

Figure 7.7: Externalized FTP Server

Approaches for Proxy Server

As described, a proxy system consists of a proxy server at the firewall. For the client side, there are three approaches for implementing the proxy.

1. **Customize User Procedure:** In this approach, the user procedures are modified to implement the proxy. This was used in the preceding discussion of proxy server. An important benefit for this scheme is that it requires no impact on the client software. Given the extensive presence of existing TCP/IP client software, this approach is quite attractive for implementing access to the Internet.

The disadvantage is that the user has to be trained for an extra step to log on the proxy server. For large sites that have been using the TCP/IP applications for a long time, this user training may be a time-consuming and expensive process.

2. **Customize Client Software:** This approach requires modifications to the client software and provides transparency to users in accessing the Internet. This transparency is attained by software at the client and the firewall that intercepts and directs the application traffic. A common implementation of such an approach is called SOCKS. SOCKS was mentioned earlier and is described later in detail.

3. Another approach is to contain all the changes in the firewall. In this case, neither the client software nor the user procedures require any changes. This approach still requires that all the messages to and from the Internet are transmitted through the firewall. Typically, a user sends a request to connect to a server on the Internet. Transparent to the user, the firewall intercepts the request, authenticates the user, verifies the request, and proceeds with the connection appropriately.

SOCKS

SOCKS provides a customized client approach for providing proxy services. In effect, SOCKS requires modifications to the client software to accommodate the interception at the firewall between the user on the private network and the server on the Internet. Typically, SOCKS is used for access from hosts on a private network to the Internet servers.

SOCKS protocol was published by David Koblas and Michelle R. Koblas (Koblas 1992). SOCKS protocol Version 4 is described in Leech (1994). SOCKS is also described in some of the security books such as Chapman (1995) and IBMFW (1995).

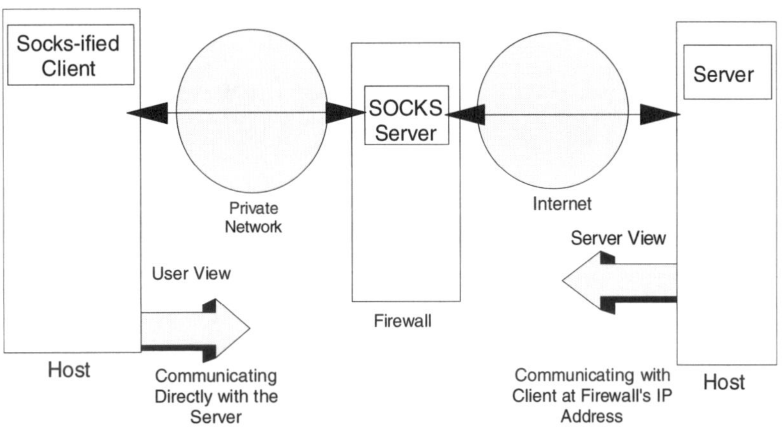

Figure 7.8: SOCKS Support in Firewalls

Figure 7.8 depicts a typical SOCKS implementation. SOCKS requires modifications to TCP/IP clients to accommodate interactions with the SOCKS server. A TCP/IP client that has been modified to handle SOCKS interactions is often called a "socksified" client. A socksified client issues SOCKS calls transparent to the user. The SOCKS server resides at the firewall and interacts with the socksified clients. There are no changes required for the server residing at the Internet.

SOCKS Version 4 (Leech 1994) works as follows. The goal for SOCKS is to provide a general framework for TCP/IP applications to securely use the services of a firewall. The protocol is independent of the supported TCP/IP application. When a TCP/IP client requires access to a server, the client code must first open a TCP/IP connection to the SOCKS server. The conventional port number for SOCKS service is 1080. If the connection request is accepted, then the client sends a request to the SOCKS server. The request includes the following information:

- Desired destination port

- Desired destination address

- Authentication information

The SOCKS server evaluates the information in the request. It either accepts the request and establishes the connection to the Internet server or denies the request. This evaluation depends on the configuration data of the SOCKS server. In either case, the SOCKS server sends a reply to the client. The reply includes information indicating whether the request was successful.

A clear advantage of the SOCKS protocol is that it is transparent to the user. The user accesses the Internet without requiring any awareness of the intervening firewall. As such, no user training is required when a firewall is installed for the private network. However, this approach requires changes to the client software. As a result, an upgrade is required for the user workstations. This upgrade can be provided either at the application level or at the underlying TCP/IP code. In the former case, each application client, such as TELNET and FTP, must be socksified. Alternatively, the SOCKS protocol can be implemented in the underlying TCP/IP stack so that it is transparent to the TCP/IP applications. As a result, each TCP/IP application can make transparent use of the SOCKS services.

Finally, it should be noted that any gateway approach relies heavily on the underlying authentication scheme. A weak authentication scheme can easily defeat the purpose of the firewall. This topic is addressed next.

User Authentication

A typical TCP/IP application, such as TELNET, requires the entry of a user ID and password. However, unless otherwise protected, the password is transmitted in the clear over the Internet. The primary concern here is with authenticating the user to the firewall. Another important concern is the authentication of the firewall administrator to the firewall.

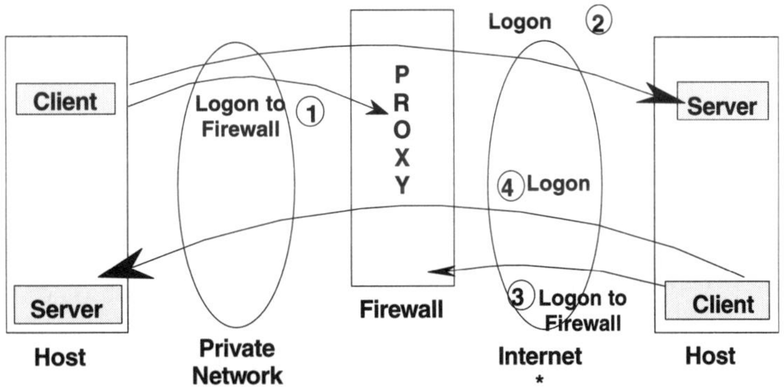

Figure 7.9: Authentification Using Firewall as the Gateway

Private Network to Internet

Consider the two scenarios for user authentication shown in Figure 7.9. The first scenario consists of steps 1 and 2 shown in

Figure 7.9. In this scenario, the client begins by sending the user ID and the password to the firewall. This exchange takes place over the secure private network. The security exposure for a password theft is arguably less in this scenario compared with the password transmissions over the Internet. Next, the user logs on the Internet host by sending the ID and password over the Internet. The topic of password transmission over the Internet is included in the next scenario.

Internet to Private Network

In the second scenario, the user logs from the Internet to a server on the private network. This is shown as steps 3 and 4 in Figure 7.9. First, the user sends an ID and a password to the firewall. However, even an encrypted password can be copied over the Internet. This may lead to a replay attack, where the intruder enters the (stolen) encrypted password and gains access to the firewall and then to the private network. In order to thwart such an attack, it is desirable to use one-time passwords. Several types of token cards are available that generate random passwords to be used only once, as described in Chapter 2. In this case, even if the password is stolen, it is of no use to the intruder, since a one-time password may not be accepted after its first use.

Authenticating the Administrator

Consider the process for a user to log on a firewall as an administrator. In late 1994, I heard of an unconfirmed story that an intruder got into a firewall as an administrator from the Internet. The intruder attempted various passwords over the Internet and at last succeeded in guessing the correct password. Assuming the firewall is residing on a UNIX system, there are two precautions for addressing such an attack.

1. The administrator should always be required to use a one-time password for gaining remote access to the firewall.

2. The (firewall) administrator logon should not be accepted from any one accessing from the Internet side. In effect, the administrator logon to the firewall is permitted only from the private network. This precaution can greatly reduce the chances of a hacker gaining administrator access to the firewall from the Internet.

Finally, the password storage files are a well-known target of attacks by hackers. The topic of securely storing passwords was addressed in Chapter 2.

Domain Name Service

A firewall can provide a modified name-server function for users residing inside and outside the private network. However, the firewall should not divulge the IP addresses of hosts inside the private network. So for inquiries from hosts on the Internet, the firewall should resolve all the names of hosts inside the private network to the IP address of the firewall. For inquiries from hosts inside the private network, the firewall provides name to address resolution for hosts on the Internet.

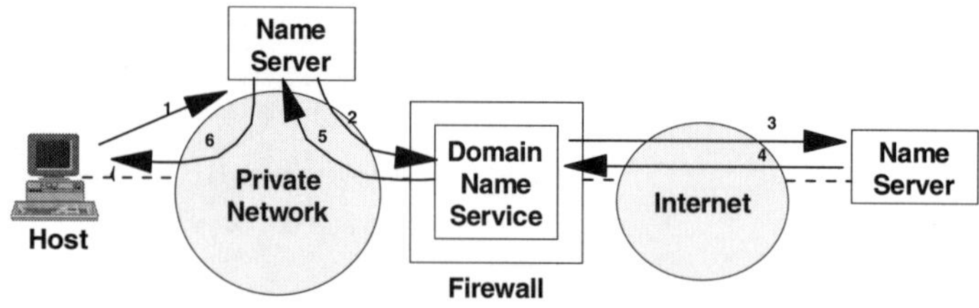

a) Name / Address Resolution Request from a Host on the Private Network for an Internet Host

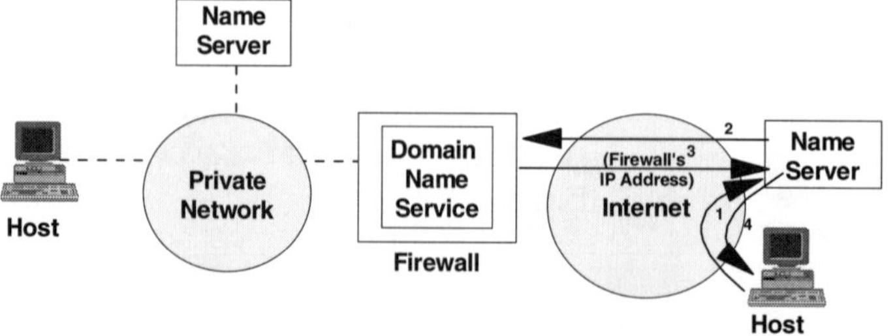

b) Name / Address Resolution Request from a Host on the Internet for a Host on the Private Network

Figure 7.10: Domain Name Service in Firewall

Figure 7.10 shows two sequences for name-address resolution. First, a client from the private network requests a name-address resolution for a host residing on the Internet. The name server on the private network forwards this request to the firewall, as shown in Figure 7.10(a). The domain name service at the firewall accesses the name server on the Internet, obtains the IP address of the requested host name, and sends this IP address to the name server on the private network. The name server on the private network forwards this response to the client that originated the request.

Next, assume that a client on the Internet requests the IP address of a host located inside the private network. The request goes to a name server on the Internet, and the name server forwards it to the firewall. The firewall responds with its own IP address, as shown in Figure 7.10(b). In this way, hosts on the Internet are aware only of the firewall's IP address for hosts residing inside the private network.

Mail Handling

E-mail (electronic mail) is one of the primary reasons for private networks to connect to the Internet. It is extensively used by Internet users to exchange information with each other. Typically, *Simple Mail Transfer Protocol* (SMTP) is used to handle mail on the Internet, although secure E-mail schemes have been developed and implemented (see Chapter 6).

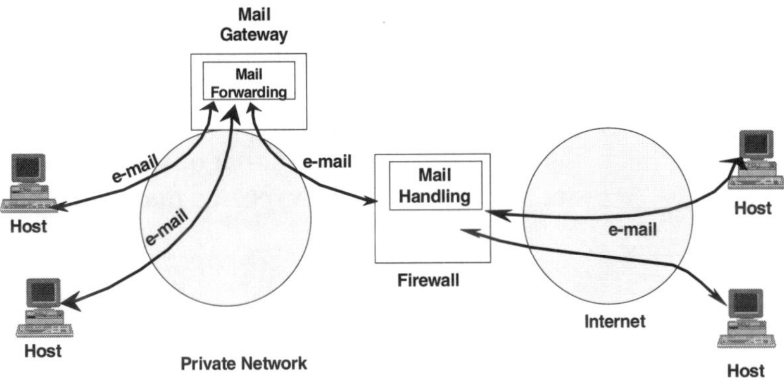

Figure 7.11: Mail Handling at the Firewall

E-mail may also need to be intercepted and forwarded appropriately. The deamon (background program running in a server) for E-mail, *SENDMAIL*, has been known to be exposed to several vulnerabilities and continues to be the target of attacks.

In order to protect the private network, one approach is to provide a mail gateway on the private network, as shown in Figure 7.11. E-mail originating from the private network is first sent to the mail gateway. The mail gateway, in turn, selects the E-mail destined for the Internet and forwards it to the firewall mail-handling program. For the E-mail received from the Internet, the firewall forwards it to the mail gateway on the private network. To the Internet users, the firewall is the only exposed mail gateway. There are some benefits to such an approach:

1. All E-mail from Internet is received by the firewall and not by the mail gateway of the private network. This is desirable, since the firewall is better equipped to handle any intrusion attempts than a mail gateway (another host) on the private network.

2. There is a single point of control of all the E-mail between the private network and the Internet. In this way, a site can implement controls to intercept and check for any viruses or other malicious software being transmitted to the private network. The mail gateway can also verify that only authorized users are allowed to send or receive mail over the Internet.

IP Security

The Internet standards community has recently developed a series of RFCs (requests for comments) to provide security mechanisms for Internet Protocols (IP).

RFC 1825 (Atkinson 1995a) provides an overview of the IP security approach, which consists of an *IP Authentication Header* and an *IP Encapsulating Security Payload* (ESP). RFC 1826 (Atkinson 1995b) describes the IP Authentication Header, and RFC 1827 (Atkinson 1995c) addresses the IP ESP. RFC 1828 (Metzger 1995) describes IP Authentication using Keyed MD5, and RFC 1829 (Karn 1995) treats the topic of ESP DES-CBC Transform.

We begin by reviewing some of the concepts, followed by their potential use in firewalls.

IP Authentication Header

The *IP Authentication Header* is intended to provide authentication and integrity between two entities supporting this header. This header can be used between hosts or *gateways*.[*] Since it does not require confidentiality, it is free from export restrictions for encryption schemes.

The IP ESP header includes a 32-bit *Security Parameter Index* (SPI). The combination of SPI and the destination address uniquely identifies a *security association*. A security association includes a variety of parameters that identify the cryptographic services applicable to the datagram. Examples of these parameters include authentication and encryption algorithms, modes of the algorithms, keys used for the algorithms, and lifetime of the keys. The IP security approach extensively uses the security association.

---

[*] According to Atkinson (1995a), a *security gateway* is a system that acts as a communication gateway between the trusted private network and the untrusted Internet network. The firewall is a security gateway.

The IP Authentication Header consists of the authentication information for the IP datagram. This information is computed by applying a cryptographic authentication function on the IP datagram. The function is computed using a secret key. According to Metzger (1995), use of the MD5 algorithm is required for support of the IP Authentication Header. IP Authentication Header should be used when users require authentication and integrity but no confidentiality.

IP Encapsulation Security Payload (ESP)

The ESP is intended to provide integrity and confidentiality for IP datagrams. ESP encrypts the data to be protected and then places it as part of the ESP portion of the datagram. ESP works in two modes, the tunnel mode and the transport mode.

In *tunnel mode*, the sender encapsulates the original datagram into ESP, obtains the encryption key (using security association), and applies the encryption transform. This encrypted ESP is placed within an IP datagram that includes cleartext IP headers. The unencrypted IP header is used to route the packet through the IP network. The receiver strips off the cleartext header, obtains the session key using the security association, and then decrypts the ESP using the session key.

In *transport mode*, only the transport layer (such as TCP or UDP) frame is encapsulated into ESP. This mode saves bandwidth because the IP headers are not encrypted.

IP Security for Firewalls

A firewall may include components to provide confidentiality and integrity, as shown in Figure 7.4. A corporate network may consist of two or more private networks that are interconnected through the Internet. The company may require data confidentiality and integrity between these networks. Another example is when a company official is on the road and requires secure communications between the hotel room and the company headquarters. Here again, the requirement is that the data traffic from the hotel room to the company headquarters should be encrypted.

The above issues can be addressed by using the IP security mechanisms. Consider the network shown in Figure 7.12a. Using ESP tunnel mode, the data traffic between the two firewalls can be encrypted. As a result, data confidentiality can be assured between the two private networks. Note that this function is transparent to the end users or host systems on the two private networks. Furthermore, no changes or modifications are required to the software on any host.

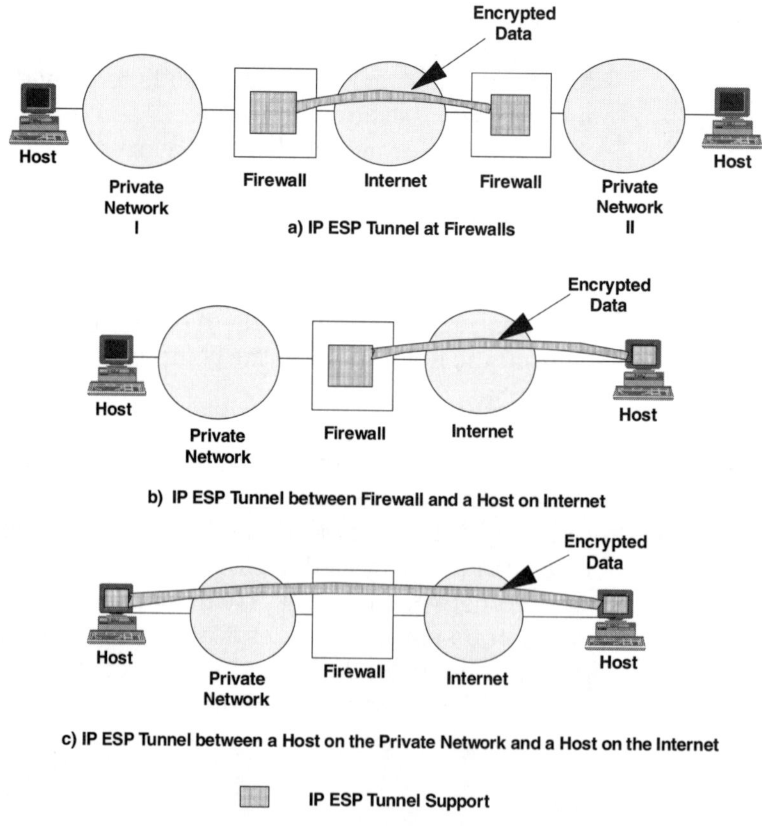

Figure 7.12: Use of IP ESP Tunnel in Hosts and Firewalls

Next, consider the requirement that the user has a secure communication from the hotel room to the company headquarters over the Internet, as depicted in Figure 7.12b. In order to provide confidentiality, the user's portable terminal (in the hotel room) and the company's firewall should support the ESP tunnel mode (or transport mode). This approach assumes that there is no firewall available at the hotel, a reasonable assumption that may change over time.

Finally, we may require *end-to-end confidentiality* between a host on the private network and another host on the Internet. This requirement can be addressed by implementing ESP tunnel mode on each of the host systems, as shown in Figure 7.12c.

Summary

This chapter started with a review of the purpose of firewalls, along with their requirements and components. In general, firewalls consist of filters and proxy servers. While filters provide limited security, proxy servers complement the protection of resources of a private network. A strong authentication at proxy servers is necessary to keep unauthorized users outside the private network. Finally, the chapter treated the topic of IP security. This approach is expected to enhance standardization across firewall products and enable firewalls to provide confidentiality and integrity.

The topic of firewall has been receiving increased attention over the last few years. Additional references on this topic include Cheswick (1994), Siyan (1995), and Chapman (1995).

Security Management

Security management pertains to the task of establishing and enforcing security policies across an enterprise. We divide security management into two distinct topics: *managing security data* and *securing management data*. Managing security data includes storage, retrieval, and maintenance of security information such as user IDs, passwords, and encryption keys. Securing management data pertains to secure storage and transmission of system management data such as alerts and alarms. Before discussing these topics, we need to address the security policies for an enterprise.

So, this chapter consists of three topics. First, it addresses the definition and implementation of security policies. Next, the topic of managing security data is presented, followed by approaches to securing management data.

Security Policies

The key objective of the *security policy* is to protect the enterprise resources, while giving due consideration to the impact on user productivity. The security policy should be uniformly enforced across the enterprise. A security policy can be incorporated in three steps.

The first step requires definition of various aspects of security policies. The second step creates the procedures and processes to enforce the security policy. The third step implements these procedures through various means including security schemes discussed earlier in this book. In the following, we address the first two steps.

Defining Security Policies

A security policy should consist of several components to address various aspects of resource protection. Some of the important areas are listed below.

1. **Accountability Policy:** This component includes the type of authentication, the password rules, and responsibilities of individuals about their assets. It defines the roles and responsibilities of the security administrator, the management, and the employees.

2. **Access Control Policy:** This policy addresses the data elements covered under access control, usage of DAC and MAC, and security classification of employees.

3. **Data Confidentiality Policy:** Policy for data confidentiality identifies the encryption requirements for each selected resource. It specifies selected encryp-

tion technologies, the key sizes, the key distribution algorithms, and the certification authority.

4. **Data Integrity Policy:** This policy describes the data integrity requirements for each selected resource. It specifies the various protocols and technologies that must be used to attain the desired levels of data integrity.

5. **Data Management Policy:** This component includes managing the company data or information assets. It specifies requirements for storage, transmission, retrieval, and maintenance of data. The information assets can be classified as follows:

- **Company Business Data:** It includes files and databases that contain the company's data such as customer database, accounts receivable, employee salaries, and sales orders.

- **Security Data:** This data includes user IDs, passwords, encryption keys, access control lists, and other information for implementation and use of security technologies.

6. **System Management Data:** System management data includes information about tracking and controlling the network. It is often desirable to store and transmit this information securely.

Establishing Security Policy Procedures

The process for establishing security policy can be described in the following steps:

1. Identify all key assets of the enterprise. Classify them based on their value to the company.

2. List the objectives for securing the assets selected in step 1.

3. Collect all of the existing information flows for each selected asset.

4. Perform risk analysis against all enterprise assets.

5. Define a set of rules to protect the selected assets against the identified risks.

6. Define the security processes using the rules from step 5.

7. Overlay the security processes on the existing processes and inform those affected by the processes.

While most of these steps are straightforward, we address the relationship of security policy to the value of the assets.

Cost Analysis

There is a certain cost associated with implementing network security to protect a company's assets. However, such costs should be balanced against the value of the asset.

Assume that there exists an asset with a value A. If the cost to penetrate the network and compromise the asset is P, then the risk factor is A/P. So, the *risk factor* of an asset is the ratio of the value of the asset to the cost to penetrate the network to compromise the asset. For a secure network, the value of P should be greater than A; or it should be more expensive to penetrate the network and steal or damage the asset than the value of the asset.

Now assume that the cost to implement the security policy that would protect the asset is N. In a well-designed network, the investment level, N, should be related to the value of the asset, A. Let us call the ratio $K = N/A$ the *investment factor*. Note that the implementation cost should clearly be less than the value of the asset, so N is less that A, as depicted in Figure 8.1.

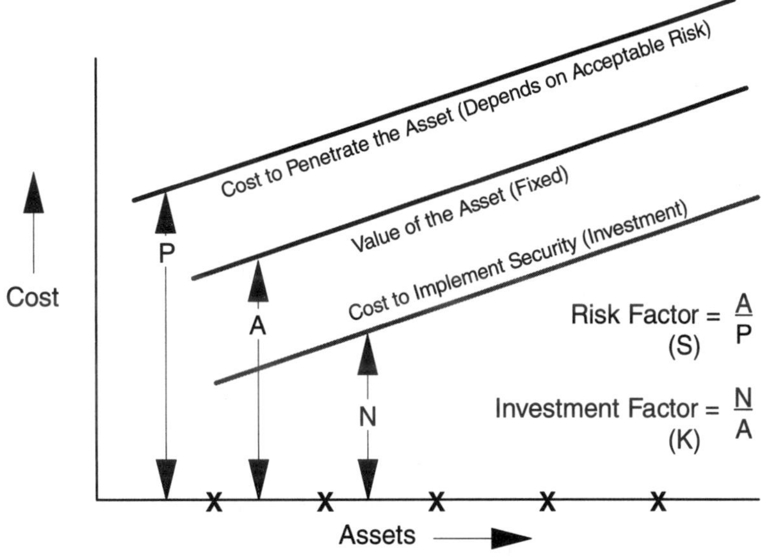

Figure 8.1: Security Cost Analysis

For many networks, the cost (*N*) to implement security and the cost (*P*) to penetrate security is fixed for all of the network assets. In such cases, it is important to evaluate the risk factor for the most critical assets.

Additional information on security policies can be found in Shaffer (1994), IBMSEC (1995), Amoroso (1994), and Russell (1991). In the remainder of this chapter, we address the topic of managing security data and securing management data.

Managing Security Data

Security data includes user IDs, passwords, access control lists, and encryption keys. A notable example of encryption keys is the storage of the private key of a user at the workstation. The private key size may vary from 512 bits to 2048 bits. So a user cannot memorize the private key, but the key is required to compute the digital signature on behalf of the user. Security information, such as the private keys, must be protected from hackers and intruders. There are hand-held cards that provide storage of security information. These cards can be carried by the user and can be plugged into a workstation. Besides key storage, some cards also offer the option of encryption algorithms. The topic of secure storage of passwords was discussed in Chapter 2.

A given enterprise may include security data for several systems from different vendors. At the same time, each system may have its own repository of security data. For example, consider the network shown in Figure 8.2. Each system has a database (security registry) for the user IDs and passwords to access that particular system.

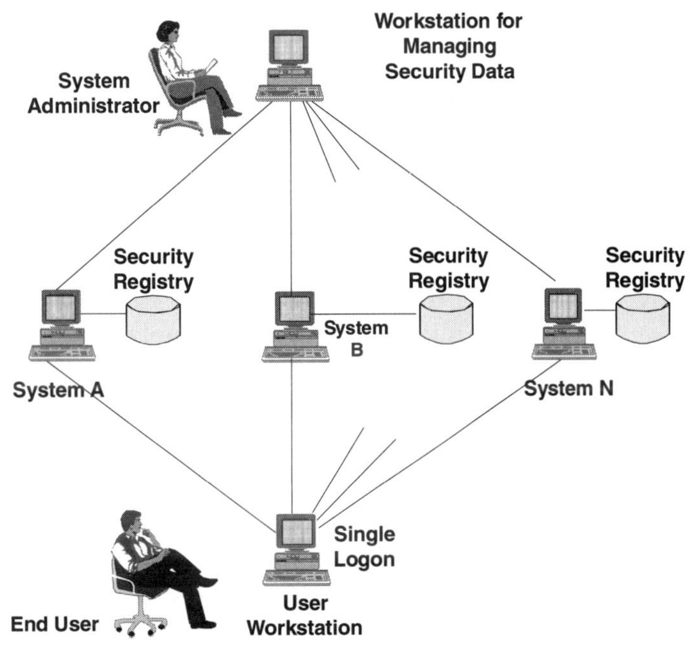

Figure 8.2: Managing Security Data

Now consider the management issues of such security data. The administrator needs to maintain and update each of the registries. Whenever an employee is hired or fired, the relevant registries should be updated within a very short time. For a company with large number of employees, such a task is highly labor intensive as well as prone to errors.

Some approaches have recently emerged to tackling the problem of managing multiple security registries. The objective is to minimize the amount of administrator intervention required in the creation and maintenance of multiple security registries. The administrator should be presented with a unified or single-system image of all the security registries. For example, the administrator can add or delete (all the entries for) a given user by executing a single update command. The process can also be automated so that no human intervention is required at all. The underlying software updates the multiple registries. While this approach offers great benefits for administrator productivity, it has the drawback of requiring a significant size of software to coordinate management of multiple registries.

OSF's DCE registry includes a set of user profile information. The DCE registry entries can be changed using the *rgy-edit* utility program. This program enables the administrator to view, add, delete, and modify information in the DCE registry database. Given the above requirements, DCE 1.1 provides *extended registry attributes* (ERA). ERA enables single sign-on by allowing secure association of additional user information to DCE registry (OSFDCE11 1995). Additional details on DCE registry can be found in Rosenberry (1992).

Security for Management Data

For any network, its management requires establishment of certain protocols between the managing hosts and the managed hosts. The information transmitted between these two entities may need to be protected. For example, no one should be capable of creating a bogus message informing that a major nuclear power plant is down or a request to shut down an airport network.

SNMP

To control TCP/IP networks, the Internet community has standardized a set of protocols. These protocols, called *Simple Network Management Protocol* (SNMP), are used to manage the components of a TCP/IP network. Over the last few years, there was a concerted effort to enhance security for SNMP Version 1 (or simply SNMP). SNMP Version 2 defines several extensions to SNMP for a variety of security services. In the following, we introduce SNMP, followed by a review of SNMP Version 2 functions.

SNMP defines the formats for information exchange between a network management station and a management agent. A management station is typically (but not necessarily) a stand-alone device that provides the interface for a human (such as a network manager) to the network management system. The management station may consist of one or more network management applications such as those for data analysis and fault recovery. A given platform, such as a router, a bridge, or a host, is managed by implementing a management agent. SNMP defines the protocols between the management station and the management agent, as shown in Figure 8.3.

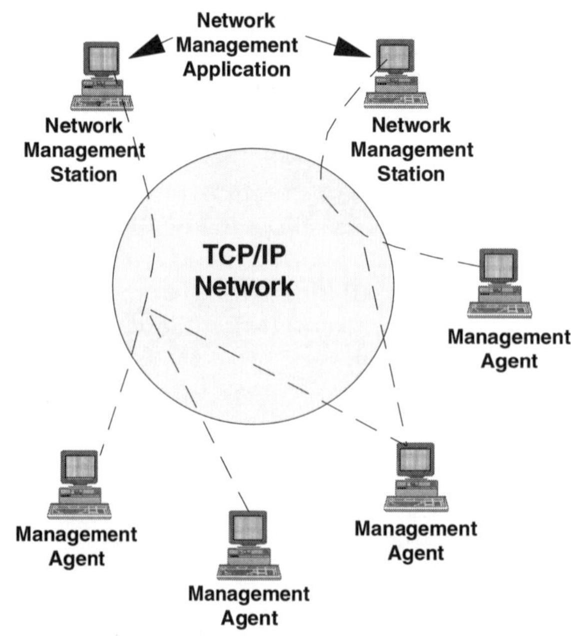

Figure 8.3: SNMP Usage in TCP/IP Network

The network resources are defined as objects. Each object is represented as a data variable. The collection of these variables is called a *Management Information Base* (MIB). An MIB describes those objects that are expected to be implemented by a managed node.

SNMP consists of the following important functions:

1. **GET:** allows the management station to retrieve the value of an object from the MIB at an agent.

2. **SET:** allows the management station to alter the value of an object at the MIB of an agent.

3. **TRAP:** allows the agent to notify the management station of an important event.

SNMP is designed to operate on top of UDP protocol. Each agent must implement SNMP, UDP, and IP.

SNMP Version 2

SNMP Version 1 had certain deficiencies, particularly the lack of security for the information exchange. There were two key security drawbacks in using SNMP V1:

1. A third party could eavesdrop on the traffic between the agent and the management station.

2. A hacker or an intruding host could initiate GET/SET commands pretending to be a management station or an agent. In this way, the intruder could read and modify an MIB.

These two security problems have been discussed in this book in other contexts. These problems can be addressed by providing confidentiality and source authentication.

In 1993, a series of Internet RFCs (requests for comments) were issued that describe *SNMP Version 2 (SNMPv2)*. RFC 1446 (Galvin 1993) describes the security protocols for SNMPv2. It specifies three security services: data integrity, data origin authentication, and data confidentiality. For data integrity, MD5 message digest algorithm is chosen. MD5 computes a 128-bit digest of the designated portion of the SNMPv2 message.

Data origin authentication is accomplished as follows. A secret value is attached to the message prior to the digest computation. This secret value is known only to the originator and the recipient of the SNMPv2 message. So the verification of the MD5 digest also validates the origin of the message.

Data confidentiality is supported through the use of Data Encryption Standard (DES) in Cipher Block Chaining (CBC) mode. The designated portion of the SNMPv2 message is encrypted and sent as part of the message to the destination.

Additional details on SNMPv2 security can be found in Galvin (1993).

Summary

Security management relies on implementation of robust security policies for an enterprise. It includes managing the security data such as passwords and keys for large enterprises. Creation and maintenance of user security data can be both cumbersome and error prone. The problem is exacerbated by the existence of several types of security registries from different vendors. This chapter also addresses the problem of securing management data, such as the SNMP protocols. SNMP Version 2 describes the security enhancements to SNMP including data integrity, data origin authentication, and data confidentiality.

Bibliography

[Ahuja 1982] Vijay Ahuja, "Design and Analysis of Computer Communication Networks," McGraw-Hill Book Company. 1982.

[Amoroso 1994] Edward G. Amoroso, "Fundamentals of Computer Security Technology," Prentice Hall, Inc. 1994.

[Atkinson 1995a] R. Atkinson, "Security Architecture for the Internet Protocol," RFC 1825. August 1995.

[Atkinson 1995b] R. Atkinson, "IP Authentication Header," RFC 1826. August 1995.

[Atkinson 1995c] R. Atkinson, "IP Encapsulation Security Payload (ESP)," RFC 1827. August 1995.

[Balenson 1993] D. Balenson, "Privacy Enhancement for Internet Electronic Mail: Part III. Algorithms, Modes, and Identifiers," RFC 1423. February 1993.

[Barlow 1993] John Perry Barlow, "A Plain Text on Crypto Policy," Communications of the ACM. Vol. 36. No. 11. November 1993. pages 21–26.

[Bellare 1995] Mihir Bellare, Juan A. Garay, Ralf Hauser, Amir Herzberg, Hugo Krawczyk, Michael Steiner, Gene Tsudik, and Michael Waidner, "iKP—A Family of Secure Electronic Payment Protocols," Extended Abstract. USENIX Workshop on Electronic Commerce. July 11–12, 1995. New York.

[Bishop 1992] Matt Bishop, "Anatomy of a Proactive Password Changer," UNIX Security Symposium. USENIX Association. Baltimore, MD. September 14–16, 1992. pages 171–184.

[Bishop 1990] Matt Bishop, "An Extendable Password Checker," Extended Abstract. UNIX Security Workshop. USENIX Association. Portland, OR. August 27–28, 1990. pages 15–16.

[Brown 1994] Patricia Brown, "ICL Extends AccessManager to Sun Platforms," Communications Week. October 17, 1994. page 4.

[Browne 1995] R. Browne, "Extended Abstract: An Architecture for Covert Channel Control in RealTime Networks and MultiProcessors," IEEE Symposium on Security and Privacy. Oakland, CA. May 8–10, 1995. pages 155–168.

[Caldwell 1995] Bruce Caldwell, "Hacking Spree Targets Citibank," Informationweek. September 4, 1995. page 20.

[Carlin 1993] Jerry M. Carlin, "UNIX® Security Update," UNIX Security Symposium IV, USENIX Association. Santa Clara, CA. October 4–6, 1993. pages 119–130.

[Carson 1990] Mark E. Carson and Wen-Der Jiang, "New Ideas in Discretionary Access Control," UNIX Security Workshop, USENIX Association. Portland, OR. August 27–28, 1990. pages 35–37.

[CERTB 1995] "Today's Challenge," CERT Brochure. CERT Coordination Center, Software Engineering Institute, Carnegie Mellon University. Pittsburgh, PA. 15213-3890. CONTACT: cert @ cert.org

[CERTFAQ 1993] CERT, "The CERT Coordination Center FAQ," Revision 7. JPO#93-025 and ESC#93-0115. cert.org:/pub/cert_advisories/01-README January 1993.

[Chapman 1995] D. Brent Chapman and Elizabeth D. Zwicky, "Building Internet Firewalls," O'Reilly & Associates, Inc. 1995.

[Cheswick 1994] William R. Cheswick and Steven M. Bellovin, "Firewalls and Internet Security: Repelling the Wily Hacker," Addison Wesley Publishing Company. 1994.

[Chokhani 1992] Santosh Chokhani, "Trusted Products Evaluation," Communications of the ACM. Vol. 35. No. 7. July 1992. pages 65–76.

[Churbuck 1995] David C. Churbuck, "Where's the Money?" Forbes. January 30, 1995. pages 100–108.

[Clark 1991] "Computers at Risk," David D. Clark, Chairman. System Security Study Committee, Computer Science and Telecommunications Board. Commission on Physical Sciences, Mathematics, and Applications. National Research Council. National Academy Press. 1991.

[Comer 1991] Douglas E. Comer, "Internetworking with TCP/IP. Volume I. Principles, Protocols and Architecture," Prentice Hall. 1991.

[Curry 1992] David A. Curry, "UNIX® System Security: A Guide for Users and System Administrators," Addison-Wesley Publishing Co, Inc. 1992.

[De Alvare' 1990] Ana Maria De Alvare', "How Crackers Crack Passwords or What Passwords to Avoid," UNIX Security Workshop. USENIX Association. Portland, OR. August 27–28. 1990. pages 103–112.

[Denning 1987] Dorothy E. Denning, "An Intrusion-Detection Model," IEEE Transactions on Software Engineering. Vol. SE-13. No. 2. February 1987. pages 222–232.

[Diffie 1976]   Whitfield Diffie and Martin E. Hellman, "New Directions in Cryptography," IEEE Transactions on Information Theory. Vol. IT-22. No. 6. November 1976. pages 644–654.

[Dunlap 1995] Charlotte Dunlap, "Netscape to Enter New Turf: Web Site Development Tools," Computer Reseller News. September 11, 1995. page 12.

[Edwards 1993] John Edwards, "Single Sign-on Technology Streamlines Network Access," Software Magazine. Client/Server Computing Special Edition. November 1993. pages 35–42.

[Ford 1995]   Andrew Ford, "Spinning the Web: How to Provide Information on the Internet," VNR International Thomson Publishing Company. 1995.

[FSTC 1994] "The Challenge - The Response," Financial Services Technology Consortium Handout. September 23, 1994.

[Galvin 1993] J. Galvin and K. McCloghrie, "Security Protocols for Version 2 of the Simple Network Management Protocol (SNMPv2)," RFC 1446. April 1993.

[Girling 1987] C. Gray Girling, "Covert Channels in LAN's," IEEE Transactions on Software Engineering. Vol. SE-13. No. 2. February 1987. pages 292–296.

[Hickman 1995] Kipp E. B. Hickman and Taher Elgamal, "The SSL Protocol," Internet Draft. June 1995.

[Hurwicz 1995] Mike Hurwicz, "Under Lock and Key," Special Report. LAN Magazine. March 1995. pages 116–121.

[Hwang 1995] Diana Hwang and Ken Yamada, "Resellers Reap High Margins, Steady Business from the Internet," Computer Reseller News. August 14, 1995. page 3.

[IBMAIX 1994] "Distributed Computing Environment 1.3 for AIX: Release Notes," IBM Corporation. GC23-2434-02. October 1994.

[IBMAIXS 1991] "Elements of AIX Security: R3.1," IBM Corporation. GG24-3622-01. April 1991.

[IBMDATAS 1977] "Data Security through Cryptography," IBM Corporation. GC22-9062-0. October 1977.

[IBMDSM 1995] "Distributed Security Manager for MVS," IBM Corporation. 1994. G221-4236-00.

[IBMFW 1995] "Building a Firewall with the NetSP Secured Network Gateway," IBM Corporation. GG24-2577-00. April 1995.

[IBMRACF 1993] "Resource Access Control Facility: Secured Signon SPE Information Package Version 1 Release 9.2," IBM Corporation. SC23-3765-00. September 1993.

[IBMSEC 1995] "IBM Security Architecture—Securing the Open Client/ Server Distributed Enterprise," IBM Corporation. SC28-8135-01. June 1995.

[IBMSLC 1994] "Network Security Program Product Guide Version 1 Release 2," IBM Corporation. SC31-6500-01. July 1994.

[IBMTCP 1990] "TCP/IP Tutorial and Technical Overview," IBM Corporation. June 1990. GG24-3376-01.

[INFOWEEK 1995] "Virus Count Up Sharply," Information Week. May 15, 1995. page 12.

[InfoSec 1994] "Securing the Infobahn," InfoSecurity Newsletter. July/August 1994.

[ITSEC 1991] "Information Technology Security Evaluation Criteria (ITSEC)," Version 1.2. Office for Official Publications of the European Communities. Luxemburg. 1991.

[Johnson 1994] D. B. Johnson, S. M. Matyas, A. V. Le, and J. D. Wilkins, "The Commercial Data Masking Facility (CDMF) Data Privacy Algorithm," IBM Journal of Research and Development. Vol. 38. No. 2. March 1994. pages 217–226.

[Johnson 1995] Johna Till Johnson and Kevin Tolly, "Token Authentication: The Safety Catch," Data Communication. May 1995. pages 62–77.

[Jolitz 1995] William F. Jolitz and Lynne Greer Jolitz, "Internet Security Breach," Dr. Dobb's Developer Update. Vol 2. No. 3. March 1995. pages 3–4.

[Kaliski 1993] B. Kaliski, "Privacy Enhancement for Internet Electronic Mail: Part IV. Key Certification and Related Services," RFC 1424. February 1993.

[Kang 1995] M. H. Kang, I. S. Moskowitz, and D. C. Lee, "A Network Version of the Pump," IEEE Symposium on Security and Privacy. Oakland, CA. May 8–10, 1995. pages 144–154.

[Karn 1995] P. Karn, P. Metzger, and W. Simpson, "The ESP DES-CBC Transform," RFC 1829. August 1995.

[Kemmerer 1983] Richard A. Kemmerer, "Shared Resource Matrix Methodology: An Approach to Identifying Storage and Timing Channels," ACM Transactions on Computer Systems, Vol. 1, No. 3, August 1983, pages 256–277.

[Kent 1993a] S. Kent, "Privacy Enhancement for Internet Electronic Mail: Part II. Certificate-Based Key Management," RFC 1422. February 1993.

[Kent 1993b] Stephen T. Kent, "Internet Privacy Enhanced Mail," Communications of the ACM, August 1993. Vol. 36. No. 8. pages 48–59.

[Klein 1990] Daniel V. Klein, "Foiling the Cracker: A Survey of, and Improvements to, Password Security." UNIX Security Workshop. USENIX Association. Portland, OR. August 27–28, 1990.

[Koblas 1992] David Koblas and Michelle R. Koblas, "SOCKS," Proceedings of UNIX Security Symposium. USENIX Association. Baltimore, MD. September 14–16, 1992.

[Kohl 1993] J. Kohl and B. Neuman, "The Kerberos Network Authentication Service (V5)," RFC 1510. September 10, 1993.

[Leech 1994] Marcus Leech, "SOCKS Protocol Version 4." Internet-Draft. Exp. December 1994.

[LeVitus 1996a] Bob LeVitus and Jeff Evans, "WebMaster Macintosh," AP Professional. 1996.

[LeVitus 1996b] Bob LeVitus and Jeff Evans, "WebMaster Windows," AP Professional. 1996.

[Linn 1993a] J. Linn, "Privacy Enhancement for Internet Electronic Mail: Part I. Message Encryption and Authentication Procedures," RFC 1421. February 1993.

[Linn 1993b] J. Linn, "Generic Security Service Application Program Interface," RFC 1508. September 1993.

[Lockhart 1994] Harold W. Lockhart, Jr., "OSF DCE: Guide to Developing Distributed Applications," McGraw-Hill, Inc. 1994.

[Loepere 1985] Keith Loepere, "Resolving Covert Channels within a B2 Class Secure System," ACM Operating System Review. Vol. 19. No. 3. July 1985. pages 9–28.

[Ludwig 1990] Mark A. Ludwig, "The Little Black Book of Computer Viruses," American Eagle Publications, Inc. 1990.

[Lunt 1990] Steven J. Lunt, "Experiences with Kerberos," UNIX Security Workshop. USENIX Association. Portland, OR. August 27–28, 1990. pages 113–120.

[Maddox 1995] Kate Maddox, Mitch Wagner, and Clinton Wilder, "Making Money on the Web," InformationWeek. September 4, 1995. pages 31–40.

[Marshall 1995] Steve Marshall, "High-tech Crooks Crack Internet Security," USA Today. January 24, 1995. page 1A.

[Mathiesen 1995] Michael Mathiesen, "Marketing on the Internet," Maximum Press. 1995.

[Metzger 1995] P. Metzger and W. Simpson, "IP Authentication using Keyed MD5," RFC 1828. August 1995.

[Miller 1967] Benjamin F. Miller, M.D., "The Complete Medical Guide," Simon and Schuster. New York. 1967.

[Morris 1979] Robert Morris and Ken Thompson, "Password Security: A Case History," Communications of the ACM. Vol. 22, No. 11. November 1979. pages 594–597.

[Needham 1994] Roger M. Needham, "Denial of Service: An Example," Communications of the ACM. November 1994. Vol. 37. No. 11. pages 42–46.

[Needham 1978] Roger M. Needham and Michael D. Schroeder, "Using Encryption for Authentication in Large Networks of Computers," Communications of the ACM. Vol. 21. No. 12. December 1978. pages 993–999.

[OpenVision 1994] "OpenVision Today," OpenVision Technologies, Inc. June 1994.

[OSF 1990] "OSF Distributed Computing Environment Rationale," Open Software Foundation. May 14, 1990.

[OSFDCE11 1995] "OSF DCE 1.1 New Features," OpenSoftware Foundation. OSF-DCE-DS-195. 1995.

[OST 1993] "In New York City Break-in, An Echo of '88 Worm Attack," Open Systems Today. November 8, 1993. page 19.

[Phillips 1995a] Ken Phillips, "Virus Whistleblowers," PCWEEK September 18, 1995. pages N1–N10.

[Phillips 1995b] Ken Phillips, "What Makes Anti-Virus Sleuth Engines Hum," PCWEEK September 18, 1995. pages N1–N15.

[Pounds 1995] Stephen Pounds, "The Latest Techno-bump on the Information Superhighway Is How to Keep Hackers out of Your Computer—and Away from Your Wallet," Palm Beach Post. March 12, 1995. page 1E.

[Press 1994] Larry Press, "Commercialization of the Internet," Communications of the ACM. November 1994. Vol. 37. No. 11. pages 17–21.

[RSA 1993] "Answers to Frequently Asked Questions about Today's Cryptography," RSA Laboratories. Revision 2.0. October 1993.

[Raleigh 1988] T. M. Raleigh and R. W. Underwood, "CRACK: A Distributed Password Advisor," Abstract. UNIX Security Workshop. USENIX Association. Portland, OR. August 29–30, 1988.

[Rescorla 1995] E. Rescorla and A. Schiffman, "The Secure HyperText Transfer Protocol," Internet Draft. July 1995.

[Rivest 1978] R. L. Rivest, A. Shamir, and L. Adleman, "A Method for Obtaining Digital Signatures and Public-Key Cryptosystems," Communications of the ACM. February 1978. Vol. 21. No. 2. pages 120–126.

[Rivest 1992a] R. Rivest, "The MD5 Message-Digest Algorithm," RFC 1321. April 1992.

[Rivest 1992b] R. Rivest, "The MD4 Message-Digest Algorithm," RFC 1320. April 1992.

[Rosenberry 1992] Ward Rosenberry, David Kenney, and Gerry Fisher, "OSF Distributed Computing Environment: Understanding DCE," O'Reilly & Associates, Inc. 1992.

[Russell 1991] Deborah Russell and G. T. Gangemi Sr., "Computer Security Basics," O'Reilly & Associates, Inc. 1991.

[Salamone 1993] Salvatore Salamone, "Internetwork Security: Unsafe at Any Node?," Data Communications. September 1993. pages 61–68.

[Schatz 1995] Willie Schatz, "The Secret to Encryption," InformationWeek. May 15. 1995. pages 74–76.

[Schneier 1995] Bruce Schneier, "E-Mail Security: How to Keep Your Electronic Messages Private," John Wiley & Sons, Inc. 1995.

[Schneier 1994] Bruce Schneier, "Applied Crypotgraphy: Protocols, Algorithms and Source Code in C," John Wiley & Sons, Inc. 1994.

[Schuman 1993] Evan Schuman, "Robert Morris in 1993: A Portrait of the Cracker as a Less Young Man," Open System Today. November 8, 1993. page 17.

[Shaffer 1994] Steven L. Shaffer and Alan R. Simon, "Network Security," AP Professional. 1994.

[Simmons 1994] Gustavus J. Simmons, "Cryptanalysis and Protocol Failures," Communications of the ACM. Vol. 37. No. 11. November 1994. pages 56–65.

[Sinha 1992] Alok Sinha, "Client-Server Computing," Communications of the ACM. July 1992. Vol 35. No. 7. pages 77–98.

[Siyan 1995] Karanjit Siyan and Chris Hare, "Internet Firewalls and Network Security," New Riders Publishing. 1995.

[Spafford 1992] Eugene H. Spafford, "Observing Reusable Password Choices," UNIX Security Symposium. USENIX Association. Baltimore, MD. September 14–16, 1992. pages 299–312.

[Stallings 1990] William Stallings, "Local Networks," Macmillam Publishing Company. New York. 1990.

[Stallings 1995] William Stallings, "Network and Internetwork Security: Principles and Practice," Prentice-Hall, Inc. 1995.

[Steiner 1988] Jennifer G. Steiner, Clifford Neuman, and Jeffrey I. Schiller, "Kerberos: An Authentication Service for Open Network Systems," Proceedings of the Winter 1988 USENIX Conference. February 1988.

[Stoll 1989] Cliff Stoll, "The Cuckoo's Egg: Tracking a Spy Through the Maze of Computer Espionage," Pocket Books, Simon and Schuster Inc. 1990.

[Strack 1990] Hermann Strack, "Extended Access Control in UNIX System V—ACLs and Context*)," UNIX Security Workshop, USENIX Association. Portland, OR. August 27–28, 1990. pages 87–101.

[Suggs 1992] Darrell Suggs, "Secure Superuser Access via the Internet," Proceedings of UNIX Security Symposium. USENIX Association. September 14–16, 1992. Baltimore, MD.

[Sullivan 1993] Kristina B. Sullivan, "Outwitting Smart Viruses," PC Week, December 27, 1993/January 3, 1994. Buyer's Guide. page 81.

[Tardo 1990] Joe Tardo, Kannan Alagappan, and Richard Pitkin, "Public Key Based Authentication Using Internet Certificates," UNIX Security Workshop. USENIX Association. Portland, OR. August 27–28, 1990. pages 121–123.

[Thompson 1984] Ken Thompson, "Reflections on Trusting Trust," Communications of the ACM. Vol. 27. No. 8. August 1984. pages 761–763.

[Tsudik 1992] Gene Tsudik, "Message Authentication with One-Way Hash Functions," INFOCOMM 1992.

[Wagner 1993] Mitch Wagner, "Possibilities are Endless, and Frightening," Open Systems Today. November 8, 1993. pages 16–19.

[Wayner 1996] Peter Wayner, "Digital Cash: Commerce on the Net," AP Professional. 1996.

[Wichers 1990] David R. Wichers, Douglas M. Cook, Ronald A. Olsson, John Crossley, Paul Kerchen, Karl N. Levitt, and Raymond Lo, "PACL's: An Access Control List Approach to Anti-Viral Security," UNIX Security Workshop. Portland, OR. August 27–28, 1990. pages 71–82.

[Wood 1995] Brad Wood, "For Your Amusement", May 5, 1995.

[Woolf 1977] Henry Bosley Woolf, Editor-in-Chief,"Webster's New Collegiate Dictionary." G. & C. Merriam Company, Springfield, MA. 1977.

[Wray 1993] J. Wray, "Generic Security Service API: C-bindings," RFC 1509. September 1993.

[Zimmerman 1995] Philip R. Zimmerman, "PGP Source Code and Internals," The MIT Press. 1995.